C

MAPS

INTRODUCTION:

Images and Myths

Mount Ebal stands at the centre of ancient Palestine, high above the green domes and minarets of Nablus; its slopes are grey and sterile, the unending stones relieved only by goats and the thornbush. From the summit the Bible lands open out in each direction: Nazareth to the north and the dim shapes of the Galilee; eastwards, across the Jordan, the Moab hills stretch in solemn line to beyond the Dead Sea; to the south lie Jerusalem and the wilderness of Judaea; westwards, through the haze, the coastal plain bends round Carmel from Acre down to Gaza and Ashqelon.

Familiar names, and a landscape that has been described so often that as early as 1821 an Englishman complained that 'the authors who have written in illustration of this small portion of the globe . . . may be thought to have so completely exhausted the subject, as to leave nothing new to be added by another'.[1] He would have been unable to write that about the population because the travellers who wrote about Palestine rarely considered its inhabitants. Perhaps, like artists, they would use them as incidental material, as drops of 'local colour' to be placed in picturesque attitudes at the side of some great ruin. But they were not interested in them as people because they were interested only in the past. Since the withdrawal of the Byzantine Empire from Syria, the West has coveted Palestine for its history. After two Eastern religions, Christianity and Judaism, had become westernized, it was claimed that the home of those religions should also be detached from the Eastern world. The Crusaders, the missionaries and the Zionists, both Jewish and Gentile, demanded Palestine for what it had been. For what it actually was, an Arab, mainly Islamic country, they did not care, and they treated its inhabitants accordingly.

Our century's ignorance has been as bad as our ancestors'. For all the invasions and changes in its rulers, the core of Palestine's population has been ethnically stable for millennia, possessing for the last thirteen hundred years a culture that has been unambiguously Arab. Yet in our own lifetime we have managed to forget it, ignore it, sometimes even to pretend that it did not exist. In the Balfour Declaration of 1917, the document which effectively decided their future, the Palestine Arabs (at that time forming ninety per cent of the population) were described merely as 'existing non-Jewish communities'. Balfour himself, as foreign secretary, admitted that 'in Palestine we do not propose even to go through the form of consulting the wishes of the present inhabitants.' Zionism, he believed, was 'of far profounder import than the desires and prejudices of the 700,000 Arabs who now inhabit that ancient land'.[2] The early Zionists were equally dismissive. According to the Russian Jew, Asher Ginsberg, they regarded the Palestinians either as 'savages who live like animals' or simply as 'non-existent'.[3] Many years later, Israel's prime minister, Golda Meir, announced that they had in fact never existed: 'There was no such thing as Palestinians. . . . It was not as though there was a Palestinian people in Palestine considering itself as a Palestinian people and we came and threw them out and took their country away from them. They did not exist.'[4] Subsequently an Israeli minister of education translated this fiction into official policy. 'It is important that our youth should know', he told Israeli schoolteachers, 'that when we returned to this country we did not find any other nation here and certainly no nation which had lived here for hundreds of years.' The Arabs whom they had encountered, he explained, were only Egyptian refugees who had arrived in the middle of the nineteenth century.[5]

This kind of propaganda could never have been really convincing outside Israel because so many people – travellers, merchants, missionaries and soldiers – had actually seen the Palestinians and knew that they existed even if they knew nothing else about them. Nevertheless, Western attitudes towards the Arabs have been conditioned almost unfailingly by ignorance or prejudice or both. Some of this has been unconscious, derived from Biblical associations – Israelites versus the Philistines, the fleshpots of Egypt and so on – and some of it is the product of a European anti-Islamic bias dating back to the Arab invasions of Spain and France in the eighth century. This bias is reflected in European literature from the *Song of Roland* to Chesterton's *Lepanto* and is well expressed by the title of a book written by the Dean of Norwich in 1697: *The True Nature of Imposture Fully Display'd in the Life of Mahomet.*

In the nineteenth century, when travellers came in increasing numbers to the Orient, Europeans began dividing up the Arabs into categories. The town Arabs, dismissed as dirty, idle and corrupt, were referred to as 'wogs' or 'gyppos'; in the words of Trollope's George Walker, they were 'a mean, false cowardly race'.[6] As a counterbalance, the desert Arab was introduced, the unfettered wanderer over great horizons, the nobleman of pure blood who cared nothing for the luxuries of the bazaar. The pasha with his belly and harem was contrasted with the hawk-faced Bedu struggling against the hardships of the desert. This romantic and largely ignorant adulation of the Bedouin was, perhaps, a particularly English cult, though it was also adopted by some Frenchmen. As the nomadic Arabs emerged as objects of unrestrained admiration, the townspeople received a still greater degree of revulsion. In the diaries and memoirs of Europeans, Bedouin worship receives almost as much space as descriptions of the squalor and vices of the cities and their inhabitants. The reaction of Sir Arthur Wauchope, British high commissioner in Palestine, was typical of this romantic fashion. On meeting an Arab delegation, he noted: 'One cannot help feeling that the very strain of noble blood which coursed through the veins of Saladin still animates the present-day sheikhs.'[7]

The writings of men like Doughty and Burton, the exploits of Lawrence and Glubb – people who knew and lived with the Bedouin instead of romanticizing about them on canvas and in verse – spread the cult of the desert Arab. It only began to fade with the coming of the oil and the revelation that a Bedu could be corrupted by material wealth as easily as anyone else. Yet it is still partly with us. Tourists in Jerusalem are carted off in air-conditioned coaches to take photographs of 'real Bedouin on camels'. And if the image is tarnished, it is too good a one to lose.

Cartoonists in the popular press frequently represent the Arabs with robes and hooked noses, usually on camels, often drawn so as to leave an impression of dirtiness.

Western attitudes towards the Arabs have undoubtedly been influenced by Zionist attempts to portray them as ignorant and backward people who needed foreign assistance in order to develop. Hence a fine Jewish scientist like Redcliffe Salaman, in the course of making remarks about the squalor of Arab villages, the filthiness of the children's clothes and the lack of education, would insist that 'the Arab is utterly incapable of developing the country alone.'[8] The Zionist leader, Chaim Weizmann, was fond of this tactic. In a letter in 1918 he decided to lecture Balfour (who had never been to Palestine) on the characteristics of the Palestinian Arab: though 'superficially clever and quick witted', he was by nature 'treacherous' and 'blackmails as often as he can'; if an official he was 'a roué', 'corrupt, inefficient, regretting the good old times when baksheesh was the only means by which matters administrative could be settled'; if a fellah (peasant), he was 'at least four centuries behind the times', and if an effendi (notable), he was 'dishonest, uneducated, greedy, and as unpatriotic as he is inefficient'.[9]

During the 1930s, when the popularity of the cinema was at its highest, films were frequently used to reinforce these ideas about the Palestinians.[10] One such film, shown in the United States in 1935, was financed by a Zionist organization, the Palestine Foundation Fund, and called *The Land of Promise*. Its one object was to contrast the decadent, backward society of Arab Palestine with the zealous idealism of the Zionist pioneers. The film begins with shots of Arabia and Egypt (though the audience is meant to believe it is Palestine) and a quick explanation: 'This is the land which God promised to Abraham. Once while the Jews lived in Islam it was the centre of a great civilization. When the Jews were driven out, the land gradually declined. Primitive life returned.' The rest of the film tells how primitive life is being erased by the hardworking Zionists. 'Where twenty years ago the soil was either marshland or just scratched with primitive plough,' everything was now different. 'A new life is starting. . . . Harvest is almost all the year round in Palestine.' Even Jaffa oranges, with which the crusaders were familiar, are claimed as a product of Jewish enterprise. 'Fields of oranges, or as they are called in Hebrew, the golden apple, cover the land where ten years ago not even thistles grew.'[11]

Such attitudes towards the Palestinians have not, however, been confined to the Zionists. They were and are widespread, and may still be found among contemporary journalists, television commentators and academics. One of the foremost American writers of the century, Edmund Wilson, could write this sort of unpleasant nonsense as late as 1956:

So the position of the Arabs in Israel – especially as one sees them in the country – is rather like that of the Navahos in the American Southwest: a once fierce but still picturesque, pathetically retarded people, cut off from the main community but presenting a recurrent problem. In a large Arab town like Acre, the squalor of the swarming streets inspires in an Israeli the same distaste that it does in a visiting Westerner. For the Jew, . . . the spectacle of flocks of urchins, dirty, untaught, diseased, bawling and shrieking and begging, in the narrow and dirty streets, inspires even moral horror.[12]

Although it is unlikely that he would do so now, Arthur Koestler could produce an even more distasteful passage in 1949. Describing the great tragedy of 1948, when more than three-quarters of a million Palestinians were turned into exile, he wrote: 'The old ones will tie a mattress and a brass coffee-pot on the donkey, the old woman will walk ahead leading the donkey by the rein and the old man will ride on it, wrapped in his keffiyeh, and sunk in solemn meditation about the lost opportunity of raping his youngest grandchild.'[13]

While the West has long viewed the Arab world with contempt, one of the most persistent contemporary images of the Palestinian Arab is quite new. To millions of people the word Palestinian now conjures up the picture of 'The Terrorist', that uncouth, shifty figure with a gun, prepared to kill people of any age, sex or colour, without apparent reason. Once again, it is an image which Zionism has sought to cultivate, because it inevitably lessens international sympathy for the Palestinians. Israel's prime minister, Menachem Begin, has called the Palestine Liberation Organization 'the blackest organization – other than the Nazi murder organizations – ever to arise in the annals of humanity'.[14] Yet the Irgun Zvai Leumi, the terrorist group which Begin himself led during the 1940s, killed as many civilians in a couple of afternoons as the Palestinian guerrillas have done in fifteen years of fighting against Israel. The blowing-up of the King David Hotel on 22 July 1948, and the massacre of the villagers of Deir Yassin on 10 April 1948, both perpetrated by the Irgun, caused the deaths of 345 people.

The Palestinian as the terrorist is less common in fiction than he is in cartoons or in letter columns in the press, but he nevertheless makes some regular appearances. He is given a star billing in Harold Robbins's dreadful 'novel', *The Pirate,* and also in a dreary thriller by Eric Ambler called *The Levanter.* The villain in the latter book, a guerrilla leader called Ghaled (the fact that this is neither a Palestinian nor an Arab name indicates the author's ignorance of his subject) is a repulsive and highly improbable person upon whom Ambler has heaped all the characteristics which Zionists like to associate with the Palestinians. He is always talking about killing Israeli civilians, bombarding Tel Aviv with Katyusha rockets or 'wading through a sea of blood'. The other Arabs in the book are older stereotypes described variously as 'stinking', 'pockmarked' or 'loathsome'.

There are between three and a half and four million Palestinians in the world today; less than one per cent are gunmen. Some of them live as a minority in Israel, others under military occupation in the West Bank and the Gaza Strip. Most are refugees, spread all over the Middle East. Yet few Palestinians have been assimilated to their host countries. The Palestinian national consciousness, the sense of identity, is far too strong. It has the vigour and the tenacity which is typically found in a people who have been robbed of their homeland.

At Bir Zeit University near Ramallah, a plaque hangs on one of the walls. The quotation is from George Bernard Shaw:

If you break a nation's nationality it will think of nothing else but getting it set again. It will listen to no reformer, to no philosopher, to no preacher, until the demand of the nationalist is granted. It will attend to no business, however vital, except the business of unification and liberation.[15]

PART ONE

Palestine and the Palestinians before 1948

1

Arab Palestine

In 1948 Palestine ceased to exist. It lost its name, it lost its territory, and it lost many of its people. Three-quarters of the land was taken by a movement which those people had opposed for half a century. Of the rest, the greater part was absorbed by the kingdom of Transjordan; only a strip of land, by Gaza, remained as Palestinian territory, and even that was controlled by Egypt. Of the inhabitants of Palestine, more than half became refugees. They went to all parts of the Arab world, to Lebanon, to Syria and to Transjordan, to Egypt and to Kuwait. A handful came to the West, to Britain, Australia and the United States. Some were lucky and were able to continue their existence in areas not taken by the Jewish state. Less than one-tenth remained in their villages and became Israeli citizens.

But the community had been broken, the nation which had struggled for birth since the death of the Ottoman Empire was stillborn. So nationhood became an idea, carried by its people into exile like the Jews who were taken to Babylon. They planned and dreamed of their return; and never did they accept that they, alone of all the Arab nations of the East, should be refused the right to decide their own future in their own land.

What sort of people are they, then, these Palestinian Arabs who, like the Jews and the Armenians, have become one of the world's dispersed peoples? In what sense do they constitute a separate people, in what way do they possess a distinct identity? Before it is possible to answer any of these questions, it is necessary to go back to a time before 1948, when the Palestinians were still living in their native land, and to look at their cultural and economic conditions, their customs and the basis of their society.

The Palestinians make no claim to racial purity. They are a people of highly diverse ethnic origins, compounded from all the conquerors of the land since the days of the Amorites and the Canaanites. Every invader until this century has, to some degree, left his mark upon the population. The people might become Aramaic speakers, they might accept Greek customs, but they remained the same people. The Canaanites and the Philistines of the tenth century BC were never deported. They remained in Palestine (which took its Arabic name, *Falastin,* from the Philistines) and their descendants formed, and still form, the core of the indigenous population.

The event which most decisively altered the character of the country was the Arab conquest of the seventh century AD. The Muhammadan Arabs brought with them their government, their language and their religion, and a majority of the inhabitants accepted all three. Palestine and its people became Arab but, once again, they remained the same people. There was little racial change in the population because the Arab conquerors were so few in number. As Professor Rodinson has explained: 'A small contingent of Arabs from Arabia did indeed conquer the country in the seventh century. But . . . the Palestinian population soon became Arabized under Arab domination, just as earlier it had been Hebraicized, Aramaicized, to some degree even Hellenized. It became Arab in a way that it was never to become Latinized or Ottomanized. The invaded melted with the invaders.'[1]

Although most of historical Palestine can be seen from one hill, Mount Ebal, the variations in land and people are remarkable. Gaza is like a town of the Nile Delta and its dark-skinned people resemble the Egyptians. In Galilee there are many with fair hair and blue eyes, whose ancestors may have been the Frankish Crusaders. In Jericho much of the population is negroid and evidently has no ethnic relationship with the nomadic Bedouin a few miles away in the Judaean desert. These are, perhaps, extreme differences; lesser ones exist in other areas. Anyone who visits places where a Palestinian population still exists in its historic setting will see them.

The present Palestinian population is estimated to be between

three and a half and four million people, which indicates that there
has been an enormous increase in population over the past seventy
years. A Turkish census on the eve of the First World War produced a figure of 630,000 Palestinian Arabs and a British census at the
end of 1922 estimated the total at about 670,000,[2] although this excluded the Bedouin, whose number was separately estimated at
71,000.[3] A second British census in 1931 indicated that the total
Arab population then exceeded 850,000 and an official estimate
for March 1947 showed another jump to more than 1,300,000.
Thus, in the thirty years between the collapse of the Ottoman Empire and the establishment of the State of Israel, the native Arab
population of Palestine doubled. And in the thirty years since
Palestine ceased to exist, the number of Palestinians has increased
by nearly three times.

From the seventh century the Sunnis, who are the largest sect of
orthodox Muslims, have formed the great majority of the population. But Palestine has always contained a large number of
minorities, some of whom arrived through historical accident.
During the 1880s Laurence Oliphant found nine distinct racial or
religious communities working on the land near Haifa. These included Muslim Serbs from Bosnia and Herzegovina who refused
to live under Austrian rule, Circassians from the Caucasus, a
Jewish settlement at Zimmarin, a nomadic tribe of Seljuk Turks
and a colony of German Templars at Haifa.[4] Other recent immigrants to Palestine included Baha'is from Persia and a few thousand Berbers from North Africa.

The Shiites, the chief minority sect of Islam, have never had
more than a few thousand followers in Palestine – their villages in
the north are an extension of the large Shia community in southern
Lebanon. The same is true of the Druzes, whose co-religionists are
concentrated in the Chouf region of southern Lebanon and in the
Jebel ed Druze in Syria. Their community in Palestine at the end
of the First World War consisted of about 7,000 people[5] spread
over a number of villages in Galilee and on Mount Carmel. With
nineteenth-century Europe, and particularly with English
travellers, the Druzes were highly popular. All descriptions of
them include adjectives like 'sturdy', 'brave' and 'independent'.
Major Conder, a British geographer in the nineteenth century,
found them 'stalwart' and 'able', 'the most interesting people in
Syria next to the Samaritans' (a tiny sect from Nablus), and only

regretted that their independent character made them unsuitable as servants.[6] Laurence Oliphant found that the Druzes were the only inhabitants 'to be relied upon' and considered them as 'by far the most agreeable class of people to live among in Palestine'.[7]

The largest and most important minority was the Christian. Estimated by the British authorities at 135,000 in 1944,[8] it has consistently formed slightly more than a tenth of the Arabic-speaking population. Some Christians are descended from converts of the third and fourth centuries who retained their religion during all the years of Islamic rule – the Atalla family, for example, lived as Christians on the same plot of land in Jerusalem for fifteen hundred years. Some are descendants of the Christian Arab tribes which fought with the Islamic armies against the Byzantine Empire in the seventh century.[9] Others have more recent origins such as a Crusading ancestry or a conversion to one of the Western churches in the nineteenth century.

Historically the Christians have been an urban community. Except in Galilee where there were a number of Christian villages, they concentrated on the towns of the west and central hill regions: Jerusalem, Jaffa and Haifa had large Christian populations and in Ramallah, Nazareth and Bethlehem Christians formed a majority. From the middle of the nineteenth century, when the Christian foreign missions began opening schools, mainly in the Jerusalem and Ramallah area, they enjoyed far higher standards of education than the Muslims. While the latter had to make do with state schools where the language of instruction was Turkish, or private Muslim schools which rarely provided secondary education, the Christians were able to benefit from such excellent schools as the Collège des Frères and St George's School in Jerusalem and the Friends Girls' and Boys' Schools set up by American Quakers in Ramallah.

The Christian community was divided almost equally between the Eastern (Greek Orthodox) Church and its Latin and Uniate rivals. The latter included the Roman Catholic Church, established at the time of the First Crusade, the Greek Catholics (converts from the Eastern Church) who were based in Haifa, and smaller groups such as the Maronites (an offshoot of the Maronite community of Lebanon), the Syrian Catholics and the Armenian Uniates. Still smaller congregations like the Copts and the Abyssinians, the Anglicans and the Syrian Orthodox clustered around

Jerusalem. Yet the predominant community ever since the failure of the Crusades has been the Greek Orthodox, a church which still suffers from an internal quarrel that has kept it politically feeble since the sixteenth century. From 1517, when the Turks took Jerusalem, the Orthodox Church in Palestine was dominated by men from the Greek community within the Ottoman Empire; since 1543 every patriarch has been Greek and so has a large majority of the bishops and higher clergy. This Greek predominance and the refusal of many of their number to learn Arabic caused such resentment among the lower clergy and laity, who were almost exclusively Arab, that the violence which broke out on several occasions (as in 1872 and 1908) had to be controlled by Turkish troops.

A large majority, around eighty-five per cent, of the Palestinian population were Sunni Muslims, most of them belonging to the Shafi rite and the remainder split between the Hanafi and the Hanbali. Although their religious centres were Jerusalem and Hebron, the Sunnis were spread throughout Palestine and dominated the political life of the region. Predominantly a rural community, unlike either the Jews or the Christians, they formed the bulk of Palestine's agricultural population at the end of the Ottoman Empire.

Unlike northern Syria, Palestine was never a land of vast estates. Certainly there were several families with about 10,000 to 15,000 acres of land and the Shawa family is thought to have owned some 25,000 acres in Gaza.[10] But most of Palestine was broken into smallholdings: half the farmers were working at subsistence level and cultivating holdings of less than eight acres. In addition, nearly a third of the rural families owned no land at all and were forced to work for their neighbours.[11] As the country population increased (at a much quicker rate than that of the towns) the average size of land holdings declined, according to British statistics, from nearly twenty acres in 1930 to about ten acres in 1944 (these figures are inflated by the inclusion of the large estates; the *median* size of holdings would have been considerably smaller).[12]

There were various systems of land tenure in Ottoman Palestine. Besides land rented from the large landowners or leased from religious charities and institutions, the most important categories of land were *mulk* and *miri*. *Mulk* corresponds roughly to the system of freehold, though under Muslim Shari'ah law the children must inherit at least two-thirds of their father's property at a ratio of two to one in favour of the sons. *Miri* was the system followed over most of Palestine. Technically the land was owned by the state and leased out to private individuals. In practice the tenants acquired ownership rights and, even though the land was never registered in their name, they were able to leave it to their descendants.

The variety of agricultural produce in Palestine was the result of sharp contrasts in climate and terrain from one part of the country to another. The Jordan valley enjoys a subtropical climate and produces dates and the fine oranges of Jericho. By the sea, near Jaffa, the Shamouti orange is grown; yet between the coastal plain and the Jordan, a distance of some thirty miles, the Judaean wilderness has its own sub-alpine conditions. From the mid-summer heat of the upper Jordan, the snows of Mount Hermon and the pines of Galilee can be seen. From the fruit-growing areas of Gaza it is a matter of miles to the Negev desert or the barren hills south of Jerusalem. The diversity of Palestinian agriculture thus becomes understandable: wine from Latrun and Bethlehem, olives from Nablus, walnuts from Jenin, wheat from Esdraelon, sesame from Haifa, almonds from Ramle, bananas from Jaffa and water-melons from Tulkarm. Palestine concentrated on arable farming for the standard of livestock was low: donkeys often had to be imported from Cyprus or Syria and the native sheep's wool was suitable only for making carpets.[13]

In spite of the variety of fruit and vegetables, Palestine has historically been a difficult land to farm. Only the coastal plain and the Vale of Esdraelon are naturally fertile. The rest consists mainly of steep limestone hills: in biblical Judaea and Samaria there is more land under rocks than there is under grass. Most of Palestine had to rely on the rains and, if these failed, there was seldom an alternative source of water. From the Mount of Olives to Jericho there is no natural water at all. Climate is also against the inhabitants and the enervating heat of the Jordan Valley, which reaches 48 °C (118 °F) in summer, is not conducive to manual labour. Apart from drought, other natural disasters in the past included occasional earthquakes and locust plagues, the latter appearing regularly every six years or so. In 1886 locusts destroyed most of the olive trees in Palestine.[14]

But there were also man-made problems. Commenting on the economic depression in 1879, the British consul in Jerusalem wrote that 'the drain of nearly all the able-bodied men for the late war, scanty harvests, insufficient rain, high prices and the ruinous loss inflicted on hundreds by the stoppage of the payment of the interest on Turkish government securities, have produced their natural consequences in widespread destitution and industrial and commercial stagnation.'[15] He went on to claim that these matters were made worse by the corruption of the Turkish administration. The Ottoman officials were, indeed, often corrupt and their systems of tax-farming and conscription concentrated on an already impoverished rural population. During the First World War the position of the fellahin further deteriorated when much of Palestine's woodland was cut down and used for fuel. Under the British mandate, living conditions improved with the introduction of health services and the beginning of state agricultural training; yet the thoroughness of British taxation methods provided an immense contrast with the inefficient ways of the Ottomans.

The Palestinian farmer was never able to operate at much more than subsistence level. The land, the climate and the Ottomans were all against him. Yet, as far as it went, agriculture was a reasonably efficient industry. As Sir John Hope Simpson's commission reported in 1930:

> The fellah is neither lazy nor unintelligent. He is a competent and capable agriculturalist, and there is little doubt that, were he given the chance of learning better methods and the capital which is a necessary preliminary to their employment, he would rapidly improve his position. . . . The ploughing of the fellah is above reproach. His field prepared for sowing is never inferior to that prepared by the most perfect implements, and sometimes it even surpasses all others. Its defect is only in its slowness.[16]

Before 1948 there were more than six hundred villages in Palestine. Many of these were independent agricultural communities which concentrated on producing enough to subsist on instead of attempting to cater for the urban markets. Given the remoteness of most villages, a farmer paid little attention to exporting his produce: he was concerned with being able to keep himself and his family. Thus he would grow a wide variety of crops in small quantities, arranging them so that they ripened in succession and thereby providing himself with food all the year round. For this type of farming, it was clearly an advantage to have parcels of land at different altitudes, as this would suit the farmer's need to diversify his crops: vegetables and citrus fruits in the valleys, olives, almonds and figs on the lower slopes and, higher up, cereals, vines and apples. During winter the farmer would cultivate crops like wheat, barley and lentils; in summer his produce would be more varied and might include tomatoes, melons and sesame. The villages were usually built on hilltops for health, climatic and security reasons. The ancient Israelites had lived on the hills on either side of the Jordan and used the valley only for farming. Similarly, the Arabs chose to live in the mountains where they were safe from malaria and Bedouin raiding-parties, descending to the valleys or the coastal plain only for the sowing and reaping of crops. During the nineteenth century, as security conditions in the region improved, the inhabitants of the Nablus mountains began building settlements on the plain to the west. By the end of the century these had become permanent villages, though their occupants retained close ties with their original villages near Nablus.

The village was usually self-sufficient economically and socially, a condition that made it both independent and introspective. Difficulties of communication and sharp differences in environment also produced strongly individualist traits. Two villages would stare at each other across a ravine yet so inbred were their inhabitants and so strong the local traditions that they might speak different dialects, cook different meals and wear different clothes. A Palestinian woman's village could be deduced from the embroidery on her dress.

The houses themselves were less individual and differed only according to region. Down the Jordan valley and along the coastal plain they were built from mud bricks;[17] in Galilee wattle and clay were used to build the walls and to cover the beams across the roof. In the hill regions in the centre of the country the houses were built of stone and, as timber was rare south of Galilee, they were given vaulted stone roofs. The architecture, however, was more uniform and a fellah's house usually consisted of a large room, split into different levels, and a courtyard. Additional rooms would be built on as the sons of the house married and increased the size of the family.[18] At harvesting a fellah would often leave his house and live on the land in a hut made of branches and rushes.

Village life revolved around the family* or clan (*hamula*), which in rural Palestine played a crucial role in both social and economic matters. Even the internal politics of the village would be conducted on family lines, the inhabitants not taking sides according to class or economic interest, but according to the position of the head of the family. As in all Arab and Mediterranean societies, the family was dominated by the men. Although kept landless until their father's death, the sons succeeded to most of the property and at the wedding of their sisters or daughters they received nearly all of the 'bride price'.[19] If there was a suitable choice, a young man was expected to marry one of his father's cousins, and, indeed, would usually be given the right of first refusal. Even if a man was not related to his bride she would almost invariably have come from his own village.

In such a society, without any sort of state or feudal security, the well-being of the family became the responsibility of its head. These duties would be various, ranging from looking after his unmarried female relations to finding jobs for his nephews and cousins. The woman's role in this society was clearly subordinate, yet it was nevertheless important and well-defined. Besides looking after their houses and children, they were required to play a significant part in the family's agricultural activities. In addition to baking the bread and storing the grain and fruit, they were expected to work in the fields and gather the harvest.

For many of the inhabitants the village frontiers were the farthest they ever went. Besides occasional visitations from Ottoman recruiting parties, the only authority seen by many villagers was the local sheikh. Before 1864 the sheikh was officially appointed by the local Ottoman governor to keep order and collect the taxes in an area usually consisting of four or five villages. In fact the appointment was a formality – the governor merely acknowledging the power of the strongest man in a district over which he himself had little real control. The sheikh was usually the largest landowner of the area who had inherited the title from his father or elder brother. In most matters he would act with almost total independence from the Ottoman authorities: he combined political

* Family here means far more than just a household. It includes all branches of the family, even distant cousins living in the same village.

predominance with military and judicial power. During the 1830s the sheikh's authority was undermined by the Egyptian occupation and, when Palestine was once again brought within the boundaries of the Empire, the Ottomans passed a series of administrative laws – included in the Tanzimat reforms – designed to strengthen the influence of the local governor in the rural areas. As a consequence of these laws the sheikhs were shorn of their military and judicial powers and replaced by a much less powerful figure, the village mukhtar. Nevertheless, the sheikhs' social standing was usually so much higher than that of the mukhtars that they were able to retain much of their authority until the British occupation in 1917.

The office of mukhtar was established in 1864. Unlike the traditional sheikh, the mukhtar's position was not hereditary: he was merely a government agent charged with a number of minor duties but possessing no independent authority. Although under the Ottomans candidates for the post were required to be literate and to possess a certain amount of property, the mukhtars were seldom either the best educated or the wealthiest members of the village. During British rule between 1917 and 1948 the property qualification was dropped and the mukhtars were given a government salary. They then became even more closely linked with the government and were consequently distrusted by their villagers.

By the turn of the century the rivalry between the sheikhs and the mukhtars was already losing its significance. Political power was moving away from the rural areas towards the great families of the cities, in particular to the old urban aristocracy of Jerusalem. This shift was encouraged by the Ottomans as the notables of the cities were easier to watch than the rural sheikhs and were therefore more inclined to co-operate with the authorities. They were thus promoted to positions of importance both inside Palestine and throughout the Empire. Palestinians served in Syria and Iraq, one became governor of Yemen and several became representatives in the Ottoman parliament.[20] The predominance of the urban families in political affairs continued during the mandate and, of the thirty-two members of the Arab Higher Committee from 1936 to 1948, only four had rural backgrounds.[21]

It was not until the nineteenth century that Jerusalem became the pre-eminent city in Palestine, although, according to Edward Lear, it was still in 1858 the 'foulest and odiousest place on earth'.[22] This new importance was partly the result of Jewish immigration and partly the consequence of the increased activity of the foreign churches. There were five thousand Russian pilgrims a year visiting Jerusalem in the 1880s[23] and, like the Jews and various Western nations, the Russians built a large compound outside the walls to the west of the city. All sorts of Christian sects poured into Jerusalem and brought with them the usual collection of cranks. One group of Swedes solemnly set off every afternoon along the Jericho road expecting to meet the Messiah.

But Jerusalem's political pre-eminence was the result of an Ottoman administrative decision to make the sanjak, or district, of Jerusalem no longer responsible to the governors of either Sidon or Damascus, as it had previously been, but to place it directly under the Sublime Porte. This development, which elevated Jerusalem to the same level as Damascus itself, also assured the city primacy over the Palestinian cities of Jaffa, Nablus and Gaza. Thus, until the disintegration of Palestine, the Jerusalem notables were the leaders of the country's population, a fact which often caused resentment among the people of other regions.

In the 1850s the British consul described the situation in Jerusalem thus: 'It should be mentioned that a close corporation of Arab families, not recognized by law, but influential by position, usurped all the municipal offices among them.'[24] Although there were old Christian families like the Cattans and the Atallas, only the great Sunni families possessed real political weight. The most important were the Husseinis, the Khalidis, the Alamis, the Nashashibis, the Jarallahs, and the Nuseibehs. The power of these families was based not so much on wealth and property (though there were families like the Abd al-Hadis who owned seventeen villages near Nablus), but on inherited prestige. The two most important posts in the Ottoman administration were the mufti of Jerusalem and the naqib al-ashraf (head of the religious endowments). Although neither of them was a strictly hereditary position only a member of one of the great families ever held them; from the eighteenth century both the Husseinis and the Alamis have at different times held each title and the Jarallahs have frequently been muftis of Jerusalem.

These families lived together in the Old City until the end of the nineteenth century. In a remarkable display of historical continuity they lived for centuries in the same places fulfilling the same duties as their ancestors. Since the seventh century the Nuseibehs have been guardians of the Holy Sepulchre (in order to avoid rivalry between the churches the honour was awarded to a Muslim); their family specialized in education and government service. The Jarallahs were a religious family who also practised law; the Khalidis, the leading liberal and reformist family, concentrated on education and politics. The Khatib family (*khatib* means preacher in Arabic) have produced the preachers and the conductors of services in al-Aqsa mosque for eight hundred years.

The second half of the nineteenth century saw rapid changes in the life-style of these families. Until then they had lived deep in the old quarters of the walled city, split up among the Muslim areas and the smaller Christian, Armenian and Jewish quarters. Now they began to move out of the city, the Alami family leading the way, to the orchards and hillsides around Jerusalem. The houses they built were of light Nablus stone, fashioned by the stonemasons of Bethlehem, with red tiled roofs and high Venetian-style windows. In 1899 the Atallas moved a couple of miles southwards and built alongside the Bethlehem road. Other Christian families followed them. Muslims like the Alamis, the Saids and the Jarallahs preferred the northern side of the city, where they built the Musrara quarter, to the west of the road to Nablus.

Western education was responsible for some of the changes, and the new American and British schools clearly influenced the ideas and manners of their pupils. One visible result was the change in interior decoration. By the turn of the century the Alami household had shed the heavy Damascus furniture with its mother-of-pearl inlay and had acquired sofas and armchairs instead of divans. In 1884 Laurence Oliphant remarked that one notable had 'so far adopted civilized habits that he sleeps on a bed himself, and not on mats on the floor, like his forefathers'. In good Victorian fashion he added: 'Women even of the poorer classes are introducing the fashion of wearing gowns, adding a table and four chairs to their domestic furniture, and have even gone the length of sleeping on bedsteads, though I have not yet pried sufficiently into nocturnal mysteries to know whether, when they go to bed, they have progressed in civilization so far as to undress.'[25]

Clothes, too, were naturally affected and in fact the divan's disappearance was largely the result of the introduction of trousers and the frock-coat which made it difficult to sit cross-legged. Major

Conder saw the occidental revolution as beginning in 1872 and as finished a decade later when the country had become 'a Levantine land, where Western fabrics, Western ideas, and even Western languages, meet the traveller at every point'.[26] Laurence Oliphant claimed that the only concession to Oriental dress which the wealthy Palestinians still made was the retention of the *tarboosh* (the red fez cap).[27] Frances Newton, writing a couple of decades later, regretted that even this had disappeared and had been replaced by the homburg.[28] At the turn of the century, Beirut had become the chief distribution centre for Western clothes, and prints, parasols and high-heeled slippers were transported down the coast to Palestine.

The Palestinian economy depended mainly on agriculture, for the country possessed no raw materials. Thus there was little opportunity for the emergence of a large entrepreneurial class. Yet there had always been a small business community based on a few minor industries, and, although its prosperity had been wrecked by the discovery of the sea route to India in the fifteenth century, it had survived in a modest way. According to C.F. Volney, Nablus was the most prosperous town in the country during the eighteenth century, depending for its wealth on wheat and olive oil.[29] Soap made from olives had always been the main manufacture of Palestine. Nablus was the centre of soap-making although there were also factories in Gaza, Ramle and Hebron.[29] Gaza was also famous for its cotton-weaving looms – according to Volney there were 500 of them – and Hebron is still known for its glass workshops.

Agriculture apart, inland Palestine was thus a place of small industries and artisan shops, many of them occupied by Christians. According to the 1931 population census, two Muslims out of three were agriculturalists, yet only one Christian in seven worked on the land. Well educated Christians entered commerce and the liberal professions: doctors, lawyers, goldsmiths, grocers, masons and ironsmiths were more likely to be Christians than Muslims. Other traditional artisans among the Christians included millers, carpenters, cobblers, potters and tanners. By contrast, government service was a career traditionally accepted by Muslim families and only rarely by Christians, though this state of affairs was reversed during the mandate.

Throughout the 1920s and 1930s, as Jewish purchases of good

farmland coincided with an increase in the Palestinian rural population, the fellahin were leaving the land in great numbers. Short of emigration, which was not an option open to many of them, the Mediterranean ports seemed to offer the only chance of a decent life. Haifa and Jaffa were the principal goals and by 1935 large shanty towns had sprung up outside both. Jaffa had become an important harbour after 1864 when it was given a lighthouse and a landing space. In 1892 its importance was enhanced by the opening of a shipping line with Liverpool, yet it remained an extremely inefficient port and it was so full of rocks that passengers and goods had to be rowed ashore in boats. Its only rival was Haifa, Acre having degenerated into a disused fortress, and during the reign (1876 – 1909) of Sultan Abdul Hamid the population of both Haifa and Jaffa increased enormously. Haifa's position was further strengthened by the massive development works undertaken during the mandate. The third most important port was Gaza. While Jaffa concentrated on the export of soap, oranges and sesame, Gaza was the main outlet for the grain produced around Hebron and Beersheba.[31] In the nineteenth century it was one of the principal suppliers of barley to the German beer industry.

Communications in Palestine were also improving in the second half of the nineteenth century. The road network, which had been originally laid down by the Romans, was being expanded and a carriageway between Jerusalem and Jaffa opened in 1867 was followed by roads in Nablus and Galilee. Even the fastidious Laurence Oliphant could write in 1885: 'I consider the road from Jerusalem to Jericho in the present day as safe as Broadway, at all events in the daytime.'[32] Railway building was also started: the Jaffa – Jerusalem line was completed in 1892, and other lines were laid from Haifa a few years later.

The Bedouin are in almost every way peripheral to a description of the Palestinian economy and social life prior to 1948, but they were nevertheless Palestinian Arabs. Frequently glorified by Europeans at the expense of the settled Arabs – 'It is only in the desert that the true Arab is to be found' is a typical remark of English travellers[33] – the life of the Bedouin was much less romantic than Edwardian ladies imagined. They had little useful contact with the rest of the population and they led very different lives. In Palestine they lived either in caves or in portable tents of black goat's hair, passing a semi-sedentary life on the edge of the desert.[34] Their relationship with other Palestinians was distant and, from the point of view of the fellahin, unpleasant. The latter's villages were built on the crests of hills rather than in the fertile valleys principally because they were easier to defend from marauding Bedouin in search of food. Often the fellahin had to pay one tribe a retainer to protect them from others.[35] One of the most beautiful of all Palestinian songs is the lament of a peasant girl who has been carried off by the Bedouin.[36]

Small groups of nomads have traditionally lived on the edges of cultivated land in Judaea and in northern Palestine. In Galilee Bedouin life centred not on camels (as it did further south) but on sheep, goats and, to a lesser extent, water buffalo. These northern groups spoke their own form of Arabic and some of them were of Kurdish and Turkoman origins. The bulk of Palestine's Bedouin, however, has always been concentrated in the Negev desert bordering on Sinai, Jordan and the Red Sea. Known as the Gaza tribes, their total number during the years of the British mandate is variously estimated at between 60,000 and 80,000.[37] Although there have been Bedouin tribes in the Negev since the fifth century,[38] their size and importance remained small until further migrations at the time of the Ottoman conquest of Palestine a thousand years later. The Turks attempted to settle the Bedouin in agricultural communities, but without success, and the principal tribes – the Tayaha with its twenty-eight sub-tribes and the Terabin with twenty-five – continued their nomadic existence until the First World War.[39] A radical change in their life-style then took place, not as a result of British rule but as a consequence of technological changes which have reduced nomadic populations all over the world. Large numbers of tribesmen found themselves forced to take up permanent agricultural work as the traditional supports of the Bedouin economy collapsed. The most important of all Bedouin industries – the rearing of camels and horses – was virtually destroyed by the introduction of the motor car. One district commissioner for Beersheba during the mandate pointed out that a camel which might have been sold for £20 or £30 in 1914 would fetch only £3 twenty years later.[40] With the establishment of the State of Israel in 1948, the Bedouin suffered further upheavals; these will be discussed in Chapter 5.

2

The Emergence of National Identity

'What are Palestinians?' once asked Mr Levi Eshkol, Israel's prime minister during the late sixties. It was not an innocent question from an inquisitive mind. Eshkol was not patiently awaiting an answer – because the question had been asked too many times before, by Zionist leaders attempting to dismiss the claims of the Palestinian people. When Einstein wanted to know what would happen to the Arabs if the Zionists' plans were successful, Weizmann pooh-poohed: 'What Arabs? They are hardly of any consequence.'[1] That has always been the Zionist line: the Palestinians are not *important* and, in order to convince others of this, Golda Meir and her colleagues have had to pretend that they do not really exist. And even if they are forced to admit their existence as people, it is not as Palestinians but as Arabs. That is why Abba Eban, in his autobiography, places the word 'Palestinians' within quotation marks.[2] The Zionists assert that the Palestinians form no nation, that they have never formed a nation, and that they are inseparable from other Arabs of the Fertile Crescent. Palestine, they declare, is an artificial entity created by the British who 'invented' the Palestinians in 1925 when the inhabitants of the old Ottoman Empire became 'redesignated'.[3] They say that the term 'Syria' included, until the First World War, the areas now known as Lebanon, Jordan and Palestine, and point out that in 1840 the Treaty of London refers to the district of Acre (in northern Palestine) as 'Southern Syria'.

Some of this is true. There never was a Palestinian national state. Nor did the people living within the borders of what was later known as Palestine previously consider themselves as members of a clearly defined geographical unit. They had their local loyalties, mainly to the sanjak of Jerusalem where most of them lived, and wider commitments to the Ottoman Empire. Those living in the north of Palestine, in the sanjaks of Acre and Nablus, were usually linked administratively to Damascus or Sidon and therefore would have felt no specifically Palestinian loyalty. The Tuqan family, for example, were spread throughout the province of Syria: originally from Hama in central Syria, one branch had settled in Nablus and another had moved south-east across the Jordan: a third remained in Syria. Since they were all living in the same province of the Ottoman Empire, they obviously never regarded themselves as being politically separated. Today the Tuqans live under three different regimes and are forced to think of themselves as citizens of different nations.

The discouragement of regional loyalties was an important component of Turkish policy in the declining years of the Empire. The Ottoman break-up was in the long run inevitable because the Western powers could not indefinitely check each other's ambitions in the Balkans and the Middle East. But the process of disintegration was slowed down by Sultan Abdul Hamid's ingenious handling of his Arab territories. In an attempt to stress the similarity of interests between Turks and Arabs, he founded mosques and schools throughout Syria and the Levant and ordered the construction of the Hejaz railway. A parliament was elected in 1877, though admittedly soon ignored, another in 1908 and a third, after the Sultan's deposition, in 1912. The deputies came from all parts of the Empire: half of them were Turks, nearly a quarter were Arabs and the rest consisted mainly of Albanians, Greeks and Armenians. By presenting themselves as rulers over a multinational empire which gave political autonomy and parliamentary representation to its minorities, Abdul Hamid and his successors were able to prolong the life of their regime. In Palestine, though the corruption of the Ottomans, their conscription demands and their taxation system caused a certain amount of resentment, the Turks attracted no popular hatred until the outbreak of the First World War. Unsurprisingly, in view of their subsequent history, many elderly Palestinians look back at the Ottoman era with nostalgia. Musa Alami, one of the most distinguished Palestinians of his generation, recalls that the Arabs regarded the Turks as partners rather than oppressors. The Ottoman garrisons were miniscule and active opposition scarce. Above all, Palestine was largely ruled by Palestinian officials. Musa Alami claims that 'a greater degree of freedom and self-government existed in Palestine than in many Turkish provinces.'[4]

The Arab nationalist movement, which, in conjunction with the British army, finally destroyed the Ottoman Empire, was initially a cultural force. If there was any political content to pan-Arab feeling at the end of the nineteenth century it was aimed not at the Turks but at Western interference in the Arab world. During the 1880s the British consul in Jerusalem reported strong anti-British feeling at the time of the campaigns against 'Arabi in Egypt and the Mahdi in the Sudan.'[5] But there was little political unrest directed against the Ottomans.

Arab nationalism, inconsistent and ill-defined though it has been from the beginning, started as an intellectual movement inspired by Arab Christians of the Levant who sought to promote Arab 'consciousness' by a revival of Arabic culture, in particular of Arabic as a language. They grouped themselves into societies such as the Syrian Scientific Society and the Society of Arts and Sciences and, even though these led on to more political organizations, opposition to the Ottoman Empire was confined to intellectual circles until the First World War. The number of Palestinians who were members of societies aiming to overthrow the Turks before 1914 can be measured in tens.[6] Ahmed Tuqan, an elderly Palestinian from Nablus who became foreign minister of Jordan, remembers the Ottomans vividly and recalls that there was no popular movement against the Turks until after the war had broken out. Had it not been for the repressive measures taken by the Turkish governor against the leaders of the nationalist movement, he believes there would have been no Arab uprising in Syria and Palestine. Even after the execution of several nationalists in Beirut and Damascus, there were numbers of Palestinians, especially from Jerusalem, who were reluctant to change their allegiance. Later, when Britain and France took control of the Middle East in the early 1920s, a large group of Palestinians, including members of most of the great Jerusalem families, clamoured for the return of Turkish rule.[7]

With the Ottoman option closed by the war, the Palestinians

turned to Arab nationalism. Aware of the threat from the Western powers, and particularly from the Zionist movement to which Britain had committed itself, they demanded Arab independence and unity with the rest of traditional Syria. As an American commission sent to the Middle East by President Wilson, reported: 'Muslim and Christian Arabs alike desired to preserve the unity of the country with Syria of which they considered Palestine to be both historically and geographically a part.'[8] While they waited for Britain to honour its pledges made to the sharif of Mecca during the war (see pages 47-8) the Palestinians were eager to be associated with the promised Arab state. Only when it became clear that the Middle East was to be carved up and that France was going to grab Syria in any event, did the Palestinians turn back from the Arab nationalist ideal and begin to concentrate on their own struggle against Britain and Zionism.

Until 1920, then, there was no popular sense of Palestinian destiny. The people had never regarded themselves as Palestinians or as separate from other Arabs. For those who lived in its sanjak and considered Jerusalem as their capital city, there was probably a feeling of cultural and economic identity, coupled with a wider political affiliation to Istanbul. It was, perhaps, like the attitude of Yorkshiremen to England for although there was no loyalty to Palestine as a geographical unit there were other ties which bound the Palestinians and kept them to some extent distinct from their neighbours.

The name Palestine, for instance, has existed in various forms since the days of the Greeks. The Greek *Palaistiné* became Latin *Palaestina* and later the Arabic *Falastin*.[9] Throughout all these ages, and until the Ottoman period, Palestine was an administrative unit subdivided into smaller areas. Under the Turkish supremacy, the sanjaks were generally kept separate, though as late as the 1850s the districts of Nablus and Gaza briefly became part of the sanjak of Jerusalem.[10] Other factors contributed to a nascent Palestinian identity: the religious celebrations at Nebi Musa, which were attended by Muslims from all over Palestine; the jurisdiction of the larger Christian communities, which took into account the historical boundaries of Palestine; the establishment in 1910 of Jerusalem as a legal centre with its own court of appeal; and the foundation, a year later in Jaffa, of the newspaper *Falastin*. Furthermore, Palestine and its inhabitants were generally regarded as distinct from their neighbours by Europe and America. In 1851 Flaubert's travelling companion, Maxime du Camp, published a book of photographs under the title *Égypte, Nubie, Palestine et Syrie* and an 1876 Baedeker was called *Palestine and Syria.* Later, during the famous correspondence between Theodor Herzl and Sultan Abdul Hamid, both men referred specifically to 'Palestine' – and neither seems to have had much doubt as to what they were talking about.

When Europe came to dispose of the Ottoman Empire after the First World War, it clearly considered Palestine as a distinct entity entitled to eventual independence and nationhood. In 1922 Britain was granted the Palestine mandate by the League of Nations. As described in Article 22 of the League's Covenant, the mandate was based on the principle of self-determination and on the provisional recognition of the Palestinian people as an independent nation: 'Certain communities formerly belonging to the Turkish Empire (i.e. Syria, Iraq, Lebanon, Transjordan and Palestine) have reached a stage of development where their existence as independent nations can be provisionally recognized subject to the rendering of administrative advice and assistance by a mandatory until such time as they are able to stand alone.'

As has happened with other peoples, nationalism among the Palestinians only emerged in the presence of an external threat. The Zionist movement, active in Palestine during the last decades of the Ottoman Empire, could be clearly seen as such a threat and was therefore partly responsible for the growth of Palestinian nationalism. Opposition to Zionism was already widespread at the turn of the century as friction developed between the Palestinian fellahin and the Zionist colonists financed by Baron de Hirsch and the Rothschild family. It became more intense as Jewish immigration increased. Although Palestine's small community of Sephardic Jews had always enjoyed good relations with the Arabs, the new immigrants were European Ashkenazim who made no attempt to integrate themselves into the existing society: they refused to learn Arabic and, as a matter of principle, they boycotted Arab shops and Arab labour. The Zionists were intent on creating their own society and they had little interest in anything else. As the Palestine correspondent of the main Zionist newspaper, *Ha'Olam,* lamented as early as 1911: 'We forgot altogether that there are Arabs in Palestine, and discovered them only in recent years. . . . We paid no attention to them; we never even tried to find friends among them.'[11]

Zionism became a political issue for the Arabs shortly before the First World War. It was discussed in the Ottoman parliament and debated in the press. In 1914 its effect on Arab public opinion made it an election issue. Raghib al-Nashashibi, one of the victorious candidates in Jerusalem, promised that 'if I am elected as a deputy I will dedicate all my strength day and night to remove the damage and danger awaiting us through the Zionists and Zionism.'[12] Awareness of the threat from Zionism and an understanding of its eventual ambition was common among the Arabs during the last years of the Empire. As one Palestinian nationalist recorded in his diary: 'I would not hate the Zionist movement but for its attempt to build its existence on the rubble of another [people].'[13]

Increasing numbers of Palestinians thus became aware of the Zionist danger and by the 1920s, despite the dissimulation practised by Weizmann and his colleagues, the Zionist programme had become pretty clear to most people. It was, after all, on the record for those who cared to look. At the Basle conference in 1897 Herzl claimed to have founded the Jewish state though one of his allies tried to 'find a circumlocution that would express all we want, but would say it in a way so as to avoid provoking the Turkish rulers of the coveted land'.[14] At the time of the Balfour Declaration, when the Zionist leaders were talking in public only of a 'national home', they were openly planning the frontiers of their future state. 'The Jewish commonwealth of Palestine is a *fact*,' wrote a leading American Zionist in 1919, 'and we are now fixing the boundaries of the state.'[15]

Israel Zangwill, one of the prophetic figures of Zionism, declared in the same year that 'The Jews must possess Palestine as the Arabs are to possess Arabia or the Poles Poland.'[16] Even Weizmann, for all his honeyed words to the British Foreign Office, was unable to pretend indefinitely that all he was aiming for was a 'national home' without political significance. In a telegram sent to an associate at the beginning of 1919, Weizmann expressed the hope that 'the whole administration of Palestine shall be so formed as to make of Palestine a Jewish commonwealth under British trusteeship.'[17] Unfortunately the telegram was seen by Lord Curzon who asked:

What is a commonwealth? I turn to my dictionaries and find it there defined: 'a state', 'a body politic', 'an independent community', 'a republic'. . . . What then is the good of shutting our eyes to the fact that this is what the Zionists are after, and that the British trusteeship is a mere screen behind which to work for this end? And the case is rendered not the better but the worse if Weizmann says this sort of thing to his friend but sings to a different tune in public.[18]

On the same day Curzon wrote to Balfour: 'I feel tolerably sure that while Weizmann may say one thing to you, or while you may mean one thing by a national home, he is out for something quite different. He contemplates a Jewish state, a Jewish nation, a subordinate population of Arabs etc., ruled by Jews; the Jews in possession of the fat of the land, and directing the administration.'[19]

This was a conclusion shared by other politicians and officials. As the chief administrator at the beginning of the mandate, General Sir Louis Bols, complained: 'It is manifestly impossible to please partisans who officially claim nothing more than a national home but in reality will be satisfied with nothing less than a Jewish state and all that it politically implies.'[20]

If this, then, was the Zionists' aim, what role did they envisage for the inhabitants of the country, the Palestinians? Again, once the foliage of deliberate deception is brushed away, the answer becomes obvious. Weizmann, momentarily losing control of his emotions, once told an English audience that the Zionists will 'finally establish such a society in Palestine that Palestine shall be as Jewish as England is English, or America is American.'[21] And how would this affect the Palestinians? Herzl had already supplied the answer twenty years or so previously: the Zionists would 'gently expropriate' Arab property and 'try to spirit the penniless population across the border by procuring employment for it in the transit countries, while denying it any employment in our own country'.[22]

'Spiriting' or expelling the native population across the border was also high on Weizmann's agenda. In 1931 he explained to the high commissioner in Jerusalem that he wanted to settle the Palestinians in Transjordan;[23] seven years later, when the Peel commission recommended handing over Galilee with its Arab majority to a Jewish state, Weizmann told the colonial secretary that he would help Britain to move the Arabs out of Galilee and across the River Jordan.[24]

Some Zionists were even blunter than this, at least to each other. Joseph Weitz, who was in charge of Jewish colonizing activities, wrote in 1940:

> Between ourselves it must be clear that there is no room for both peoples together in this country. . . . We shall not achieve our goal of being an independent people with the Arabs in this small country. The only solution is a Palestine, at least Western Palestine (west of the Jordan river) without Arabs. . . . And there is no other way than to transfer the Arabs from here to the neighbouring countries, to transfer all of them; not one village, not one tribe should be left.[25]

A British Zionist, Lieutenant-Commander the Hon. J.M. Kenworthy, M.P., trumped even this. At a discussion of the Royal Institute of International Affairs in January 1931 he advocated still wider Jewish expansion. 'Why', he asked, 'should not the Jews be allowed to settle in Transjordania [sic], a fertile, sparsely inhabited area which they should be allowed to colonize as the Americans colonized the land to the west of New England?' If they encountered hostility, 'They could easily defend themselves there as the Americans had defended themselves against the Red Indians.'[26] It hardly needs adding that the fate of the Palestinian Arabs was of as much interest to Kenworthy as the fate of the Red Indian tribes.

While the intricacies of Zionist diplomacy in the West were largely unperceived by the Palestinians, there was enough evidence on the ground for them to know what was going on. Besides, few Zionists took much trouble to hide their intentions. In a passage that became widely circulated, Sir Alfred Mond (later Lord Melchett) wrote: 'The day in which the Temple will be rebuilt is nigh, and I shall work for the rest of my life to rebuild Solomon's Temple in the place of the Mosque of Aqsa.'[27] Since the mosque is on the holiest Islamic site outside Arabia, the Palestinians were justifiably anxious about the fate of their holy places. All through the mandate period they were given other glimpses of the Zionist programme. The 1926 edition of the *Encyclopaedia Britannica* announced that 'The Jews are looking forward to the redemption of

Israel . . . [and] the restoration of the Jewish state.'[28] A previous edition (1919) had described the Jewish national flag as the flag of the state of Palestine and, when asked for an explanation, the editor admitted that 'its inclusion was somewhat premature'.[29] In 1945 there was a near riot in the Ramallah Friends Boys' School when the American Consulate presented the library with a copy of *Compton's Encyclopaedia* – again with the Star of David as the Palestinian flag.[30]

The most disturbing feature from the Palestinian point of view was the manner in which the Zionists were able to establish their independence from the government and from the indigenous society. Even under the Ottomans they had recorded several gains: they had begun their own schools, established their own bank and set up their own civil courts. Soon after the war they founded the kibbutz movement and established the Hebrew University and the Federation of Hebrew Labour. Already, by 1920, the Zionists had set up the framework of a self-contained community, to the anger and frustration of the Arabs. Sir Louis Bols enumerated the causes of Arab discontent in a dispatch in 1920: 'The introduction of the Hebrew tongue as an official language; the setting up of a Jewish judicature; the whole fabric of government of the Zionist Commission of which they [the Arabs] are well aware; the special travelling privileges to members of the Zionist Commission; this has firmly and absolutely convinced the non-Jewish [i.e. Arab] elements of our partiality.'[31] At the same time a British commission of inquiry, investigating the Jaffa troubles of the year before, reported: 'The fundamental cause of the Jaffa riots and the subsequent acts of violence was a feeling among the Arabs of discontent with, and hostility to, the Jews, due to political and economic causes and connected with Jewish immigration, and with their conception of Zionist policy as derived from Jewish exponents.'[32]

As the Zionist – Palestinian enmity revolves above all around the question of land, it was natural that the land issue should have come to dominate all others. Land sales to Jews had begun before the First World War with the connivance of the Ottoman authorities, who hoped they would thereby attract Jewish capital to their exhausted economy.[33] These sales were concentrated mainly in the fertile valleys in the north and along the coastal plain. During the 1920s the Zionists continued buying land in these regions, expanding around the Bay of Haifa and also into Galilee. They registered their largest deals with the Beirut families of Sursock and Tayyan who owned enormous estates in the Vale of Esdraelon and the Wadi Hawarith. It was non-Palestinian absentee landlords such as these who gave the Zionists wide areas of the most fertile land in Palestine. According to Dr Ruppin of the Jewish Agency, ninety per cent of all land bought before 1929 came from absentee landlords.[34]

When the Beirut merchants, who had bought land as an investment following the Ottoman Land Code of 1858, had been bought out, the Zionists turned their attention elsewhere. One suitable target was the Eastern Orthodox Patriarchate, which had suffered a financial disaster after the Bolshevik revolution of 1917. Stripped of its property inside Russia and denied the donations previously sent by the Russian Church, the Patriarchate was forced to sell much of its property in Palestine in order to remain solvent. Another target was the Palestinian aristocracy itself. While its members lambasted anyone found selling land to the Zionists and even formed organizations such as 'The Arab Company for the Return of the Lands in Palestine', some of them were secretly selling off pieces of their own properties. As the German consul in Jerusalem drily pointed out in 1933, the Arab leaders 'in daylight were crying out against Jewish immigration and in the darkness of the nights were selling lands to the Jews'.[35]

From the time of the first land sales in 1878 until the outbreak of the Palestinian revolt in 1936, the Zionists acquired over half their land from absentee landowners, a quarter from the Palestinian landlords, and most of the rest from churches and foreign companies.[36] Only a small fraction, less than one-tenth, was bought from the fellahin and, in most cases, the sales were forced upon them. When the British closed the Ottoman-sponsored Agricultural Bank, they virtually prevented the fellah from obtaining credit: he was then forced either to sell a part of his land in order to develop the rest or to turn to moneylenders who were likely to charge some thirty per cent interest – an impossible rate for most farmers.[37] In many instances, therefore, the fellahin had no option but to sell their land. As Sir John Chancellor, the high commissioner, explained in a letter for King George V in May 1930: 'They [the fellahin] are not free agents in the matter: they are distressingly poor and are heavily in debt to usurious moneylenders. When they are pressed by their creditors, and a Jewish land broker appears with money in his hand, the Arabs have no alternative but to sell their land in order to clear themselves of their liabilities.'[38]

Zionism's goal and its justification – summed up in Zangwill's slogan, 'A land without people for a people without land'[39] – was based from the beginning on an immense fallacy. The land was never without people; even in 1891 the Russian Jew, Asher Ginsberg, wrote that it was difficult to find any uncultivated farmland in Palestine.[40] Forty years later Sir John Hope Simpson reported to his government that there was not enough farming land even for the rural Arab population.[41] As Sir John Chancellor informed the king: 'The facts of the land situation are that all the cultivable land in Palestine is now occupied; and no more land can be sold to the Jews without dispossessing Arab cultivators and creating a class of landless peasants – a process which has already begun.'[42]

A year later he wrote with still greater urgency: 'Palestine is now full: without infringing that part of the Mandate which requires us to safeguard the rights of the existing non-Jewish communities, we cannot allow any more Jews to enter the country. . . . If . . . Jewish immigration on a large scale is allowed . . . we shall be forcing on the country at the point of British bayonets an alien population which is antipathetic to the indigenous population.'[43]

In 1930 Chancellor had stressed 'the need for taking measures to ensure the Arab agricultural population shall not be dispossessed of their land by the sale to the Jews'.[44] This was indeed the heart of the problem, for, while the fellahin were generally able to hold on to their own property, they had no control over land on which they were only tenants. Consequently, in all the large deals between the Zionists and the landowners it was the fellahin who were the losers. The Jews acquired the land, the landlords took the money and nobody paid attention to the fate of the tenants. When the Lebanese Sursocks sold 60,000 acres in the Vale of Esdraelon between 1912 and 1925, they pocketed nearly three-quarters of a million pounds and went happily back to Beirut. Twenty-one Arab villages were flattened and their 8,000 inhabitants evicted.[45] As eviction orders increased over the following years, British police were used to force villagers from their homes. There was never a chance for them to remain on the land as tenants of the new Jewish owners because this was expressly prevented by the Zionist organizations. The constitution of the Jewish Agency, for example, declared that 'it shall be deemed a matter of principle that Jewish labour shall be employed [on Agency property]'; land was leased by the Jewish National Fund on condition that it was cultivated 'only with Jewish labour', and the Palestine Foundation Fund insisted that their settlers 'hire Jewish workmen only'.[46] Even in private Jewish businesses Arab labour was usually boycotted. In March 1949 the *Jewish Frontier* announced that 'unemployment among Jews at the end of 1938 was much reduced owing to the replacement of Arab labour in plantations, increased security measures and public works. . . . This year for the first time only Jewish workers are employed in Jewish-owned orange groves.'[47] Arnold Toynbee had foreseen this several years previously. 'All the Palestinian land which is purchased by Jewish funds is becoming . . . an exclusive preserve for the Jews,' he told an audience at the Royal Institute of International Affairs in 1931.[48] 'You see what this means,' he continued. 'It means what in South Africa is called segregation.'

Throughout the 1930s dispossessed fellahin made the one-way journey to the coast in search of work. They settled in shanty towns of tin and petrol cans on the edges of Jaffa and Haifa. During the brief building booms they found work; for much of the rest of the time they remained unemployed, their prospects diminished by the refusal of Jewish concerns to employ them. In 1927 a riot broke out at Petah Tikwa when Arab labourers were prevented from picking oranges bought by Arab businessmen.[49] Racial tension snapped later in Jaffa when a Jewish contractor, who was building, on behalf of the government, three schools for Arabs in an Arab city, refused to employ a single Arab labourer.[50] A striking example of this Zionist attitude is contained in an incident at a forest planted in honour of Herzl near Lydda. When it was learnt that the trees had actually been planted by Arabs, they were immediately uprooted and replanted by Jews.[51]

Jewish competition also affected other sections of the population, particularly the largely Christian artisan and merchant classes. The great waves of immigration forced up prices and the new Jewish industries, which were granted protective tariffs to keep them competitive, also contributed to the steep rise in the cost of living. As wages for Jewish labourers were very much higher than those for Arabs — according to the government handbook their agricultural wages were at least sixty per cent higher and the industrial earnings for unskilled workers one hundred per cent higher[52] — the burden of Zionism was once again being placed upon the poorer Arab classes.

Apart from all the economic problems which they brought with them, it was the insensitivity, the alien quality of Zionism, which the Arabs most resented. The majority of Zionists simply refused to consider the feelings of the Palestinians. They landed in a conservative, mainly Islamic country and seemed to go out of their way to upset the inhabitants. Colonel Walter Stirling, who was chief staff officer under Lawrence in Damascus, described how shocked the Arabs were on seeing Jews of both sexes swimming naked.[53] In Safad, Laurence Oliphant found it strange that the Jews should refuse to change any of their Ashkenazi habits even though they were living in a predominantly Muslim town.[54] Few Zionists were prepared to compromise and integrate themselves into the existing Palestinian society. Stirling recorded a couple of incidents when Zionist colonists refused to put up the signposts of the Palestine Postal Department simply because, in addition to English and Hebrew, they were also written in Arabic.[55] Sir John Chancellor summed up this attitude in his May 1930 dispatch to the King's private secretary: 'What makes them [the Zionist Jews] very difficult to deal with is that they are regardless of the rights and feelings of others and are very exacting in pressing their own claims. Even as a minority of the population of Palestine the Jews adopt towards the Arabs an attitude of arrogant superiority, which is hotly resented by the Arabs with their traditions of courtesy and good manners.'[56]

It was this arrogance and exclusiveness above all that convinced the Palestinians that the Zionists were the enemy. Freya Stark described it well during the Second World War:

This feeling of exclusion haunts one through all the Zionist endeavour in Palestine: it spoils the atmosphere of the agricultural colonies, where Arab labour is nearly all shut out; it spoils the hotels where Arab service even in laundry or garden . . . would be 'disapproved of'; it infuriates you if you happen to dislike the Jewish wine and ask for the Catholic, which is hardly ever obtainable.[57]

One of the leading socialist pioneers of Zionism, David Hacohen, recalls with shame how, in the early years of the mandate, he had:

> to defend [to my English and other friends] the fact that I would not accept Arabs in my trade union, the Histadrut; to defend preaching to housewives that they not buy at Arab stores; to defend the fact that we stood guard at orchards to prevent Arab workers from getting jobs there. . . . To pour kerosene on Arab tomatoes; to attack Jewish housewives in the markets and smash the Arab eggs they had bought; to praise to the skies the Keren Kayemet (Jewish National Fund) that sent Hankin to Beirut to buy land from absentee effendis and to turn the fellahin off the land – to buy dozens of dunums* from an Arab is permitted, but to sell, God forbid, one Jewish dunum to an Arab is prohibited; to take Rothschild, the incarnation of capitalism, as a socialist and to name him the 'benefactor' – to do all that was not easy. And despite the fact that we did it – maybe we had no choice – I wasn't happy about it.[58]

At first the Palestinians listened to Zionist claims to their land with disbelief. They formed over ninety per cent of the population and their ancestors had lived there for thousands of years; moreover, the last of the great civilizations to which they had belonged, the Arab, had enjoyed thirteen hundred years of almost uninterrupted existence in Palestine. It seemed inconceivable that the land should now be taken away from them and given to an alien people with an incomparably weaker historical claim. H.G. Wells found the plan equally astonishing: 'If it is proper to "reconstitute" a Jewish state which has not existed for two thousand years, why not go back another thousand years and reconstitute the Canaanite state? The Canaanites, unlike the Jews, are still there.'[59]

Besides historical arguments and claims deriving from their actual possession of the land, the Arabs also argued that they had been promised Palestine by the British in 1915 in return for Arab help against the Turks. The correspondence between the sharif of Mecca (Sharif Hussein) and Sir Henry McMahon acting on behalf

* A dunum is a measure of land area equal to 1,000 square metres, or about a quarter of an acre.

of the British government, in which this promise is alleged to have been made, has been analysed and discussed at length over the past sixty years and there is little to be gained in repeating the arguments made by both sides. It is well known that in his letter of 24 October 1915 McMahon promised that, subject to certain modifications, 'Great Britain is prepared to recognize and support the independence of the Arabs in all the regions within the limits demanded by the sharif of Mecca.' The modifications referred to the land 'lying to the west of the districts of Damascus, Homs, Hama and Aleppo'. As no part of Palestine lies to the west of these districts, and as McMahon neither mentioned nor disputed Sharif Hussein's claim to the area, the Arabs believed that Palestine should have been included in the area in which Britain had promised an independent Arab government. This view is supported by a Foreign Office minute of 1918: 'Palestine was implicitly included in King Husein's [sic] original demands and was not explicitly excluded in Sir H. McMahon's letter of 24.10.15. We are, therefore, presumably pledged to King Husein by this letter that Palestine shall be "Arab" and "independent".'[60]

Throughout the mandate period the Arabs argued that Palestine had been pledged to them in 1915 and thus they refused to recognize a second promise made by Arthur Balfour, the British foreign secretary, in a letter to Lord Rothschild two years later. They rightly believed that the establishment of a Jewish national home in Palestine, as envisaged by Balfour, was inconsistent with their aim of a Palestine that was to be Arab and independent. They also saw that Balfour's pledge to do nothing 'which may prejudice the civil and religious rights of existing non-Jewish [i.e. Arab] communities in Palestine' would be impossible to keep if the Zionist programme was to be implemented. As Lord Grey, the former Liberal foreign secretary, pointed out in the House of Lords in March 1923: '[The Balfour Declaration] promised a Zionist home without prejudice to the civil and religious rights of the population of Palestine. A Zionist home, my Lords, undoubtedly means or implies a Zionist government over the district in which the home is placed, and if ninety-three per cent of the population of Palestine are Arabs, I do not see how you can establish other than an Arab government, without prejudice to their civil rights.'[61]

The instinctive Arab reaction to the Balfour Declaration and the establishment of the mandate was to denounce both and to refuse to co-operate with the British authorities. The Palestine leaders believed they could force Britain to repudiate the Declaration simply by refusing to acknowledge its validity. Although they rejected violence as a means to back up their position, they remained uncompromising in attitude and stuck rigidly to three basic demands: the termination of Jewish immigration, the abrogation of the Declaration, and the establishment of Arab independence. It was in this spirit that they boycotted the elections to the proposed legislative council in 1923. When it became obvious that they were not able to change British policy by these methods and that, in addition, they were throwing away an opportunity to have some influence over their own future, the Palestinians altered their tactics. While continuing to voice their total rejection of Zionism and British policy towards it, they came to the conclusion that they would only achieve political concessions through co-operation with Britain. They had many sympathizers in Parliament, particularly in the House of Lords, and they hoped that British public opinion would swing their way and force the government to reconsider its policy. And indeed, as the mandate progressed, many British politicians and officials in Palestine and in London came to the conclusion that it was unworkable. Sir John Chancellor, high commisioner between 1928 and 1931, predicted continuous conflict unless the government accepted its obligations towards the Arabs:

The facts of the situation are that in the dire straits of the [First World] War, the British government made promises to the Arabs and promises to the Jews which are inconsistent with one another and incapable of fulfilment. The honest course is to admit our difficulty and to say to the Jews that, in accordance with the Balfour Declaration, we have favoured the establishment of a Jewish national home *in* Palestine and that a Jewish national home in Palestine has in fact been established and will be maintained; and that, without violating the second part of the Balfour Declaration, and without prejudicing the interests of the Arabs, we cannot do more than we have done.[62]

From the first years of the mandate, the Palestinian leadership was split into two factions, each of them pro-British in sentiment and each headed by one of the great Jerusalem families. Haj Amin al-Husseini was the man whom Britain chose to build up as the major political figure in Palestine. Selected as mufti by Sir Herbert Samuel in 1921 after an extraordinary piece of ballot-rigging by the British (Haj Amin had in fact only come fourth in the ballot), he was given additional power when the Supreme Muslim Council was established a year later with himself as president. A strong nationalist, Haj Amin was a man of talent and huge ambition. He was also stubborn, narrow-minded and unteachable: he never listened to advice and he was sadly lacking in political judgement. Nevertheless, through his exalted religious status, the great prestige of his family, and his own strong personality, he was able to attract the most determined Palestinian nationalists to his side.

The other party, known as the Opposition and led by the mayor of Jerusalem, Raghib al-Nashashibi, was a much looser formation which owed its tenuous unity not to any particular man nor to any particular ideology, but simply to the hatred and mistrust which so many of the Palestinian landed class felt for the mufti. As Nashashibi told Colonel Kisch of the Jewish Agency, he opposed Haj Amin al-Husseini much more strongly than the Zionists did themselves.[63] The Opposition detested the mufti's autocratic methods, his intransigence and his refusal to make political concessions. As a group it was less fervently nationalist than Haj Amin's following and more willing to co-operate with the mandate authorities. Its leaders were sufficiently practical to understand that the Jewish national home had become established and hoped to limit its scope rather than abolish it altogether. Although realistic in their politics, many of them were rightly suspected of collaboration with the Zionists. It is clear that they readily accepted Jewish funds for their newspapers and to subsidize their political activities; moreover, most of the Palestinian landowners involved in land sales with the Jews were followers of Raghib al-Nashashibi and included members of his own family.

Jerusalem was, of course, the political centre but the Husseini – Nashashibi rivalry was repeated throughout the country, the businessmen and landowners tending to ally themselves with Raghib al-Nashashibi, the intellectuals in general siding with the mufti. Although political leadership was ususally in the hands of the Muslims, the Christian communities also took part in politics.

Many of them, especially among the Protestants and the Greek Orthodox, were active in the national struggle as writers and journalists – most of the newspapers in Palestine were owned by Christians – and also as members of delegations sent to Britain and Europe to explain the Arab point of view. In some ways the Christians felt themselves to be more threatened by Zionism than the Muslims. Like the Jews, they were predominantly an urban community and therefore likely to suffer from Jewish competition. Furthermore, the areas where the Zionists were most enthusiastic about acquiring land – Galilee and Esdraelon – contained large Christian populations.

While the Jerusalem families quarrelled repeatedly during the 1920s, their disagreements with each other and with the British were never violent during this period. They retained their basic positions against Zionism, taking either the Husseini or the Nashashibi line, but there were no steps towards countering the movement with force. The dispute over the Wailing Wall and the 1929 riots were violent, isolated incidents and should not be seen as part of the later armed struggle. In the years before 1935 both factions advocated moderation and attempted to persuade the British to grant them self-governing institutions. This moderation was chiefly based on the belief that the Zionist enterprise was winding down. After the initial excitement following the Balfour Declaration and the setting up of the mandate, the Zionists began to lose momentum: contributions from the Jewish diaspora started to fall off and the Jewish Agency was forced to cut its budget. This coincided with a sharp drop in Jewish immigration so that in 1928 the number of new arrivals was exceeded by Jews emigrating to other countries. By 1930 the annual total of immigrants was less than 5,000.[64] In the circumstances it is understandable that many Palestinians should have felt that Zionism was not a threat worth fighting about.

The situation was altered dramatically by the rise of anti-Semitism in Europe and the enormous increase in Jewish emigration to Palestine which it produced. In 1934 more than 45,000 Jews entered the country and a year later the figure was up to 66,000.[65] For the Palestinians, Zionism had again become a danger. Pressure on the small landowners and fellahin to sell their holdings was stepped up and dispossession again became frequent. Moreover, as even the urban Jewish economy began to insist on solely Jewish labour, the evicted or dispossessed fellahin were rarely able to find employment in the towns of the coastal plain.

As the British made no moves towards limiting the number of immigrants, the Palestinians turned to more active forms of protest. In the autumn of 1933 large demonstrations took place in Jerusalem and Jaffa and a number of Arabs were killed by the police. As Sir Arthur Wauchope, the high commissioner, reported, 'A genuine national feeling is growing constantly more powerful in Palestine and more bitter against [the] British government.'[66] He understood the reason: the Palestinians were becoming more radical in their demands as they became more desperate about the threat of Zionism. This feeling was not confined to the traditional leadership but was shared by most sections of the community. Indeed, by the mid-1930s the Arabs of Palestine were showing clear signs of frustration with the leadership of the bickering Jerusalemite families and their failure to achieve anything at all in the struggle against Britain and Zionism.

At times the Husseini – Nashashibi rivalry seemed to take precedence over all other issues and the two families and their supporters spent most of the local elections smearing each other with accusations of selling land to the Jews and collaborating with the British authorities. Since the franchise in the towns of Palestine was limited to the men of property, most of these elections were won by the Nashashibis. But in 1934 the Khalidis, one of the most prominent of the Jerusalem clans, deserted the Nashashibi party and caused the defeat of Raghib al-Nashashibi who was standing for re-election as mayor of Jerusalem. It was symptomatic of the decline of the Opposition. The Arab moderates, who had flourished before Hitler's rise in Germany gave the Zionist movement an invigorating boost, were forced to give way, their much-vaunted policy of co-operation shown up as valueless. The Husseini faction, with its tougher political stance, was thus able to dominate its rival. Even so, the mufti's despotic methods and his inability to listen to anyone turned many people against him and assisted the establishment of several new political parties. However, with the exception of the Independence (Istiqlal) Party, these were soon exposed as being merely instruments for the advancement of a particular notable and his family, and they enjoyed little popular support. During 1935 and 1936, when the Palestinian national struggle began to gain ground, the inadequacy of the traditional leadership became apparent. Although the mufti provided direction of a sort, it was not what the people then required. Wauchope made the obvious comparison between the 'tenacity of the villagers' in their opposition to Britain and 'the feebleness and a lack of any great qualities of leadership' among the prominent Arabs.[67]

The Palestinian rebellion, which grew out of a series of minor incidents in 1935 and 1936 into a serious military confrontation in 1937 and 1938, was not begun by the Arab leaders. It was a genuinely popular war which the Jerusalem leaders spent trying to catch up with rather than direct. In a report of a meeting with the high commissioner in May 1936, it is stated that: '[Raghib al-Nashashibi said that] the tension in the country was great and the attitude of the leaders was dictated by the pressure brought to bear upon them by the nation. The people . . . at the present time were ruling the leaders and not the leaders ruling the people.'[68] Although the Husseinis were able to come to terms with the revolt and became directly involved in it, the Nashashibis failed. Eventually they opted out of the struggle, became allied with Emir Abdullah of Transjordan, and resigned themselves to the dismemberment of Palestine which they rightly foresaw would benefit them at the expense of the Husseinis. Even now it is difficult to judge which tactics were right for that time. It has been argued that if the Palestinians had adopted a more violent attitude towards the British mandate when it was first established, then the Zionist programme would never have had the chance to establish itself and would soon have been abandoned by Britain. It has also been claimed that the Palestinians should have done exactly the opposite. Had they co-operated with Britain, had they presented their case to the royal commissions sent out to investigate various 'disturbances' in Palestine and participated in the elections to the legislative council, then they might have succeeded in placing themselves in a position where they could have influenced British policy. Had they fought for the possible and not the unattainable, Britain might have accepted their position and put an end to Zionism's creeping success. Musa Alami, who believes not only that the Jewish national home was a fact which should have been recognized, but also that if it had been recognized it could have been limited, sees the 1930s as a series of wasted opportunities: 'There were so many mistakes which we made, so many times when things could have been different — and better — had we taken a different line, had we been more realistic. But our leaders thought they had a duty to reject every suggestion. They refused to talk to the royal commissions. It became almost a religion to say no, no, no!'[69]

By 1935 the traditional Palestinian leadership had forfeited the allegiance of its followers. The huge increases in the numbers of immigrants and the land transfers that accompanied them created a new feeling of militancy which the Jerusalemites were unable to control. Britain's refusal to make concessions either on immigration or on the setting up of self-governing institutions and the discovery in October 1935 that the Jews were smuggling weapons through the port of Jaffa, contributed to this mood and convinced many Arabs that only through violence could they hope to hold on to their homeland. The first skirmish took place in November when a small band of Arab guerrillas was caught by British troops in the hills around Jenin. The leader of the band was Izzedin al-Qasim, a puritanical religious sheikh whose followers consisted of dispossessed fellahin from the slums of Haifa and villagers from the surrounding countryside. Although al-Qasim was killed in this first incident, he is today regarded by the Palestinian guerrillas as their founder.

Al-Qasim's short campaign was followed by a general strike in the spring of 1936, but the damage which this did to the Palestinian rural economy and the fact that the Jewish community was so self-reliant that it was largely immune to economic pressure, ensured its failure. By early summer the Arabs had decided to fight. Small military units were formed in the mountainous regions of central and northern Palestine, from where they began a campaign of sabotage against roads, bridges and pipelines. The fighting was at its most intense in northern Galilee but spread also into southern Galilee and the Nablus hill-country. Towards the south, around Jerusalem, Hebron and Beersheba, and along the coast between Gaza and Jaffa, the revolt was generally contained by the British forces.

Over the following two years the rebellion became more threatening and the size of the Arab forces grew. At their peak the guerrillas numbered some 3,000, though they were supported by many more part-time fighters and sympathizers in the villages. In the summer of 1938 they were at the height of their power, controlling most of the hill-country and the towns of Nablus and

Ramallah. In October they briefly occupied the Old City of Jerusalem.

The growth of the rebellion in 1937 — 8 was in part prompted by the royal commission's recommendation of July 1937 that Palestine should be partitioned. Galilee, with its Arab majority was to be handed over to the proposed Jewish state; Jerusalem, Bethlehem and a corridor to the sea were to remain under the mandate, and the rest of Palestine was to be united with Transjordan under Emir Abdullah. Few Palestinians were prepared to accept the loss of historic Arab towns such as Acre and Safad and one consequence of the proposals was to bring the Husseini family and their supporters firmly on to the side of the rebellion. Most of the Nashashibi faction, however, which was closely linked to Abdullah, supported the scheme as it seemed the best means of ensuring the downfall of the mufti and of preparing for their eventual domination of Palestinian — Transjordanian politics. Thus they seceded from the Arab Higher Committee, which had been set up at the beginning of the revolt in order to give the Palestinian leadership the mask of unity, and proclaimed their intention of co-operating with Britain. The rebels, backed and to some extent now led by the mufti, reacted by terrorizing the Nashashibis and their allies. Many charged with supporting partition or lacking in enthusiasm for the rebellion were murdered during the next two years and others fled the country. This in turn produced a reaction led by Fakhri al-Nashashibi, the nephew of Raghib. He supervised the organization of armed bands in different regions whose duties were to protect the Nashashibi supporters and help the British in hunting down the insurgents.

The rebellion lost a part of its momentum when the Woodhead commission of November 1938 came out in opposition to the previous partition plan. It ended the following year, damaged by its own disunity and destroyed by British troops. In this, the first incarnation of the Palestine resistance movement, it is estimated that there were some 20,000 Arab casualties. Of the 5,000 or so killed, three-quarters died on the battlefield. Perhaps 1,200 were victims of terrorism by Jews and other Arabs and 112 were executed by the British.[70] Most of the casualties were fellahin or urban slum-dwellers recently arrived from the countryside — for it was in a very real sense a popular war, not one directed from above. Analysing the social and economic backgrounds of nearly

300 rebel officers, an Israeli historian, Professor Porath, has found that a large majority were Muslim villagers and points out that the ratio of countrymen to townsmen would have been even higher if it had been possible to examine the records of the ordinary guerrillas.[71] In his study he also finds that the Druze community generally opposed the revolt and that the Christians, though prominent among the nationalist intellectuals, took little part in the fighting. The role played by the large landowning families – with the exception of the Husseinis – was equally limited. Although the Arab Higher Committee was sufficiently active for Britain to declare it illegal and deport some of its members to the Seychelles, the impetus of the revolt clearly came from elsewhere.

For the Palestinians, the rebellion was a catastrophe. It weakened and divided them and the divisions were still there when they had to fight the Zionists ten years later. Yet it is difficult to condemn their resort to arms. They had watched while their country was filled with foreign settlers and their land taken away from them. They had appealed to their trustee, Britain, to safeguard their rights, and that trustee had ignored them. A majority in their own country, denied the right to exercise any control over their future, they were pushed into stating their position through violence. As one member of Parliament said in the House of Commons in 1938:

There are no Arab members of Parliament, there are no Arab constituents to bring influence upon their members of Parliament. There is no Arab control of newspapers in this country. It is impossible almost to get a pro-Arab letter in *The Times*. There are in the City no Arab financial houses who control large amounts of finance. There is no Arab control of newspaper advertisements in this country. There are no Arab ex-Colonial Secretaries. . . . Only violence brought their claims to our attention.[72]

PART TWO

The New Diaspora

3

The Exodus 1947 – 1948

Great Britain retained the Palestine mandate for nine years after the defeat of the Arab rebellion. It was a period dominated by the Second World War and by the murderous assault launched against the British in Palestine by Jewish terrorist groups. The assassination of Lord Moyne in Cairo by the Stern gang, the blowing up of the King David Hotel, and the execution of British soldiers by Menachem Begin's Irgun Zvai Leumi, were the most notorious episodes in this campaign. In a situation that showed no hope of improvement, the British, weakened by war and bullied by the United States, whose insistent and open partisanship on the side of Zionism made it impossible to carry out a balanced policy in Palestine, finally decided to abdicate. They announced their intention to relinquish the mandate and left the problem in the hands of the United Nations.

In point of fact the fate of Palestine was decided by one member rather than by the U.N. as a whole. The United States, which had opted for partition and the creation of a Jewish state, was determined to force its policy through the General Assembly. When it became uncertain whether the scheme would attract a sufficient majority, the Americans reacted strongly. Haiti, Liberia, the Philippines, China, Ethiopia and Greece – all of which opposed partition – were given concentrated doses of political and economic pressure.[1] All, except Greece, were 'persuaded' to change their minds. The delegate from the Philippines was placed in a ridiculous position: after making a passionate speech against partition, his country ended up by voting in favour of it.[2]

The partition scheme that was forced upon the General Assembly in November 1947 was very different from the plan produced by the royal commission ten years previously. Under the latter the Palestinians had stood to lose their most fertile lands along the coast and in Galilee but they would have held on to the bulk of their homeland. In the U.N. plan the Zionists were granted nearly sixty per cent of the country including eastern Galilee, the coastal plain stretching from a point just north of Isdud (Ashdod) nearly as far as Acre, the Vale of Esdraelon and the rich farmlands running along the Jordan from south of Beisan (Bet She'an) to Tiberias, and almost the whole of the Beersheba district from the Dead Sea to the Gulf of 'Aqaba. The Arab allotment consisted of western Galilee, an enclave at Jaffa, the Gaza Strip and the central hill-country from Jenin down to Beersheba. Jerusalem and Bethlehem were to be excluded from both states and placed in an international zone.

Despite large-scale immigration, the Jews still formed less than a third of Palestine's population in 1947. Only in one sub-district, that of Jaffa (in which Tel Aviv was situated), were they in a majority and in no sub-district did they own more land than the Arabs.[3] The absurdity of the plan can be demonstrated by the fact that even in the proposed Jewish state there were more Arabs than Jews. In eastern Galilee, compromising the sub-districts of Safad, Tiberias and Beisan, the Jews formed only a quarter of the population and in the Beersheba area an Arab population of 103,820 was expected to submit to 1,020 Jews.[4] This last stretch of territory, an Arab area inhabited almost exclusively by Arabs, was given to the Zionists not because they had any sort of claim to it but simply because they wanted a port on the Red Sea. The British, who had blundered their way through the mandate attempting to fulfil promises which one of their own high commissioners recognized were 'inconsistent . . . and incapable of fulfilment' (see page 49), had at least tried to be impartial. The American-dominated United Nations made no effort at all. Questions of right and principle were forgotten and the idea that a people should have some say in determining its own future was completely discarded.

It is often stated that if the Palestinians had accepted partition, they wouldn't have lost even more of their territory in the war; and if they had later accepted the armistice frontiers of 1949, they wouldn't have lost the few remaining fragments of their homeland in 1967. But everyone should have seen that they could never have accepted partition in the first place. How could any people, however moderate and reasonable, be expected to surrender voluntarily the greater part of their country? Eamon De Valera, president of Ireland, saw clearly that it was impossible. To one visitor who had solicited his support for partition he replied: 'I read the Old Testament many years ago. I am afraid I have forgotten many things I read; but one passage I recall clearly. It is the story of Solomon's judgement of the two women who desired the same baby. I remember how when Solomon ruled that the baby be divided the real mother screamed, "No! No! Give the baby to the other woman!" That is my answer to partition. The rightful owners of a country will never agree to partition.'[5]

The partition plan was thus rejected out of hand by the Palestinians. In practice it was also rejected by the Zionists. Although the Jewish Agency decided ostensibly to accept the resolution, many Zionists did not even bother to pay lip-service to it. Israel's present prime minister, Menachem Begin, then announced: 'The partition of the homeland is illegal. It will never be recognized. The signature by institutions and individuals of the partition agreement is invalid. It will not bind the Jewish people. Jerusalem was and will for ever be our capital. Eretz Israel will be restored to the people of Israel. All of it. And for ever.'[6] The man soon to become prime minister, David Ben-Gurion, was equally unwilling to accept the U.N.'s decision on Jerusalem: 'Tens of thousands of our youth are prepared to lay down their lives for the sake of Jerusalem. Everything possible will be done for Jerusalem. It is within the boundaries of the State of Israel just as Tel Aviv is.'[7]

Other leaders were less blatant about it but even a casual glance at Zionist military plans for the spring of 1948 indicates what little respect they had for the proposed partition boundaries. In particular, it is clear that they were not prepared to recognize the international status of Jerusalem or Arab rule in western Galilee.

The Israeli version of the 1948 war is contained in a government handbook published by the Israel Information Service in 1967: 'If the Arab states had not waged open war on Israel on the morrow of its re-establishment [sic] in May 1948, the Arab refugee issue would never have arisen.'[8] This is such a ridiculous fabrication that it is difficult to see how anyone could ever have been deceived by it. On the day Israel proclaimed its independence there were already 300,000 Palestinian refugees, and Zionist forces had occupied large chunks of territory designated for the proposed Arab state as well as parts of Jerusalem intended for international administration. At midnight on 14 May, when the last British soldiers were departing and the new state was proclaimed, the Zionists had captured the Arab quarters of west Jerusalem and infiltrated the Old City; they had taken Jaffa and opened a corridor between the coast and Jerusalem; and they had destroyed dozens of Arab villages. In early April their most well publicized crime had been committed: the massacre of 254 civilians of the village of Deir Yassin. Although the killers were members of Begin's Irgun gang, the operation was carried out with the encouragement of the Jerusalem commander of the Zionist regular forces (the Haganah).[9] Deir Yassin was eighteen miles *outside* the borders which the Zionist leaders pretended to have accepted in the partition plan.

The first stage of the 1948 war, the Zionist offensive which ended on 15 May, unfolded much as its planners had intended. The Zionist strategy, a series of connected operations under the title Plan Dalet, has been well described by Lieutenant-Colonel Netanel Lorch, recently director of information at the Israeli Foreign Ministry, and by Yigal Allon, a former foreign minister and commander of the Haganah in 1948.[10] It had two objectives: the consolidation of territory intended for the Jewish state and the expulsion of its Arab inhabitants; and the seizure of specific areas promised to Arab Palestine, whose population was also to be driven out. Allon has explained why the Arab areas were attacked: 'The strategic considerations which had underlain the plan of Zionist settlement decided in large measure the fate of many regions of the country, including areas largely or entirely settled by Arabs, such as Tiberias, Tsemah, Bet She'an, Acre, Haifa, and Jaffa, all of which were surrounded by Jewish villages.'[11]

Acre and Jaffa were supposed to be in the Arab state and they were attacked and occupied, and most of their inhabitants ejected, *not* because the Arab states had 'waged open war on Israel' but because, as one of the most senior Israeli field commanders admitted, they were near Jewish settlements. The fact that the United

Nations had planned to leave these towns under Arab control, and that Allon and his colleagues had said they would accept that plan, was not something, apparently, which it was necessary to consider. The Zionists wanted Jaffa and Acre and so they took them. It was part of Plan Dalet. So was the capture of Haifa, the occupation of all Galilee, and the assault on Jerusalem. Not all the operations in the plan were successful – the Latrun villages blocking the main road between Jaffa and Jerusalem were never taken nor was the Old City itself – but it achieved a good deal. By 15 May, when the Arab states 'waged open war on Israel', and thus, according to the Israel Information Service, began the whole problem, the Zionists had already seized large areas intended for the proposed Arab state and uprooted a mass of refugees from their homes.

The first stage of the war was almost entirely one-sided. The Haganah was able to field 30,000 front-line troops backed up by 32,000 garrison forces, 15,410 settlement police and the 32,000 men of the Home Guard.[12] Besides these, there were the two terrorist groups, the Irgun, whose members totalled 5,000, and the Stern gang, with 1,000 'fighters for the freedom of Israel'.[13] The opposition to them in the first round was pitiful. The mufti and his supporters in the Arab governments do not appear to have foreseen the need for an army. In December 1947 they decided to raise an irregular force of volunteers from various Arab countries which they infelicitously called the Arab Liberation Army. Composed of some 5,000 men, it performed dismally throughout the war in Palestine: it never won a battle and, after a series of early setbacks, it usually withdrew before being forced into a confrontation. Recent research into its operations in Galilee indicates that its effect on the civilian population was generally demoralizing.[14] Besides this force, the defence of Palestine in the pre-15 May stage was undertaken by the villagers themselves who defended their homes as best they could with antiquated weaponry. There was no strategy, no co-ordination between them. They had been disgracefully deserted by their leaders, most of whom were living in safety in Beirut, Cairo and Damascus. Only two members of the Arab Higher Committee, Ahmed Hilmi and Dr Hussein Fakhri Khalidi, remained in Palestine during the war. Only one Jerusalem notable, Abdel Qader Husseini, took part in the fighting; and he was killed, long before 15 May, during the Zionist assault on Kastel.

It was not only the leadership which, as so often before, let the Palestinians down; the response from the Arab states was equally inadequate. With the exception of Transjordan, none of them seem to have had any idea about what fighting a war entailed. The recently established Arab League, consisting of Egypt, Iraq, Syria, Lebanon, Saudi Arabia, Transjordan and Yemen, did not feel that actual fighting would be necessary. Its political committee believed that 'massing present Arab forces on the borders would suffice to convince the big countries to intervene and force Israel to comply with Arab demands'.[15] Even when it became clear that they would have to fight, the Arab states remained remarkably complacent; Syria offered a brigade of 1,876 men, Lebanon a battalion of 700.[16] When Glubb Pasha, commanding Transjordan's Arab Legion, told the Secretary-General of the Arab League that the Zionists had 65,000 men under arms, the latter replied: 'I expect it will be all right. I have arranged to get up seven hundred men from Libya.' On being asked how they were to be armed, he answered: 'I have sent a man to buy seven hundred rifles from Italy.'[17]

The entry of the Arab armies into Palestine on 15 May did, however, bring an end to the first Zionist offensive. Although the motley collection of Syrian and Lebanese troops in the north were unable to salvage the remains of Galilee, the presence of a brigade of Egyptian soldiers in the south and the activities of the Arab Legion around Jerusalem took the pressure off the Palestinian villagers. After a fortnight's fighting a battalion of the Arab Legion had cleared the Haganah out of the Old City, while another held the vital defile at Latrun some miles to the west of Jerusalem. This was the most important strategic prize in Palestine, as the Israelis recognized when they captured it in 1967 and demolished the surrounding Arab villages. But in 1948 it was held, against repeated assaults, by the Arab Legion; had it fallen, the Zionists, or Israelis as they had now become, could have penetrated the Ramallah area to the north of Jerusalem and turned the whole Arab position.

But the entry of the Arab armed forced only temporarily halted the Israeli success. When the first truce was called, on 11 June, the Israelis took the opportunity to reorganize their forces and bring in large quantities of arms from Czechoslovakia. The Arabs did nothing at all. Believing, for some reason, that there would be no more fighting, no steps were taken to increase either the size or the efficiency of the armies. Nor was any attempt made at liaison between them: for the entire duration of the war, the Egyptians refused to divulge any details of their plans, tactical or strategic, to their neighbours at the front, the Arab Legion.[18]

During the third round, which took place between truces in mid-July, the Israelis concentrated on selected targets in the Arab areas. The twin towns of Lydda and Ramle, on the coastal plain east of Tel Aviv, were captured on 12 July and emptied of their inhabitants within a few hours. This was followed by yet another unsuccessful attack against the Arab Legion at Latrun. Four days later, Nazareth, the last Arab town in the north, fell and serious resistance in Galilee came to an end. The final phase of the war took place in October when the Israelis broke through the Egyptian positions in the south and captured Beersheba. The Egyptian troops were bundled back to Gaza and the front south of Jerusalem was abandoned. Had it not been for a detachment of the Arab Legion, the Israelis would certainly have captured Hebron. A few days later the remnants of the Arab Liberation Army were finally chased across the Lebanese border and the fighting ended. By the end of 1948, Syria, Lebanon and the Arab Liberation Army had abandoned the struggle while the Egyptian forces, which had lost almost the whole of southern Palestine, were cooped up in Gaza. Only the Arab Legion and an Iraqi force to its north remained in position and they were hardly in a state to take on the entire Israeli army. When the Iraqis, too, announced their intention of leaving, Transjordan was forced to sign an armistice, even though this meant abandoning a series of villages a few miles from the coast. None of these had been captured by the Israelis and all of them had been intended for the Arab state. But the Israelis demanded them as the price of peace and Transjordan was in no position to argue.[19]

The only surprising thing about the 1948 war is that the Israelis did not take over the whole country, since this was obviously their intention. Two Zionist writers have since revealed that the operation designed to capture the whole of eastern Palestine was abandoned late in 1948 in deference to world opinion. The Israeli leaders were apparently unwilling to risk their position 'on the uncertainties of yet another military operation, which would greatly intensify the Arab refugee problem'.[20] Later they seemed to regret their caution. In 1964 Israel's retired prime minister, Ben-

Gurion, implied it was the fault of the generals: 'Israeli territory might have been greater if General Moshe Dayan had been chief of staff during the war of 1948.' General Allon put the blame on Ben-Gurion: when the prime minister ordered a cease-fire, he claimed, 'We had been on the crest of victory . . . from the Lītāni [river in Lebanon] in the north to the Sinai desert in the south-west. A few more days of fighting would have enabled us . . . to liberate the entire country.'[21] To observers it must have seemed odd that the Israelis should have been so dissatisfied with their achievements. At the end of 1948 they controlled more than three-quarters of Palestine and were contemplating taking the rest.

As far as the Palestinians were concerned, the military defeat was not the most important feature of the disaster. They had, after all, been defeated in 1938 and most of them were able to carry on their lives in much the same way as they had done before. But this war was different: more than half of the people were uprooted from their land, turned into refugees and refused the chance to return home. This dispersion, this mass exodus to neighbouring countries, is the central feature of modern Palestinian history. No one can understand the Palestinians today, their ideas, their aspirations or their behaviour, without understanding the tragedy at the root of the Palestinian problem and why it happened.

Why did they leave? What could have induced a nation of peasant farmers and small-town artisans to abandon their land and their houses? For many years people in the West believed the official Israeli version, alleging that the exodus followed 'express instructions broadcast by the president of the Arab Higher Executive (the mufti)'.[22] Many still do: letter writers to the *Guardian* and the *Daily Telegraph* repeatedly quote this even now. A prominent English Zionist told me in 1979: 'Arab leaders broadcast to the Arabs in the Haifa and Galilee areas that they should evacuate Palestine, or Israel as it had then become, and return with the conquering armies when they would be awarded the spoils of victory.'[23]

It is an extraordinary accusation, it has been shown to be false time after time, and it is difficult to see what the Zionists hope to achieve by endlessly repeating it. The logic seems to be that if they can prove that the Palestinians left of their own free will, then this somehow invalidates their right to return home. It is difficult to see why it should. People all over the world leave their homes in time of war and for a variety of different reasons. Yet, whatever the cause of their flight, they all have the same right to return home afterwards. In any case, not one piece of evidence was ever produced to substantiate the allegations about the broadcasts. Attempts to establish the truth in this matter were made independently by two scholars in the 1950s, Dr Walid Khalidi and Dr Erskine Childers. Childers went to Israel in 1958 as a guest of the government and tried to find evidence of the broadcasts. As the Israelis were unable to produce it, he decided to examine the American and British monitoring records of all Middle East broadcasts throughout 1948. He reported: 'There was not a single order, or appeal, or suggestion about evacuation from Palestine from any Arab radio station, inside or outside Palestine, in 1948. There *is* repeated monitored record of Arab appeals, even flat orders, to the civilians of Palestine *to stay put.*'[24]

Additional evidence of the attitude of the Arab leadership is contained in a letter from the Arab Higher Committee, dated 8 March 1948, which specifically asks Arab governments to co-operate in preventing Palestinians from leaving their country. The letter says: 'The Arab Higher Committee has resolved that it is in the interests of Palestine that no Palestinian should be permitted to leave the country except under special circumstances, such as for political, commercial or extreme health reasons.'[25] Meanwhile, in Jerusalem itself, Ahmed Hilmi and Hussein Khalidi actually issued orders forbidding anyone to leave the city without a permit.[26]

Not only is there no evidence to substantiate the allegation that the Arabs left as a result of orders broadcast by their leaders: there is overwhelming evidence which indicates that the real responsibility for the refugee problem lies with the Zionists. As Count Bernadotte, the mediator sent out to Palestine by the United Nations, said shortly before his assassination by Zionist terrorists: 'The exodus of Palestinian Arabs resulted from panic created by fighting in their communities, by rumours concerning real or alleged acts of terrorism, or expulsion.'[27]

Expulsion was the commonest method, employed against the populations of Haifa, Lydda, Ramle and many villages in Galilee. In Haifa, according to the semi-official Zionist paper, *Palestine Post* (now the *Jerusalem Post*), 'Haganah forces in a thirty-hour battle . . . crushed all resistance, occupied many major buildings forcing thousands of Arabs to flee by the only open escape route – the sea.'[28] Two Zionist writers, Jon and David Kimche,

have described what happened to the inhabitants of Lydda and
Ramle:

> [On 11 July, Dayan and his troops] drove at full speed into Lyd-
> da, shooting up the town and creating confusion and a degree of
> terror among the population. . . . Its Arab population of
> 30,000 either fled or were herded on to the road to Ramallah.
> The next day Ramle also surrendered and its Arab population
> suffered the same fate. Both towns were sacked by the vic-
> torious Israelis.[29]

Terrorism and the massacre of civilians were other techniques
used by the Zionists. According to the Kimches again, the killing
of unarmed villagers began in December 1947, soon after the U.N.
debate.[30] It was a standard method used in forcing the Galilee
Arabs to escape across the Lebanese or Syrian borders. At Ain al-
Zeitouneh, thirty-seven boys were taken as hostages and never
seen again; the other inhabitants were taken to the edge of the
village and told to leave.[31] An inhabitant of Safsaf (now called Sif-
sufa) has described what happened to her village when Israeli
troops captured it in October 1948:

> 'As we lined up, a few Jewish soldiers ordered four girls to ac-
> company them to carry water for the soldiers. Instead they took
> them to our empty houses and raped them. About seventy of
> our men were blindfolded and shot to death, one after the
> other, in front of us. The soldiers took their bodies and threw
> them on the cement covering the villages's spring and dumped
> sand on them.'[32]

Similar atrocities took place in more than a dozen villages of
Galilee,[33] and also near Hebron. According to one Israeli soldier, a
member of the Mapam Party, Israeli troops committed a horrific
massacre at the Sunni village of Duwayma, between Hebron and
the coast:

> They killed some eighty to one hundred Arabs, women and
> children. The children were killed by smashing their skulls with
> clubs. . . . In the village there remained Arab men and women
> who were put in the houses without food. Then the sappers

came to blow up the houses. One officer ordered a sapper to put two old women into the house he was about to blow up. The sapper refused, and said that he will [sic] obey only such orders as are handed down to him by his direct commander. So the officer ordered his own soldiers to put the old women in and the atrocity was carried out. Another soldier boasted that he raped an Arab woman and then shot her. Another Arab woman with a day-old baby was employed in cleaning jobs in the yard. . . . She worked for one or two days and then was shot together with her baby. . . . Cultured and well mannered commanders who are considered good fellows . . . have turned into low murderers, and this happened not in the storm of the battle and blind passion, but because of a system of expulsion and annihilation. The less Arabs remain, the better.[34]

These massacres were calculated to panic the neighbouring villagers into flight. After 254 civilians in Deir Yassin 'had been deliberately massacred in cold blood', as Jacques de Reynier of the Red Cross described it,[35] the wretched survivors were publicly paraded through Jerusalem[36] in order to spread terror among other sections of the population. Arthur Koestler called the bloodbath of Deir Yassin 'the psychologically decisive factor in this spectacular exodus', and it was expertly exploited by the Zionists. A Christian missionary in Jerusalem recalls a loudspeaker blasting out this message to the Arab population: 'Unless you leave your homes, the fate of Deir Yassin will be your fate.'[37] And according to Menachem Begin, who was responsible for the massacre, the Arabs of Haifa fled to their boats crying 'Deir Yassin!'[38]

'The affair of Deir Yassin', wrote Jacques de Reynier, 'had immense repercussions. The press and radio spread the news everywhere among Arabs as well as the Jews. In this way a general terror was built up among the Arabs, a terror astutely fostered by the Jews. . . . Driven by fear, the Arabs left their homes to find shelter among their kindred; first isolated farms, then villages, and in the end whole towns were evacuated.'[39]

Psychological pressure was a vital ingredient in the Zionist offensive and was often more effective than terrorism. It has been well documented by Israeli officials. Harry Levin, who was an experienced journalist then employed in the Jewish broadcasting service in Jerusalem and who later became Israel's first ambassador

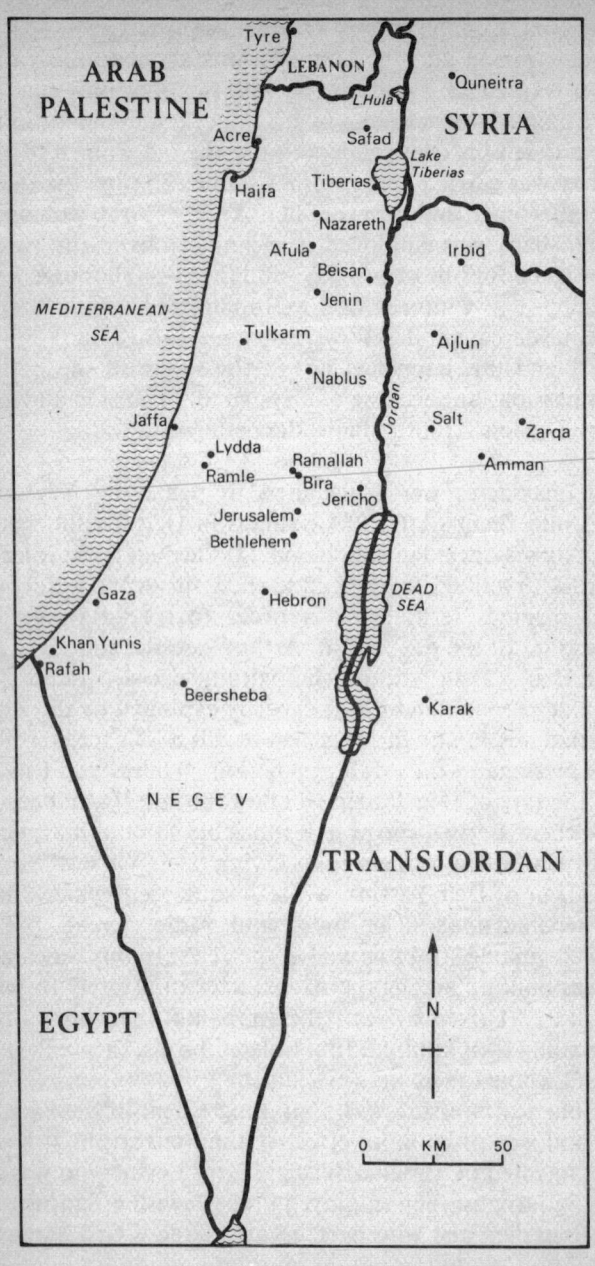

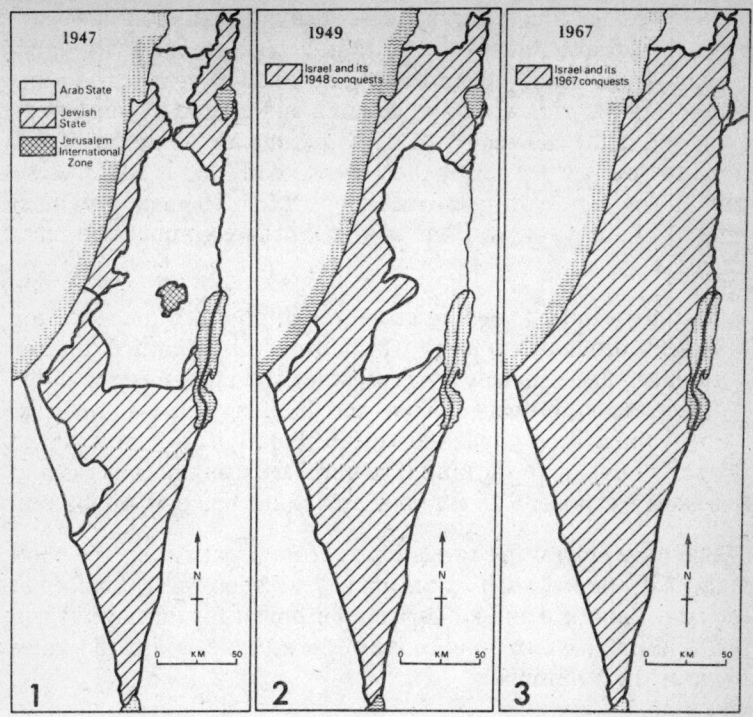

THREE STAGES IN THE CONQUEST OF ARAB PALESTINE

1   The U.N. Partition Plan 1947

2   Israel as it emerged after the 1948 War

3   Israel with its 1967 conquests

to New Zealand and Australia, described one feature of it: 'Near-by, a loudspeaker burst out in Arabic, Haganah broadcasting to civilian Arabs, urging them to leave the district before 5.15 a.m. "Take pity on your wives and children and get out of this blood-bath," it said. "Surrender to us with your arms. No harm will come to you. Or get out by the Jericho road, that is still open to you. If you stay, you invite disaster".'[40] Leo Heiman, an Israeli veteran of the 1948 war, has written of more complicated tech-niques:

> As uncontrolled panic spread through all Arab quarters, the Israelis brought up jeeps which broadcast recorded 'horror sounds'. These included shrieks, wails and anguished moans of Arab women, the wail of sirens and the clang of fire-alarm bells, interrupted by a sepulchral voice calling out in Arabic: 'Save your souls, all ye faithful. The Jews are using poison gas and atomic weapons. Run for your lives in the name of Allah!'[41]

The most interesting revelation is from Yigal Allon, the com-mander of the Haganah forces in Galilee. Allon was a member of the Israeli political and military establishment for thirty years and the following passage is indicative of the attitudes of Israeli leaders towards the Palestinians:

> We saw a need to clean the Inner Galilee and to create a Jewish territorial succession in the entire area of the Upper Galilee. . . . We therefore looked for means which did not force us into employing force, in order to cause the tens of thousands of sulky Arabs who remained in Galilee to flee. . . . We tried to use a tactic which took advantage of the impression created by the fate of Safad and the [Arab] defeat in the area which was cleaned by Operation Metateh [the seventh operation in Plan Dalet] – a tactic which worked miraculously well!
>
> I gathered all the Jewish mukhtars, who have contact with Arabs in different villages and asked them to whisper in the ears of some Arabs that a great Jewish reinforcement had arrived in Galilee and that it is going to burn all the villages of the Huleh. They should suggest to these Arabs, as their friends, to escape while there is still time. . . . The tactic reached its goal com-pletely. The building of the police station at Halsa fell into our hands without a shot. The wide areas were cleaned.[42]

The passage is worth quoting at length because an Israeli leader, a former foreign minister and deputy prime minister, is here admitting something which Israeli propaganda still denies. According to the propaganda version, the flight of the refugees followed 'express instructions broadcast' by the mufti. Throughout her life Golda Meir claimed that the refugee problem was not Israel's responsibility and Zionist apologists in the Western press still trot out the myth about the broadcasts. Yet here a leading Israeli statesman explains in detail how he personally contributed to the refugee problem. Admittedly he does not mention the massacres; that would have been too much to expect. But he makes it clear that the Arabs did not leave of their own accord or in deference to the mufti's wishes; they were quite definitely expelled. Moreover he reveals the Zionists' motive behind the expulsion and, perhaps unconsciously, their real attitude towards the Palestinians. Three times in those two paragraphs he talks about expelling the Arabs; but instead of using phrases like 'drive out' or 'get rid of', he uses, on each occasion, the verb 'to clean', as if the Arabs, although its natural inhabitants, were somehow polluting the land. When he 'cleaned' the Galilee of Arabs, Allon was, and knew that he was, quite literally treating them like dirt. It was a phenomenon which Asher Ginsberg had recognized fifty years before; many visitors to Israel recognize it today.

In 1979, Allon's deputy at the time, Yitzhak Rabin, added more evidence to the story of the refugees. Rabin, who was afterwards chief of staff and prime minister, recounted in his memoirs how Ben-Gurion ordered the expulsion of the inhabitants of Lydda and Ramle:

We walked outside, Ben-Gurion accompanying us. Allon repeated his question: 'What is to be done with the population?' BG waved his hand in a gesture which said, 'Drive them out.' . . . The population of Lod [Hebrew word for Lydda] did not leave willingly. There was no way of avoiding the use of force and warning shots in order to make the inhabitants march the ten to fifteen miles to the point where they met up with the Legion.

Thus, in one blow, an Israeli politician demolished the chief Israeli myth. Other Israelis were horrified and a cabinet censorship committee quickly had the passage removed. Had it not been for the translator of the book, who leaked the story to the *New York Times,* the admission might never have been made public.[43]

There were, of course, some Israelis who refused to accept the lie about the refugees and who did their best to expose it. After Nathan Chofshi had read an article by Rabbi Mordechai Kaplan which merely parrotted the official version of the exodus, he wrote to the *Jewish Newsletter* (9 February 1959):

> If Rabbi Kaplan really wanted to know what happened, we old Jewish settlers in Palestine who witnessed the fight could tell him how and in what manner we, Jews, forced the Arabs to leave cities and villages which they did not want to leave of their own free will. Some of them were driven out by force of arms; others were made to leave by deceit, lying and false promises. It is enough to cite the cities of Jaffa, Lydda, Ramle, Beersheba, Acre, from among numberless others. . . . We came and turned the Arabs into tragic refugees. And still we dare slander and malign them, to besmirch their name; instead of being deeply ashamed of what we did, and trying to undo some of the evil we committed, we justify our terrible acts and even attempt to glorify them.[44]

The exact number of refugees was never accurately established. The U.N. Economic Survey Mission's report in 1949 put the total at 726,000; the Refugee Office of the U.N. Palestine Conciliation Commission placed it at 900,000. The answer is probably somewhere in between. By the winter of 1948, therefore, when the fighting was over, perhaps 800,000 Palestinians had become homeless; some had found shelter with relatives in other countries, most were camping out in Lebanon, Syria, Transjordan or in the two fragments that remained of their homeland, the Gaza Strip and the Jerusalem hinterland, henceforth to be known as the West Bank of the Jordan. They expected to remain refugees for weeks, at worst months, and that afterwards they would be allowed home. The United Nations, which had contributed so much towards the establishment of Israel, now asked the Zionists to take the refugees back. The U.N. mediator in Palestine, Count Folke Bernadotte, reported to the U.N. secretary-general: 'It would be an offence against the principles of elemental justice if these victims of the conflict were denied the right to return to their homes while Jewish immigrants flow into Palestine, and, indeed, offer at least the threat of permanent replacement of the Arab refugees who have been rooted in the land for centuries.'[45] The General Assembly agreed with Bernadotte and its resolution of December 1948 recommended 'that the refugees wishing to return to their homes and live at peace with their neighbours should be permitted to do so at the earliest practicable date, and that compensation should be paid for the property of those choosing not to return'.[46]

The Israelis, however, who had taken a lot of trouble to drive the Arabs out, were predictably reluctant to accept them back again. The new foreign minister, Moshe Shertok, explained that the proposal was impossible: writing to Bernadotte as early as 1 August, he declared that 'the reintegration of the returning Arabs into normal life, and even their mere sustenance, would present an insuperable problem'.[47] Why it should have been insuperable is not clear. After all, the U.N. partition plan, which the Israeli leaders claimed to have accepted, envisaged that the Jewish state would have as many Arabs as Jews in its population. Shertok was writing only three weeks after the expulsion of the inhabitants from Ramle and Lydda. Apart from the fact that these towns had been looted, which might have made life temporarily uncomfortable, it would have been perfectly possible for the Arabs to have returned to their homes and carried on as before. If 'reintegration' was merely going to mean a return to the *status quo ante,* it is difficult to see how this would have presented 'an insuperable problem'. But the Israelis remained adamant; the Arabs were not coming back. The General Assembly repeated its resolution and Israel repeated its refusal. 'Israel categorically rejects the insidious proposal for freedom of choice for the refugees,' Ben-Gurion said later in the Knesset.[48] Today, thirty-two years after, the United Nations still annually reaffirms that resolution and annually Israel takes no notice.

Israeli leaders pretended that the Arab exodus was totally unexpected. 'Pre-State Zionism could not even have conceived of such a thing,' wrote Ben-Gurion in 1952.[49] Weizmann termed the exodus 'a miraculous simplification of Israel's tasks'.[50] But was it really such a miracle and had Zionism really never conceived of such a thing? Hadn't Herzl wanted to 'spirit the penniless population across the border'? Hadn't Weizmann suggested the Arabs should be resettled in Transjordan? Hadn't numerous Zionists from Zangwill to Begin known all along that the Arabs would have to leave? How else would Weizmann have achieved his aim of making Palestine as 'Jewish as England is English'? No, 1948 was not an undreamed-of miracle; it was a deliberate and logical step in the progress of Zionism. Another step was taken in 1967 when the remaining regions of Palestine were seized and a few more areas scrubbed 'clean' of Arabs. A second refugee problem was created and history repeated itself. And were the refugees allowed back this time? 'No, no, of course not. Surely you must understand? They would have presented an insuperable problem.' Or as Dayan put it with more honesty on American television when asked whether Israel could not absorb the refugees and the inhabitants of the conquered territories: 'Economically we can but I think that is not in accord with our aims in the future.'[51]

4

The Exiles

All through the fearful, parched summer of 1948 the Palestinian exodus continued. It was leaderless and disorganized, long columns of men and women of all ages making their way to the nearest point of refuge. They carried their smaller children, a few provisions, perhaps a bundle of bedding – and the keys to their houses; for they all thought they would be returning, whether their side won or lost, after the fighting. Many families still have those keys.

Some went just a few miles inside the Lebanese border and waited for the fighting to end; as the weeks dragged on, and they became desperate for food and water, they walked to Tyre and Sidon; later, most of them went to Beirut. Others went to Syria, usually to Damascus, though a few stayed on the Golan Heights, condemned to live in sight of their homes on the other side of Lake Tiberias. Large numbers fled to areas of unoccupied Palestine, though many of them were moved on two or three times before they were allowed to settle down. Jaffa residents, who had escaped from their city before its capture in May, took refuge in Lydda or Ramle. In July they were expelled again with 60,000 others and forced to struggle up the hills to Ramallah, a town already full of refugees from West Jerusalem. When the Israelis seemed poised to take Ramallah as well, many took off again and crossed the Jordan. In the south of Palestine more than 200,000 refugees arrived destitute in the heavily populated Gaza Strip.

So the Exile began, with all the misery, homelessness and humiliation which it entailed and continues to entail. Only a

Palestinian can describe the desperation he has experienced by being stateless, of not belonging; the indignity of being a refugee, an outsider in every country he is allowed to visit; the feeling that he is where he is only on sufferance, that he is living on charity and will be thrown out if he misbehaves himself; the humiliation of being an alien, of being made to wait interminably for work permits and visas because he has no passport of his own; above all the longing to return home. Fawaz Turki, in his book *The Disinherited*, has described with dry irony how he was deported from London, without ever having left the airport, bearing a piece of paper pronouncing him 'of dubious nationality' and thus ineligible for permission 'to enter Her Majesty's realm'. 'Her Majesty's realm did not need a permit', he added, 'when it entered mine and robbed me of my nationality.'[1]

The Palestinians became a nation of wanderers. They travelled restlessly over the Arab world and beyond, alternately suspected and ignored, seeking vainly for a way to satisfy their overwhelming sense of identity and to reconcile it to their present circumstances. Wherever they went, they remained, by need and by inner compulsion, Palestinians, and the longer the exile went on the more intense the identity grew. Theo Canaan tried to re-create the architecture of Jerusalem in Lebanon. For many years Jabra I. Jabra wrote short stories about Bethlehem and Jerusalem from his exile in Baghdad; later he turned to novels, endlessly writing of the predicament of the Palestinian exile in the Arab world.[2] Tawfiq Sayigh died in California, the poetry to which he had devoted his life dominated by the theme of exile.

Perhaps it was inherent in their role that the intellectuals should spend the rest of their lives roaming the world, searching for something which they would never find; and it was always a doomed quest, for none of them were able to rid themselves of their troublesome identity and acquire another people's. Walid Khalidi, whose family had lived in Jerusalem for over a thousand years, travelled to England and became a don at Oxford. He spoke and wrote English better than most British academics but he remained a Palestinian and an Arab. When Britain collaborated with the Israelis over the Suez invasion in 1956, he resigned his post and went to Beirut.

It was perhaps easier for the businessmen, the merchants and traders. Their yearning for Palestine was no doubt as strong and as

sentimental as the intellectuals', but they were not searching for a
role; they already had one. The increasing importance of oil and
the economic expansion of the Arab world provided unexpected
opportunities for the Palestinian commercial and professional
classes. Many of them took part in the great boom in Beirut which,
following the collapse of Alexandria and the alienation of Haifa,
had become by the 1950s the greatest port in the eastern
Mediterranean. Palestinians became prominent in the Lebanese
world of banking and commerce and a few were able to integrate
themselves into Lebanese society. They opened businesses, set up
banks and ran their own construction companies.

Fuad Es Said is a good example of a Palestinian businessman
who managed to build a second life in Beirut. In 1948 he left Jaffa
with his young family to stay with his wife's relatives in Lebanon.
He expected to return home within a fortnight, back to the old
family house surrounded by orange groves. But he was not allowed back, and today, thirty-two years later, he still hasn't seen his
old home. In the disaster he lost everything he had — except for the
contents of two suitcases. The family settled in Beirut and slowly
he began to build up an import business. Through hard work he
became very rich and a respected figure in Beirut. At the same time
his wife came to be recognized as one of the most distinguished
women of modern Lebanon. She worked for the Red Cross and
the American University; she also ran the Ba albek International
Festival and was presented with the O.B.E. by the British ambassador. To all appearances, the Es Saids had become a Lebanese
family, and yet they never forgot that their home was in Palestine.
Like so many Palestinians, Fuad Es Said had that strange
masochistic tendency, which became both a need and an obsession, to talk about his homeland and to describe at length the
beauty of Jaffa and its orange groves. And like so many others, he
always talked of Jaffa as if it were still the charming old port of the
1940s and not the disgrace it is today — a derelict and neglected
suburb of Tel Aviv, whose orange groves have been uprooted and
filled with concrete.

Yet all these groups — the intellectuals, the businessmen and the
professionals — were in fact the lucky ones. They had skills to offer, they were able to support themselves — they could, at any rate,
choose their place of exile. That was something denied to perhaps
four-fifths of the population. These last formed the backbone of

Palestinian society, the fellahin and their dependants, the unskilled workers, the dispossessed peasants who had been living in the shanty towns of Haifa. They had little to offer their host countries, who had enough agricultural labourers and unskilled workers of their own. So, when it became clear that there was to be no quick return home, they went into the refugee camps and, for the most part, they stayed there.

The camps were set up, with the help of the United Nations Relief and Works Agency for Palestine Refugees in the Near East (U.N.R.W.A.) on any available land; several were grouped around the large cities – Amman, Beirut and Damascus – where there might be some chance of finding a job. In Jordan some of them were placed in the desert, and in other countries, on rough, barren land or on old campsites once used by the French and British armies. At the beginning, the refugees were herded into barracks, several families to a room, or packed closely in tents donated by the Red Cross and similar bodies. Musa Alami recalls that terrible winter of 1948 – 9 and remembers seeing twelve people with their heads in a tent and their legs in the rain outside. Four years later a majority of the camp refugees were still living in tents.[3] Conditions in these places were, without exception, disgusting; in 1955 an American rabbi compared them, unfavourably, with the Jewish refugee camps in Germany.[4] Food rations were miserable – as an U.N.R.W.A. report described it, 'enough to ward off starvation, little more'. There was little sanitation, no sewage system and only basic medical facilities. According to U.N.R.W.A. statistics, Qalandia camp outside Ramallah had an infant mortality rate of 172 per 1000 for babies in 1954 – 5.[5]

Qalandia is better today. The tents have gone and so have the public latrines. Gradually, during the 1950s, the U.N.R.W.A. hut spread over the camps. It came in three sizes – 3 metres by 3, 3 metres by 3½, and 3 metres by 4.2 – depending on the size of the family, plus a few square metres of 'backyard' behind, where the refugees might keep a goat or a few chickens, or even build on another room. Further improvements have been made over the years – most camps have electricity and running water at communal water points – but they do little to reduce the wretchedness and despair. Moreover, as a result of the high birth rate, many camps have become dangerously overcrowded: al-Karam camp, which U.N.R.W.A. had designed for 5,000 people, had a population of 17,000 by 1975.[6] In the camp at Dheisheh, midway between Bethlehem and Hebron, there are several families with twelve children and one with seventeen – and even families of this size are expected to live in the U.N.R.W.A. hut.

Nobody who has ever visited a Palestinian camp can forget the things he has seen or the desperation he has sensed: the squalid sheds, their roofs of tin or corrugated iron weighted down with stones to stop them blowing away; the walls of squashed petrol cans, a few plants growing in rusty tins, the clouds of flies, the stink of animals and excrement; the long lines of women, queuing up for rice, or kerosene, or a few kilos of flour; above all the faces, of women, worn and vacant, exhausted by years of carrying water and heavy loads, of children, wide-eyed and dirty, of men who push past sullenly, saying nothing.

Wavell camp is situated in al-Beqa´a valley in Lebanon, near the great Roman temples at Ba´albek. It was an old army barracks surrounded by refugee shelters, a neglected and desolate spot. Little has improved for its inmates since 1948. In 1975 there were still no doors to the building or to the latrines and the roof leaked in several places. The narrow rooms had been partitioned off with cement blocks and pieces of cardboard. In each there lived one family no matter how many people it contained. In some cases people had lived huddled together in the same room for fifteen years. They received basic rations of flour, sugar, rice and fat, and nothing else. The children were undernourished and many of them had influenza; in the camp there was nowhere for them to play. For the men there was no work either there or at Ba´albek, and it was a long journey to any major town.

Refugee life means, first of all, degradation. It means farmers, who once worked their own lands, having to choose between unemployment and selling lottery tickets; it means women having to wait in queues for handfuls of rice and sugar; it means children standing in bare feet along the airport road in Beirut, trying to sell chewing-gum to passing motorists. It means fear and insecurity. It means the intense and perpetual humiliation of constant interference from another country's police force. It means being exposed to the mockery and derision of local inhabitants, who would never allow the refugees to forget that they are aliens. Fawaz Turki remembers a street entertainer in Beirut who told his monkey to show the crowd 'how a Palestinian picks up his food rations'.[7] Another camp dweller recalls jeering Lebanese children who asked him to show them his tail. And the people of south Lebanon, who before 1948 were a good deal more backward than the Palestinians, referred to the Ain al-Hilweh camp near Sidon as 'the zoo'.[8]

Perhaps the most demoralizing feature of camp life was the lack of employment opportunities. It is often said that the host countries could and should have done more to find work for the refugees. Yet the Palestinians of the camps are mainly farmers or unskilled labourers who arrived in Jordan, Syria and Lebanon at a time when the inhabitants of these countries were already leaving the land in great numbers and searching for work in the cities. The population of Beirut has increased tenfold since the 1930s; by 1970 the city was one of the four or five most overcrowded in the world and contained nearly half the population of the country. This was caused primarily by the agricultural depression in the fifties and sixties which drove tens of thousands of small farmers to seek easier work in the capital.

The situation is similar in Syria. Many people in the West, such as Mr Walter Laqueur, the director of the Institute of Contemporary History in London, have advocated resettling the Palestinians in underpopulated areas in Syria where they can begin farming again. But they seem unaware of the fact that Syria cannot even deal with its own rural inhabitants. The population of Damascus is over two million and growing; hundreds of farmworkers, unable to find work in the countryside or in the provincial towns, are arriving there every week.

In these circumstances the refugees were naturally unable to continue working on the land. The best they could hope for was unskilled work in the construction industry, the most expanding section of the Lebanese economy until 1975. Even this was unsatisfactory: since many refugees were unable to acquire a work permit, employers felt they were justified in paying low wages; besides, over three-quarters of the refugees employed by other people were paid on a daily basis and could be sacked without notice. For those unable to set themselves up as artisans or small shopkeepers inside the camp, the only other sort of jobs to which an uneducated refugee could realistically aspire were as nightwatchmen, concierges or fruit and vegetable sellers working from barrows.

Something else which the advocates of resettlement fail to appreciate is the opposition of the Palestinians themselves to all designs to plant them permanently outside Palestine. The refugees do not want to go anywhere except their homeland. They are proud of the fact: they often claim that they are the first refugees in history who refused to accept refugee status and resettlement. This is something which Americans and Europeans seem unable to understand; they argue that after thirty-two years the refugees should now cut their losses and go off and live in northern Syria or Iraq and start again. Anyone who says that has probably never met a refugee, certainly not one who lives in a camp. To a Palestinian it is inconceivable that he should go anywhere but home and the idea of the Return has been the principal thing he has dreamt, thought and talked about for three decades. He admits that he personally may not see the Return and that is why he has told his children and grandchildren to re-bury his body in Palestine whenever they do go home. That is why a Palestinian child, who has never seen Palestine, will know all about his village or town. Go to Qalandia camp and ask the five-year-olds where they are from and they will tell you 'from Lydda' or 'Ramle' or any of the villages of the coast. They have never been to Lydda or Ramle but they have been told from birth about that July day when Moshe Dayan herded their parents and grandparents along the hill road to Ramallah.

In 1954 John Foster Dulles told an audience at the American University of Beirut that the Palestinian problem would be solved when the generation of exiles was replaced by its children because they would feel no attachment to their homeland.[9] He probably believed this to be true and, like the Israelis, he no doubt hoped it would be. But we now have a third generation of refugees and no serious observer would deny that the Palestinians' attachment to their land has intensified during the exile. As they themselves point out, if Palestine can mean so much to the Jews of the diaspora who hadn't seen it for 2,000 years, what can it mean to a people who actually remember it?

Inside the camps the refugees are organized according to where they came from in Palestine. Families who were neighbours in a Galilean village were later neighbours in the Lebanese camps. There they would continue to speak in the same dialect, cook the same dishes, sew the same embroidery. They guarded their culture closely and made no concessions to any other. That is why the sense of being Palestinian is so strong. That is why they have refused to be taken off and resettled in Syria or elsewhere.

Resettlement was one of U.N.R.W.A.'s early projects. The agency officials acted from the best of motives: they saw the wretched lives which people were leading and they wanted to improve them, to take them out of the disgusting, stinking slums where they lived and give them the opportunity to begin another life. And the Palestinians reacted with fury. They accused U.N.R.W.A. of trying to weaken their resolve and make them forget Palestine. They accused the agency of being a collaborator with the U.S.A. and Israel, of trying to make their exile permanent, and they told the officials that they were determined to stay in their slums and wait to go home. U.N.R.W.A. abandoned the project but ran into similar difficulties elsewhere. On one occasion, the agency decided to brighten up a part of the Borj al-Barajneh camp outside Beirut by planting a few trees. The following day the children of the camp uprooted all the trees and destroyed them. They didn't want trees in the camp because trees implied permanency. And their stay there was only temporary, they told you, because soon they would be going home.

A generation has grown up which has known no other life than the camps, and another has been born. Over half the refugees are under eighteen, brought up in this atmosphere and nurtured on hatred for the people who forced them to live like this. Education is the best escape route (the resistance movement is the other) and their parents recognize this. A successful education means a decent job, decent wages, financial security for the whole family. It also carries no implication of permanent resettlement outside Palestine. This is partly why the refugees have so many children: they reason that one of them will either win an U.N.R.W.A. scholarship or get the chance of a place in a vocational training centre. That means a job in the Gulf or Saudi Arabia and remittances back to their parents whose life will be made slightly more comfortable while they wait for the return.

Realizing that the Palestinians must have employment wherever they live, U.N.R.W.A. decided to make education its first priority. The agency handles primary and lower secondary education, subsidizes higher secondary education in governmental private schools and contributes a number of university scholarships each year. Perhaps the most important aspect of U.N.R.W.A.'s work is the courses it runs at vocational training centres in Jordan, Lebanon, Syria and the West Bank. After 1948 the governments of Syria and Jordan took on much of the refugees' education themselves; in Lebanon, however, which decided to preserve the Palestinians' alien status, the refugees were not admitted to state schools. U.N.R.W.A. thus had to educate them entirely by itself and, as a consequence, its schools in Lebanon became overcrowded and education standards were lower than in the other countries. As far as university education was concerned, Syria, Jordan and Egypt were the countries most open to students. Today there are about 40,000 Palestinians studying in universities around the world. While Egypt and Jordan account for the bulk of them, about 15,000 are at universities in the West. Most of the latter are engaged in specialist studies, such as computer science and microbiology, which are not yet available in the Arab world.

U.N.R.W.A.'s various training programmes provide intensive courses in practical fields and are greatly sought after. The vocational training centre in Damascus has 2,000 refugees applying annually for 250 places. These centres concentrate on preparing their students so that they will find jobs afterwards. Thus the Qalandia V.T.C. offers two-year courses in welding, plumbing, machine tools, auto-mechanics and other activities likely to procure them employment in the Gulf and elsewhere. Nearby, at the Ramallah Women's Training Centre, students are trained as nurses, pharmacists, clothes makers and secretaries – once again, the emphasis is on useful, practical skills which will make the exile more bearable. According to the principal of the Damascus V.T.C., nearly two-thirds of his students go to the Gulf countries; the remainder find work in Syria and a few join the resistance. He points out that his best students are invariably from the camps. U.N.R.W.A. has given them the chance to escape and few of them will throw it away.

The Palestinians have emerged during the exile as the best educated of all the Arab peoples, and they have a higher proportion of university students than either Britain or France. Education was the only thing left to them, the only way they could show people who did have countries that they were no better than the Palestinians. So they seized it, as a badge of pride as well as an investment for the future, and never let it go. Today Palestinians are in leading academic positions throughout the Middle East and in the West as well. Arnold Toynbee once called them the 'un-acknowledged pace-setters of the Arab world' and compared their expulsion from their country to the expulsion of the Greeks from Byzantium in 1453.[10]

Employment opportunities for the refugees varied considerably in each of the three host countries. Transjordan, which absorbed East Jerusalem and the West Bank and became known as Jordan, finished the 1948 war with a Palestinian majority. The Palestinians, both refugees and inhabitants of the West Bank, became citizens of the Hashemite Kingdom and immediately began to participate in the government of the country. The alliance between King Abdullah and the Nashashibi family was renewed and most of the Palestinian notables became supporters of the regime. Although there was usually tension between the refugees and the Bedouin supporters of the King, large numbers of Palestinians found work in Jordan and some of them joined the army and the civil service. Amman, which had been a large village in 1948, was built and inhabited almost exclusively by Palestinians.

In neither Syria nor Lebanon were the refugees given citizenship, although in Syria they were allowed to enter the army and government service. The 300,000 or so Palestinians in Syria today – perhaps a third of whom are refugees from the Jordanian and Lebanese civil wars – enjoy the same rights as the Syrians except that they do not have a passport. They have the same law and the same opportunities and they do not need work permits. In Lebanon, which admittedly was unable to support its own population, the situation has always been worse. There the Palestinians were regarded as non-nationals; they had to apply for work permits, which were often not granted, and they were prohibited from entering the army or the government. Yet, curiously, Beirut was the city in which the Palestinians were most successful. It was the only city in the Arab world which allowed virtually unrestricted freedom of speech and so it became the intellectual capital of the region. Palestinian academics gathered there, several of them working as political scientists, economists and historians at the American University; bodies like the Institute for Palestine Studies, the Palestine Research Centre and the Lebanese Association for Information on Palestine were also set up. In the business world, individual Palestinians were notably successful in construction and banking: two of the most remarkable banks which operated from Lebanon – the Arab Bank and the Intra Bank – were founded and directed by Palestinians. Most important of all, Beirut became the capital of the resistance movement and the headquarters of the Palestine Liberation Organization.

Yet, inevitably, career opportunities in the host countries were limited and from the beginning Palestinians had gone elsewhere to look for work. Perhaps 60,000 have emigrated to the West, the largest number going to the United States and most of the others to Britain, Australia, Canada or Brazil. Several hundred natives of the town of Beit Jala live in Latin America, dispersed over Chile, Bolivia, Peru, Ecuador, Honduras and Nicaragua. According to its mayor, Bethlehem has more than a hundred graduates with doctorates working in the United States. Most Palestinians in the West work in the professions or as academics. Far larger numbers, though, have gone to other parts of the Arab world, usually to the Gulf. If Beirut is the political and intellectual centre of the diaspora, Kuwait is its commercial base. Palestinians began arriving in Kuwait soon after 1948, in time to take part in the great oil boom. The last population census, published in 1975, gave their numbers as 204,000, and today there are more than a quarter of a million.[11] Comprising twenty per cent of the population, they form by far the largest of the non-Kuwaiti communities and the enormous role they have played in the building of the state is acknowledged by the Kuwaitis themselves.

Although only a handful have been given Kuwaiti nationality, most Palestinians have gone there, travelling on a Jordanian passport or a Syrian or Lebanese *laissez-passer,* in the hope of remaining there – at least until their future as a people is decided. By contrast with their compatriots in the Levantine countries, the Palestinians in Kuwait are almost uniformly prosperous (manual labourers in Kuwait tend to be Egyptians, Iranians, Pakistanis or Koreans). More than half of them are in the private business sector, usually in partnership with Kuwaitis, and control vast enterprises such as the Consolidated Contractors Company which now operates as far afield as Mauritania and the Sudan. But there are 21,000 Palestinians in the civil service and they easily outnumber Kuwaiti nationals in the teaching and medical professions.[12] They do not become ministers or heads of department but in government, as in business, the most active brains are Palestinian. Nevertheless the Palestinian community is not wholly welcomed by the

Kuwaitis because of its usually radical politics. It also suffers a certain amount of discrimination. For example, as the standard of education is much higher among Palestinians than among Kuwaitis, the government has had to pass legislation which gives job preference to its own nationals in various fields.

Palestinian communities have sprung up in all the Arab countries of the Gulf with the exception of Oman which excludes them. The largest and fastest growing is in the United Arab Emirates; about 60,000 Palestinians are thought to live in Abu Dhabi and Dubai, although the government refuses to break down its 826,000 population into countries of origin.[13] In social terms it is similar to the community in Kuwait: doctors, clerks, contractors, skilled workers such as electricians, mechanics and so on. Many of them are senior officials (though never the most senior) in ministries and embassies abroad. Even more than in Kuwait they dominate the native community and the contrast between them is visible. The Palestinians are fair-skinned and wear Western clothes; they move faster and speak a very different Arabic from the dark Arabians in their immaculate white robes. Some Palestinians feel that they are resented, which is perfectly possible, since there is a sort of colonialist relationship between them and their hosts. But they have never had the kind of problems in the Gulf which they have had to face in Jordan or Lebanon. On only one occasion have Palestinians been subjected to any sort of police pressure in Abu Dhabi. This was in 1977 when a Palestinian gunman killed an under-secretary from the U.A.E. Foreign Ministry – probably by mistake; the real target was almost certainly the Syrian foreign miniser, Abdul Halim Khaddam, who was near him at the time.

Many of the Palestinians living in the Gulf are very rich indeed. There is no income tax in these countries and some businessmen earn £100,000 a year. But that dubious equation which plays such a part in American foreign policy – as material wealth rises, nationalism diminishes – doesn't apply here. These businessmen still feel the pull of their homeland; they send contributions to the Palestine National Fund or the Palestine Red Crescent (the Palestine equivalent of the Red Cross) and some of them are members of the Palestine National Council (a sort of parliament in exile). They are paranoiacally aware of their statelessness and they yearn for a country to which they can belong. Even if they were to continue living in Abu Dhabi or Qatar or Bahrain, they would still need somewhere with which they could identify. Their attachment to their homeland is as strong as ever and they show it by the way they bring up their children. Like Palestinian children throughout the diaspora, these know where they come from in Palestine; in Kuwait many of them attend schools run by the P.L.O.

This sense of attachment — so ineradicable that it has defeated all attempts at resettlement — is difficult for a non-Palestinian to describe. It can, perhaps, be only really understood by listening to a Palestinian talking about his homeland. Abdullah Haman is now the U.N.R.W.A. area officer for the Hebron district in the West Bank. Before 1948 he was living in the orange-growing belt near Jaffa, in a village between Rehovot and Rishon le Zion. Forced from his home by one of the earliest operations of Plan Dalet, he became a Jordanian citizen and settled in Hebron. In 1967 the Israelis overran his second home, in the process opening up the border that separated him from his old village. Soon afterwards, with that compulsion common to so many Palestinians, he made the journey to his former home. His house and those of his relations had long been destroyed but the citrus groves were still there and he stood and watched their harvesting. He describes the experience with tears: 'You cannot imagine the pain of going back to your childhood home, of seeing your orange groves as you remembered them, heavy with ripe fruit. You cannot know the agony of seeing other people manhandling your trees and of knowing that you are a stranger there, forbidden to touch even one orange.'

In a small shop near the Azem palace, deep in old Damascus, an old Palestinian worked until recently, selling copper pots and inlaid wooden boxes. He came from near Rosh Pinna in eastern Galilee and was forced into exile when Yigal Allon decided to 'clean' the area of Arabs. But every year, on the anniversary of his exile, he travelled to Quneitra and climbed the Golan Heights. At a spot between Hula and Lake Tiberias he halted and looked down at his home in the plain below — a small dot some five or six miles away. Then he prayed that he would be allowed back. He did this for nineteen years until in 1967 the Israelis took the Golan as well and even that consolation was denied him. But until the day of his death he shared the same hopes as every other Palestinian — that one day they would let him go home.

Palestinian poetry also expresses this sense of attachment; much of it, indeed, is concerned with little else. Arabic, more than most languages, suffers in translation and there is little point in discussing the merits of this poetry here. But it is of interest because it illustrates so well the Palestinians' attitudes towards their homeland. Modern Palestinian poetry, which one critic has termed 'the poetry of occupation',[14] can be said to have originated with the works of Tawfiq Zayyad, Samih al-Qasim, Selim Jubran, Fouzi al-Asmar, and Mahmoud Darwish – all of them, except al-Asmar, Arab members of the Israeli Communist Party (see Chapter 5). Their influence on Palestinian poets in the diaspora has been immense, and since 1967, a generation of younger poets, writing in similar style, has grown up under Israeli occupation in the West Bank and Gaza.

Palestinian poetry is lyrical, written in unrhymed verse, and concentrates on imagery. Jerusalem and the land of Palestine recur in poem after poem: Palestine as an idea becomes a lover or a mother, its fate compared to the rape and disgrace of a woman. Sometimes, as in poems by Fadwa Tuqan and Tawfiq Zayyad, its tragedy is illustrated by the Crucifixion. The land of Palestine is represented by the olive tree but other symbols include orchards, orange trees and lilies. The Palestinian's relationship to his land, to the soil itself – a relationship which is organic and inalienable – is well expressed in Selim Jubran's poem, 'Announcer for the Wind and Rain':

> You can uproot the trees
> From a mountain embracing the moon
> In my village
> You can plough all the houses of my village
> Without a trace,
> You can take my rebec
> And burn it, having cut its string,
> You can . . .
> But you cannot strangle my tune
> For I am the lover of the land
> Singer for the wind and rain.[15]

The same feelings are described in Fouzi al-Asmar's poem, 'The Impossible'. It was written while he was in prison in Israel in 1970.

He was held without trial for fifteen months and repeatedly told
that he would only be released if he left the country. This is his
reply:

> Don't ask me the impossible
> Don't ask me to hunt stars, walk to the sun.
> Don't ask me to empty the sea, to erase the day's light
> I am nothing but a man.
>
> Don't ask me to abandon my eyes, my love,
> the memory of my childhood.
>
> I was raised under an olive tree,
> I ate the figs of my orchard
> Drank wine from the sloping vineyards
> Tasted cactus fruit in the valleys   more, more.
>
> The nightingale has sung in my ears
> The free winds of fields and cities have always touched me
> My friend
> You cannot ask me to leave my own country.[16]

5

The Arabs in Israel

In the Knesset debate on the Citizenship Law of 1950, the Israeli minister of the interior referred to the Palestinians still remaining within the frontiers of the new state as 'foreigners'. It was an odd way to describe a people who had lived for centuries in the same place, but even the Palestinians themselves, in the post-war years, must have felt that they were almost foreigners in their own land. Less than a tenth of their number remained in Israel and even some of these were refugees who had fled their homes to areas later captured by the Israeli army. The 1948 war had transformed them from being part of a large majority to minority status; after the first waves of Jewish immigration in the early fifties they formed barely ten per cent of the population.

150,000 Arabs were resident in the State of Israel as it emerged from the 1949 armistice agreements. Most of them were in the north, in Galilee and the district known as the Triangle; a few thousand, mainly Bedouin, remained in the south; but in the centre, where the towns of Jaffa, Lydda and Ramle still stood, there were hardly any Arabs at all. The survivors owed their preservation to a number of reasons. In Lydda a few hundred people were allowed to stay because they worked for the railway and would therefore be useful to the Israelis.[1] To the north the villagers of Furaidis had a traditional friendship with the settlers of Zikhron Ya'aqov and were thus protected[2] — as were the Druzes from Mount Carmel whom the Zionists had long cultivated. The Palestinians of the Triangle became inhabitants of the state when their area was ceded to Israel at Rhodes, and in Galilee a number of Arabs remained simply because their area was too large for the Israelis to 'clean' thoroughly. As for Nazareth, the surrender of the largely Catholic town without a shot made it difficult for the Zionists to treat its population too roughly.

The Rhodes agreement left the Arabs dazed and demoralized. Many of their relatives had joined the exodus and they had no idea to which country they had gone or even if they were still alive. Thirty thousand Arabs were refugees inside Israel, where many had fled to Nazareth and were now refused permission to return to their villages. Suddenly the Arabs found themselves dominated by the movement they had feared and opposed for decades. They were placed under military rule and forbidden to move outside their areas without permits; in Lydda they were unable to walk outside their own quarter alongside the railway which was soon to be known as the 'Arab ghetto'.[3] Israel and the Zionist movement were now their masters and even their children were made to sing the *Hatikva* (the Israeli national anthem) each morning in school.[4] Throughout the country the Palestinian community was in chaos, from the Bedouin tribes of the Negev, which had lost eighty per cent of their numbers, to the Greek Catholics in Galilee who had lost nearly all their priests.

Before the experience of the Israeli Arabs can be described, Israeli attitudes towards them must be understood. When Israel's first prime minister, David Ben-Gurion, read out Israel's declaration of independence, he talked about liberty and equality for all citizens, and so on. But it was rhetorical and meaningless and he knew it. Ben-Gurion didn't like the Arabs and he was delighted that so many had left the country. However, he would have preferred to have thrown them all out because, like Weizmann, he wanted a state 'as Jewish as England is English' or, like Dayan, 'a Jewish state like the French have a French state'. When he drove around the Galilee in the 1950s, he was so disgusted by the sight of Arab villages in the distance that he said: 'Whoever tours the Galilee gets the feeling that it is not part of Israel.'[5] In 1958, according to the Israeli newspaper *Ha'Aretz,* he 'refused the identity card issued to him because it was written in Arabic as well as Hebrew'.[6] Commenting on this report, Uri Avneri, editor of *Ha'Olam HaZe* and now a member of the Knesset, wrote:

Ben-Gurion has always been utterly reactionary in his opposition to anything Arab. The prime minister has never visited an Arab town or village since the establishment of the state.* When he visited the Jewish town of Upper Nazareth, he refused to visit Arab Nazareth, only a few hundred metres away from the Jewish town. In the first ten years after the establishment of the state, Ben-Gurion did not recieve a single delegation of Arab citizens.[7]

It may be argued that this was the attitude of one man and so it was. But he was the most powerful leader in Israeli history and these views were shared by most of the Israeli Establishment. The country's second most powerful figure since independence, Mrs Golda Meir, once admitted that she could not sleep at night because she was kept awake by 'the thought of all the Arab babies who were being born at that moment.'[8]

In October 1973 the British M.P., Robin Maxwell-Hyslop, told the House of Commons about the attitude of David Hacohen, then the influential chairman of the Knesset Foreign Affairs Committee:

Six weeks after that war [June 1967] six hon. members of this House, three from each side, including myself, went to Israel and to Jordan as the guests of those countries. There was a horrifying moment for me. We were all present as guests at lunch of the Foreign Affairs Committee of the Knesset in Jerusalem. After lunch the chairman of the Foreign Affairs Committee of the Knesset spoke with great intemperance and at great length to us about the Arabs. When he drew breath I was constrained to say, 'Doctor Hacohen, I am profoundly shocked that you should speak of other human beings in terms similar to those in which Julius Streicher spoke of the Jews. Have you learned nothing?' I shall remember his reply to my dying day. He smote the table with both hands and said, 'But they are not human beings, they are not people, they are Arabs'. He was speaking of the Arab refugees.[9]

It is often said that Israeli attitudes towards the Arab population were conditioned by feelings of insecurity and the enmity of the

---

* The following year he did in fact visit the Druze village of Jalis in a helicopter. In Israel, however, the Druzes are not classified as Arabs (see pages 111–2).

Arab world. That may be so. The fact is that, for whatever reasons, hostility and prejudice towards the Arabs formed the basis of Israel's attitude towards its minority population right from the establishment of the state. Only if this fact is recognized can the problems of the Palestinians in Israel, as described in the following pages, be properly understood.

On 21 May 1948, six days after the declaration of independence, Israel declared a state of emergency. As it is still in force today, the government can continue using the Defence (Emergency) Regulations 1945, which it inherited from the mandate government. Under these regulations military rule was imposed on all the Arab centres of population and was not abolished until 1966. The powers of the military governors were enormous and they were used extensively. Freedom of movement for the Arabs was almost totally restricted in the first ten years of the state and a man wanting to travel from a Galilee village to nearby Haifa to look for work had to apply several days in advance for a military permit. Within the regulations Arabs could be exiled, with no reasons given, to remote parts of the country and made to report several times a day to the nearest police station. They could also be arrested and detained, for an unlimited period, without being charged. The poet, Fouzi al-Asmar, was imprisoned without trial for fifteen months and only released after representations had been made on his behalf from abroad. Even then he was kept under house arrest in Lydda for another year while the Israeli authorities repeatedly 'encouraged' him to leave the country.[10]

As if the mandate regulations were not bad enough, the powers of the military government were supplemented by the Law and Administration Ordinance which enabled the minister of defence to authorize 'defence areas' and 'security zones' whenever it suited him. It was under this ordinance that most of the expulsions of villagers and the expropriation of their land was carried out. All the minister had to do was to declare such and such a 'security zone', prohibited to all except the military and the police, and the inhabitants of the zone could be evicted. This happened to several tribes of the Negev Bedouin and to various villages in the Galilee, including Iqrit, Kafr Birim, Majdal and Umm al-Faraj.[11]

These regulations, then, provided the *legal* framework for Israel's treatment of its Arab minority. By any standards they were oppressive and it is interesting to read what one Zionist lawyer, Mr

Ya'acov Shimshon Shapiro, had to say about the mandate regulations in 1946: 'The system established in Palestine since the issue of the Defence Laws is unparalleled in any civilized country; there were no such laws even in Nazi Germany. . . . It is our duty to tell the whole world that the Defence Laws passed by the British mandatory government of Palestine destroy the very foundations of justice in this land.'[12] Mr Shapiro later became attorney-general and minister of justice in Israel but, curiously enough, he saw no need to repeal them. Laws, which are apparently so odious that they did not exist 'even in Nazi Germany' evidently became quite tolerable when applied to Arabs.

Any visitor to Israel, provided he is not accompanied by a guide from the Ministry of Information, will notice that the Arabs of the country are an underprivileged minority. The discrimination against them is blatant and institutionalized. As Mrs Shulamit Aloni, member of the Knesset and leader of the Civil Rights Movement in Israel, said in the Knesset in October 1975: 'In the twenty-eight years since the creation of the State of Israel we have not yet learned that one should behave towards Arabs as citizens with equal rights and duties and treat their problems like those of all citizens, directly and without discrimination.'[13]

Education is a major grievance. Standards of education are very low among the Arab population partly because there are not enough schools and partly because the existing ones are so poorly equipped. At the village of Deir al-Asad in Galilee there are 1,300 pupils attending elementary school – enough, one would imagine, to justify a secondary school. But there isn't one there or anywhere nearby – except in Karmi'el which is only open to Jews – and anyone who wants to go to secondary school from Deir al-Asad has to commute long distances, at considerable expense, either to Acre or Nazareth. In these circumstances it is hardly surprising that two-thirds of Arab children never get beyond the elementary level. As for the schools that do exist, many of these are disgraceful. There is an appalling shortage of facilities and almost all schools lack sports fields, libraries and laboratories. In Nazareth the classrooms are makeshift affairs, housed in rented buildings and scattered all over the city.

Israel's neglect for Arab education can be measured by the number of university students; although the Arabs form fifteen per cent of Israel's population, they comprise less than three per

cent of the country's university students.[14] This neglect is inten-
tional: Israel does not want a well educated minority. As Mr Uri
Lubrani, formerly adviser to the prime minister on Arab affairs,
once explained: 'It would have been better, perhaps, if there were
no Arab students. If they remained hewers of wood it would
perhaps be easier to rule over them.'[15] Apart from the need to keep
the Arabs in a state of ignorance so that they will continue to provide Israel with a large fund of unskilled labour, the government's educational policy is clearly designed to limit any feelings
of national consciousness among the Palestinians. To this end,
Arab schoolchildren were made to sing the Jewish national anthem. To assist this attempt at cultural domination, not a single
Arabic book was published in Israel during the first ten years of
the state.[16] School curricula are brought in to bolster this policy.
Arab children at secondary school study both Hebrew and Arabic
literature, but, while they are made to study Zionist poets like
Bialik, Shim'oni and Y.L. Peretz, the only Arabic poems they can
read deal with nature, love and similar subjects.[17] Similarly, they
spend 256 hours studying the oral Jewish tradition and the Bible
(presumably so that they learn that Palestine does not, in fact,
belong to them) and only thirty hours on the Koran.[18] Furthermore, Jewish history is given more time than Arab history,[19] and
the great eras of the latter are omitted from school textbooks.[20]
The only thing an Arab schoolchild will learn about Saladin is that
he had a Jewish physician, Maimonides.[21]

Labour is another of the basic Arab grievances. Farming had
always been the backbone of the Palestinian economy and even in
1948 a majority of the Arab population worked in agriculture. But
the expropriation of land, which followed the war and which will
be discussed later, destroyed the livelihood of many of the surviving Arabs and drove them to the towns in search of work. The
Israeli writer, Aharon Cohen, has described their position:

The Arab worker who managed to find a job in the first ten
years after the establishment of Israel was restricted to unpleasant jobs that Jewish workers would not accept, like in sewage
or building. The wages paid to Arab workers never equalled
those paid to Jews, even if the Arab was doing the same work.
In practice many jobs were closed to Arab workers and
employees. The Arab worker who found a temporary job in a

remote Jewish colony could be dismissed on the grounds that he was 'not organized'.[22]

'Not organized' meant that he did not belong to the Histadrut, the General Federation of Labour in Israel – which was not surprising as, until 1962, no Arab was allowed to become a member of this all-powerful trade union body. Even when Arabs were allowed to join the Histadrut, their position improved only marginally and still today most of the menial jobs in Israel – dishwashing, road-mending, garbage-collecting and so on – are performed by Arabs.

Some Arabs still work in agriculture, not usually as farmers or tenants, but as labourers on Jewish farms. Officially this is highly disapproved of as only Jews are allowed to work on land owned by the state or the Jewish National Fund (i.e. about ninety per cent of the country). In December 1974 the Israeli minister of agriculture declared that 'the domination of Jewish agriculture by Arab workers is a cancer in our body.'[23] A few months later, his ministry and the Settlement Department of the Jewish Agency began, according to the Israeli newspaper *Ma'ariv,* 'a vehement campaign to eradicate the plague of land-leasing and orchard-leasing to Bedouin and Arab farmers in the Western Galilee'.[24] Nevertheless, because Arabs are much cheaper to employ than Jews and also because they can be dismissed without problems, both the 'cancer' and the 'plague' still continue.

The expansion of the Israeli economy and the decrease in Jewish immigration from abroad produced jobs for most of the Arab population, even if they were largely menial ones. They did not, however, improve the position of the Palestinian intellectuals, who were often unable to gain employment, firstly because they were Arabs, and secondly because they were considered politically 'unsound'. Even if they managed the first hurdle, which many did not, the second produced a variety of complications.

Fouzi al-Asmar lost his first job at a printing house run by the socialist party, Mapam, because he refused to become a party member; later, when he was turned down by the Bank Leumi le-Israel, he was told by an official of the L.T.M. (the police special branch) that he would never get a job until he changed his political line (a moderate form of Arab nationalism).[25] When Muhammad Mi'ari was appointed lecturer at Haifa University, the Ministry of

Defence tried to persuade him to become an informer. When he refused, the ministry informed the dean at Haifa that he was a security risk and should not be accepted as lecturer. Only when Mi'ari caused a public outcry was he reinstated.[26]

The appointments page of the Hebrew newspaper, *Yedi'ot Aharonot,* demonstrates another method of job discrimination against Arabs. About ninety per cent of the jobs offered are reserved for 'army leavers only'. As no Arabs, unless they are Druzes, do military service, this is a none-too-subtle means of ensuring that they don't apply for most of the jobs.

Discrimination against the Arab areas, particularly in the sphere of housing, is another cause for complaint. It is here that the anti-Arab policy of the government is at its most blatant. Not only are Arabs forbidden to live on land owned by the Jewish National Fund, they have also had to endure the expropriation of their own lands so that new towns can be built in which only Jews can live. The two most notorious examples of this are the towns of Karmi'el and Upper Nazareth. Karmi'el is a hideous town of uniform tower blocks stuck insensitively on to the Galilean landscape. It was built by Arab labour on land expropriated from three Arab villages yet no Arab can either live or open a business there. When two Arab businessmen tried independently to get permission to build factories on the town's industrial site in 1972, it created an uproar among the inhabitants. The latter claimed that Karmi'el was part of a project to 'Judaize the Galilee', that they had been promised it would remain an exclusively Jewish town, and that it would be intolerable if Arabs were allowed to live there. The government accepted their arguments, and permission to the businessmen was refused.[27] On another occasion, when one man agreed to rent his villa to an Arab from a nearby village, most of the residents signed a petition demanding rescission of the agreement as 'a matter of principle'.[28]

The problems of the Arab town of Nazareth, and its relationship with its Jewish neighbour, Upper Nazareth, illustrate the difficulties with which the Israeli Arabs are constantly confronted. Nazareth is the largest Arab town in Israel and its population is split evenly between Christians and Muslims. Its pre-1948 population of 14,000 was swollen by 10,000 refugees from rural Galilee and since then the population has grown to 45,000. Today it is a shoddy, overcrowded and neglected town. Partly because its council is controlled by the Communist Party but mainly because it is Arab, the government is not interested in Nazareth's development. The town receives no development funds and has no industry; the few factories it possessed during the mandate were closed down in the fifties. This attitude forces eighty per cent of the labour force to seek work outside the town, usually in the Jewish factories of Haifa. As for public housing, this simply does not exist. According to a report in the Israeli newspaper, *Ha' Aretz,*

The Ministry of Housing has not built a single apartment in Nazareth since 1966. Nazareth requires every year an addition of 400 – 500 residential units to keep housing conditions at their present level, and without taking into consideration the housing requirements for the absorption of young people migrating to Nazareth from the neighbouring villages.[29]

The situation is exacerbated by the presence of Upper Nazareth on a hill overlooking the old town. During the fifties, land was expropriated from several villages and from Nazareth itself in order to build an exclusively Jewish town in an otherwise Arab area. Work was begun on the site without the mayor of Nazareth being consulted or even invited to look at the plans. Today it has a Jewish population of 16,000 yet its budget allocation is higher than that of the Arab town whose population is nearly three times greater. Upper Nazareth has several factories – textiles, food industry, and car assembly plants – and no unemployment. It also has scores of empty flats, but, because they are built on land owned by the Jewish National Fund, Arabs are forbidden to buy these – even if the land was taken from them in the first place. When a few Arab families disregarded the law in 1975 and either bought or rented several flats, pandemonium broke out among the Jewish population. According to the Israeli newspaper, *Ma'ariv,* 'The residents complain that the situation is intolerable . . . [and] threaten to abandon the town en masse and move to neighbouring cities – if nothing is done to prevent the penetration of Arab families into that section of the city [i.e. Upper Nazareth], and in particular into the housing blocks where they live.'[30]

Arab rural areas suffer in the same way as Nazareth. According to one member of the Knesset, not more than one per cent of the money allocated to local development goes to the Arab sector.[31]

Another, Mrs Shulamit Aloni, declared in 1975 that 'a comparative analysis of the budget of the local municipalities for the year of 1974 – 75 in the Jewish and Arab sectors demonstrates clearly gross discrimination against the Arab sector.'[32] She went on to point out that while the Arab town of Shafa'amr, with a population of 15,000, had a budget of 3.9 million Israeli pounds, and the Arab village of Kafr Kanna had a budget of 1.2 million for its 7,000 people, the Jewish town of Migdal Ha'Emek (12,000 inhabitants) received 15 millions and the settlement of Azatah (now called Netivot), with a population of only 5,500, was allocated 17 millions. In other words, for every pound spent on an inhabitant of the Arab village of Kafr Kanna, twenty-two were spent on each Jewish settler at Azatah.

This discrimination is obvious to anyone who takes the trouble to compare an Arab village with a Jewish settlement. The settlements are usually hideous but they are at least planned and they are given basic amenities – roads, water, electricity and so on – before the settlers move in. The Arab villages are totally unplanned and lack many important facilities. They had to wait years for electricity and many of them still don't have it. No Arab village has either a sewerage system or a network of paved roads. Telephones and health centres are also non-existent and there is not one public library in any Arab town or village in Israel.

The issue which has always overshadowed all others for the Arabs is the expropriation of their land. The great confiscations took place soon after the 1948 war when nearly a million acres of Arab land were expropriated. Since then, according to Israeli statistics, a further 440,000 acres have been seized, excluding the areas taken from the Bedouin in the Negev.[33] How has this come about? What pretexts have the Israelis used to grab all this land? The early methods were crude: under the Defence (Emergency) Regulations 1945, expulsions and expropriations could be carried out 'for security reasons'. Israeli soldiers could merely enter an Arab village, as they did at Ashqelon in 1950, round up the inhabitants and take them to the frontier – and no questions were asked. 'Security' was the excuse. Once these expulsions had taken place, the villages were usually destroyed and their lands given to a nearby kibbutz or moshav. (A kibbutz is a Jewish collective farm and a moshav is a smallholders' co-operative.)

This method was employed at several villages in northern

Galilee. Two of the most notorious incidents took place at the Greek Catholic village of Iqrit and the Maronite village of Kafr Birim. In the autumn of 1948, after the fighting in Galilee was over, Kafr Birim was occupied by the Israeli army. A few days later the inhabitants were informed that they would have to leave their homes temporarily as military operations were expected in their area. They were reluctant to do this and only moved to some nearby caves after a promise from an official at the Ministry of Police and Minorities that they would soon be allowed to return home.[34] This promise was repeated a few months later by the prime minister's adviser for Arab affairs.[35] But nothing happened. The villagers waited another three years and then took their case to the Supreme Court which ruled in their favour. The army, however, refused to implement the court's decision and, in September 1953, it mined the village and ordered the Israeli air force to drop incendiary bombs. Every building was destroyed except the church. Most of the land was given to the recently established Kibbutz Birim, the rest to a moshav settlement of Iranian Jews.

The fate of Iqrit was similar. The Supreme Court recognized the villagers' right to return to their land and denied that the army had any right to prevent it. In giving its verdict, the court pointed out that the miltary governor had not even issued an expulsion order. The military governor therefore rectified the omission and Iqrit was declared a 'security zone' forbidden to civilians.[36] The villagers complained once again to the Supreme Court but, before it had time to consider the case, the military acted. On Christmas Day 1951 army sappers blew up every house in the village. They even took the mukhtar of Iqrit to a hill overlooking the village and made him watch the demolition.

The inhabitants of both villages continued to live in the area (although they were supposed to be security risks) and some of them even became labourers on the kibbutz and the moshav which had displaced them. But they refused to surrender their claim to the land and only a few accepted compensation. In 1972 they began lobbying again. Dayan had just abolished security zones within the state's 1949 boundaries since they were no longer necessary (Israel having greatly extended its borders in 1967) and the villagers believed there was no legal obstacle to their return. In August of that year they occupied the ruins of their homes before being forcibly removed by the police. The affair caused a major political debate, with most of the opposition parties siding with the villagers. When the government refused to change its policy on the issue, Menachem Begin, the leader of the right-wing coalition Gahal, was particularly critical. 'An injustice has been done to the residents of Kafr Birim,' he declared. 'This is a mistaken decision.' In the election campaign of 1977 Begin went even further. He specifically promised the villagers that they would return home if he was elected. As prime minister this proved a huge embarrassment to him and he tried to postpone taking a decision for as long as possible. It was left to his agriculture minister to reveal in January 1979 that the special cabinet committee on Iqrit and Kafr Birim had decided that the villagers would not return.[38]

Most of the expropriations, however, were completed within the framework of civilian law. In the early years of the state the government passed a great many laws, all of them designed to make the expropriations appear legal and respectable: the Law of Acquisition of Absentee Property, Emergency Articles for the Exploitation of Uncultivated Lands, the Law for the Requisition of Land in times of Emergency, the Law for the Acquisition of Land and so on. Even these didn't cover all the needs of the government and in some cases it resorted to simple confiscation. In order to acquire land for the building of Karmi'el in 1962, the minister of finance merely issued a decree ordering the confiscation of 1,350 acres of land belonging to three Arab villages. This move completely destroyed the economy of one village, Deir al-Asad, which lost all of its best arable land as a result.[39]

These sets of laws sound harmless enough but the problems begin with their definition. The Emergency Articles for the Exploitation of Uncultivated Lands are all very well but what exactly do they mean? The title sounds reasonable but how was 'uncultivated' defined? In most cases it was quite simple. The military governor would designate a piece of land as a 'defence area', to which civilians were denied entry. The owners of the land were thus unable to farm it and so it became derelict. Then the Ministry of Agriculture stepped in, declared it uncultivated and ordered its expropriation. The Law of Acquisition of Absentee Property was even more invidious since it gave the state powers to confiscate all Arab land unless the owners could first produce documentary evidence showing that the land was actually theirs and secondly prove that they had not left their place of residence between 29 September 1947 and 1 September 1948 to go anywhere outside Jewish control. As most of the land was never registered but was farmed by families through hereditary right, it was obviously impossible for many people to prove that they were the owners. Furthermore, as is normally the case in wartime and was particularly so in this war, many people did leave their places of residence; and, since they were Arabs, it was natural that they fled to areas controlled by other Arabs. According to Israeli law, they thus became absentees even if they never left the area which later became Israel. Mahmoud Safadi was a businessman with property from Tiberias. When Yigal Allon began his notorious 'cleansing' operation in eastern Galilee, he left his home and went to stay with relatives in Nazareth, which was then under Arab control. He thus became an absentee, although he had never left Israel, and lost all his property.

These laws affected all sections of the Arab community. Under the Law of Acquisition of Absentee Property, the Islamic Waqf, or Religious Muslim Trusteeship Fund, lost all its property in Israel. At the same time the Supreme Muslim Council was abolished and its role assumed by a Jewish official. It is not exactly clear why this happened or how a religious charity could be deemed to be 'absent'. Nevertheless, all the Waqf's property was confiscated and some of it was sold or demolished. All but a half acre of the Muslim cemetry at Jaffa was expropriated in order to build the Tel Aviv Hilton and lay out the grounds for the Independence Gardens. Into the remaining half acre all the bones from the rest of the graveyard were placed, but even this was later used for a new road complex.

The victims of these laws also included the Bedouin of the Negev. In 1948, about 59,000 of the 70,000 tribesmen left the Negev.[40] Some, like 6,000 members of the Azazma tribe, were expelled, while others left of their own accord and went to Sinai or Transjordan. The war destroyed the tribal structure of those who remained, and all but two of the sub-tribes lost large numbers of their members. The survivors lost nearly all their cultivable land and most of their pasture; they were then removed to an area north-east of Beersheba and forbidden to stray outside it. 'In view of the great strategic importance of the Negev', announced the Israeli ambassador to Britain in 1958, 'and the need for special security arrangements', etc., '. . . it has therefore been found necessary to restrict the movements of the Bedouin in the Negev to a defined area.'[41] The government's policy, then, was to treat the Bedouin as the Americans had treated the Red Indians: to crowd them into reservations that kept getting smaller for 'security reasons', and encourage them to settle down. The process is called 'relocation', one of the many euphemisms employed by Israeli officials.

Today the Negev tribes have a population of 40,000, and Israeli policy towards them has changed. The government's industrial plans and the gradual withdrawal of the armed forces from Sinai have given the Negev a new importance. In practice this means that the nomadic life of the Bedouin will have to stop and they will be made to settle down in the new urban centres which the government is building for them. But the path from the desert to the town is too short for the Bedouin and they insist that, if they have to settle, it will be as farmers rather than industrial workers. To this the officials reply that there is not enough water but they do not explain why there is abundant water for the Jewish settlements and none for the Bedouin.[42] Since the tribesmen are not co-operating with the government, the latter has established a unit called the Green Patrol which is meant to harass the Bedouin and prevent them grazing their flocks on state-owned land. But in practice, according to Israeli civil rights supporters, the purpose of the Green Patrol is to reduce the tribal flocks and to drive the herdsmen off their lands. As a reporter on the *Jerusalem Post* noted in February 1979: 'Reports of bullying and intimidation by patrolmen carrying out evacuation edicts recur with alarming frequency. Units have been known to swoop down on encampments, confiscating or scattering herds, destroying property, and threatening women and children with loaded pistols.'[43]

Perhaps the people who suffered most from the various laws of expropriation were the Muslim villagers of the Triangle. This is the district bordering the plain and the Samarian foothills a few miles inland from the coast which stretches from Herzliyya to Zikhron Ya'aqov. These villages had been established in the nineteenth century by inhabitants from the Nablus mountains. In the 1947 partition plan they were assigned, with the whole of Samaria, to the proposed Arab state. During the war they held out against the Zionists and were never captured, though much of their land nearer the sea was occupied by the Israeli army. At the armistice the inhabitants discovered to their astonishment that most of the villages had been annexed by Israel rather than by Jordan which controlled them. This was Israel's price for peace and, as neither the United States nor the United Nations was prepared to exert pressure on the new state, the Jordanians were forced to agree.

The border decided at Rhodes was drawn quite arbitrarily. No respect was paid to village boundaries and many people were separated from their lands; the villages of Barta a and Beit Safāfa were cut into two bits, leaving members of the same family on different sides of the barbed-wire fence and unable to communicate. The fate of the village of Tayibe – the 'model' Arab village to which Israeli government guests are taken to see how the Palestinians 'thrive' under Israeli rule – was more typical. During the fighting the Israelis captured the village lands but not the village. With the news of the armistice the inhabitants were furious that they had been simply handed over to Israel but were understandably relieved that they were to be reunited with their lands. Or so they thought. However, the Law of Acquisition of Absentee Property, which was passed in 1950 but made retroactive, was specially devised to take care of cases like this. Although they had not moved from their village, the inhabitants were declared 'absentees' and their land 'abandoned property'. According to the villagers, they lost 8,000 of their 11,000 acres.[44] There was a similar tale for all the Triangle villages. Tira, some four miles to the south-east, retained only 1,500 acres from an original 8,500.[45]

It was not hard to find the reason behind Israel's expropriation policy. Since only six per cent of Palestine legally belonged to Jews at the time of independence, the government obviously had to steal most of the rest if it wanted to create the kind of Jewish state which the Zionists had in mind. And this is what it did. It even produced a press release in 1953 to show that all but twenty of the 370 Jewish settlements established during the previous five years had been built on 'absentee' property.[46] General Dayan described the process to an audience in 1969:

Jewish villages were built in the place of Arab villages. You don't even know the names of these Arab villages, and I don't blame you, because these geography books no longer exist. Not only do the books not exist, the Arab villages are not there

either. Nahalal [Dayan's own village] arose in the place of
Mahlul, Gevat [a kibbutz] in the place of Jibta, Sarid [another
kibbutz] in the place of Haneifa, and Kfar-Yehoshua in the
place of Tel-Shaman. There is not one single place built in this
country that did not have a former Arab population.[47]

Now, after more than thirty years and the establishment of
settlements in the West Bank and Gaza, as well as in Syrian
and Egyptian territory, many Israelis admit that they don't need
any more land. But expropriation still continues, this time with a
political motive. Most Israeli Arabs, who now number 550,000,
live in Galilee. In 1948, when vast numbers of Arabs were expelled,
the Jews became a majority in the area; but by 1978, as a result of
its enormously high birth rate, the Arab population had overtaken
the Jewish. The issue has become a very emotional one in the
country because the U.N. never intended western Galilee to be part
of Israel in the first place. It was supposed to become a part of
Arab Palestine and, if the plan of a Palestinian state was ever to
become a reality, the Galilee Arabs might easily demand inclusion
in it – especially if they formed a majority of the area's inhabitants.

Thus the programme, 'the Judaization of the Galilee', was launched. Its purpose was to ensure that the area would never be
dominated by the Arabs and, to this end, Karmi el and Upper
Nazareth were built. More recently, when the issue became particularly sensitive, a frantic drive for new settlements – always at
the expense of Arab land – was begun. On 31 January 1979 the
minister of industry and commerce told the Knesset that the
government had given top priority 'in all ministries' to the (Jewish)
development of the Galilee, and reported that ten settlements had
been established in the region since the government had taken office (in May 1977).[48] A fortnight later the minister of agriculture,
General Sharon, announced that twenty-nine settlements would be
started in Galilee during the following three months. He added
that 'since the 1930s there hasn't been as pressing a desire for
settlements as there is now.'[49]

Anyone travelling in Galilee is aware of the meaning of Judaization: the surviving Arab villages are usually on high ground, on
rocky hillsides, surrounded by a few terraces of olive groves;
beneath them, covering the fertile ground in the valleys, sprawl the

kibbutzim and moshavim, property of the Jewish National Fund. One thing may puzzle the traveller: the prevalence of the cactus plant, often in the most unlikely places, in the middle of fields or near the Jewish farms. The explanation is a strange one: the cactus is a persistent plant and, however many times it is destroyed, it usually reappears. It is a traditional feature of the Arab village and the cacti are still reappearing in the places where the villages used to stand. Before 1948 there were 475 Arab villages within the borders of what became the State of Israel; of these, 385 have been destroyed by the Israeli authorities.[50]

The Israeli policy of expropriation destroyed the Arab agricultural economy: there was simply not enough land to sustain it. In 1948 the average amount of arable land for each village was about 2,280 acres; by 1974 it had diminished to 500 acres. Before 1962 the village of Deir al-Asad was self-sufficient in food. It produced enough meat, fruit, wheat and vegetables and sold the surplus in Acre or Nazareth. In 1962 its land in the Majd al-Kurum valley was confiscated for the Karmi'el project, and the village was stripped of its most fertile acres. Only the hill land to the north, consisting mainly of olive groves, remained. In one blow the economy of Deir al-Asad was ruined. Today only ten per cent of the labour force can work on the land; over eighty per cent commute daily to the factories of Haifa or work as labourers on Jewish farms.[51] It is the same with all the other villages. The most depressing sights in all Israel are the long lines of buses standing outside every Arab town and village between five and six in the morning, picking up the thousands who have been deprived of work in their own places.

The reactions of the Israeli Arabs to this systematic onslaught on their lives and even on their identity have been varied. It must be remembered that they have lived and are living in very different circumstances from other Arabs. They have always been ruled by outsiders – the Turks, the British and the Israelis – and few of them have ever seen an Arab city under Arab administration. For most of the last thirty years they have been demoralized and on the defensive, almost anxious not to attract attention. They realize that their situation is anomalous, and that an Arab minority inside a state almost permanently at war with the Arab world is bound to be regarded with suspicion by the government of that state. They know that many Israelis consider them a 'fifth column', and that some, like Tel Aviv's deputy mayor, David Shikma, call periodically for their expulsion.[52] It is this background which has produced such contrasting attitudes towards the Zionist state — attitudes which, while never affectionate, range from total rejection to resigned acceptance and even collaboration. According to a public opinion poll published in the summer of 1979, half the Arabs of Israel do not recognize Israel's *right* to exist, and nearly two-thirds of them believe that the Zionist movement is racist.[53] Many of them would concede that the state is not going to vanish and even that it is dangerous to go on trying to reject it, but none can forget that its creation was an injustice done to their people.

These attitudes of acceptance or opposition usually have personal origins; there do not appear to have been any divisions between social classes or regions or between the rural and urban populations. As rough generalizations, though, it can be said that the merchants and businessmen have tended to be less hostile to the regime than the intellectuals, while Muslims have been more firmly opposed than the Druzes or the Christians. But the diversity of attitudes and the impossibility of generalizing about them can be demonstrated by the frequency of divisions within families. One of the best examples of this is the Fahoum family from Nazareth. Of five brothers, one was appointed mayor of Nazareth by the Israelis and another became a Knesset member affiliated to the largest Zionist political party; on the other side, one brother became a leader of the nationalist coalition, the Arab Front, during the 1950s, while a fourth was a founder member of the Palestine Liberation Organization and later became chairman of the Palestine National Council.

The Arabs who accept Israel and actively co-operate with it can be divided into two categories: those who have actually been bought by the regime and those who feel there is no sensible alternative. The latter have a defeatist attitude, a sort of Vichy response to something they are certain will always defeat them; and, like the Vichy men, they loathe other people who insist on carrying on the struggle. They say: 'Israel is here to stay and therefore we had better make the best of it. We are Israeli citizens and, if we want to improve things, we must be loyal to the state. In our situation we have to be realistic. To go on insisting about our rights which we lost over thirty years ago merely gives the Israelis an excuse to go on persecuting us.' Twenty years ago this view had a lot more support than it does today. Had these pessimists been able to extract some real concessions from the government, they might have retained some credibility. But the Israelis refused to help them and continued with policies which are at the root of Arab discontent – discrimination in general and land expropriation. The natural result of all this has been vastly increased support for the radicals and nationalists among the Arab population, particularly for the Communist Party.

The Arabs who have been bought by the regime are a mixed bag. At the bottom are the informers or paid collaborators. These are usually from the lowest levels of society and their job is the same as police spies anywhere. During the military government, their duty was to report daily on all activities of the village, particularly those dealing with cultural or political matters. At a different level are the village leaders and mukhtars. These did not receive salaries like the informers and they were not active collaborators. Nevertheless, they were usually among the most conservative elements within the Arab population and, in return for certain privileges they were granted by the government, they could usually be relied upon to dampen any signs of nationalism or opposition. This method, though, has been declining steadily over the years. Formerly the Israelis would 'fix' the leading family of a particular village and most of the inhabitants would fall into line. But now, as the social organization of the village disintegrates and power is no longer concentrated in the hands of one or two families, the quislings are disappearing.

A third group supporting the regime has consisted of urban notables and politicians. Most of these have been affiliated to the largest political party, the Israel Labour Party, although because they are Arabs they were not allowed to become members of it before 1973. The party was formed in 1968 by the merger of three Labour groups, Mapai, Rafi and Ahdut'Avoda. In one form or another the party formed the government of Israel from 1949 to 1977.

Some of the Arab supporters of the Israel Labour Party stand in the Knesset elections and three or four of them are usually elected. As far as the party is concerned, they have only two functions: to persuade Arabs to vote for the party at the elections and to toe the line afterwards. During the military government the first function was made easier by the pressure Mapai officers exerted on Arab voters. At one election, all the Arabs in Lydda voted for Mapai except for one couple who voted for Mapam (the United Workers' Party). The husband was later arrested, told by the military governor, 'I'll teach you to vote for Mapam,' and then beaten up.[54]

The Arab Knesset members affiliated to Mapai have always been considered a disgrace by large numbers of Israeli Arabs. They have rarely made speeches on sensitive issues and on one occasion, when the Knesset was evenly divided on the subject of whether to retain the notorious Defence (Emergency) Regulations, Arab members voted against their abolition. Today they are more despised than ever before and a diminishing number of Arabs vote for them either in local or national elections. They began their careers claiming that acceptance of Israel and co-operation with the authorities formed the only possible basis for coexistence between Jews and Arabs, and for many years they managed to persuade people that they were the true representatives of the Arabs who were fighting for their rights from within the government. But the continuous encroachment on Arab rights by successive governments which they voted for in the Knesset undermined their position and drove many of their supporters into the radical camp.

One such victim was Saif al-Din Zuabi, a large landowner from Nazareth and a former mayor of the city. In 1949 he was elected to the Knesset as a Nazareth Democrat (affiliated to Mapai) and he remained there for most of the next three decades. He was in fact one of the few supporters of Mapai who did speak on Arab issues and in the fifties he openly attacked the Nationality Law and the Law of Acquisition and spoke in favour of the repatriation of refugees. Yet no one who was an active supporter of Golda Meir's party could retain a large body of Arab supporters indefinitely and in 1975 he was decisively defeated in elections for mayor of Nazareth. In a direct election he received only twenty-four per cent of the vote while his Communist opponent, Tawfiq Zayyad, polled sixty-three per cent. Disillusioned by his failure, he resigned from the Knesset in 1979, blaming both Arab and Jewish extremists for the failure to achieve a satisfactory form of coexistence.

A very different group of Israeli supporters are the Druzes. Officially the state does not recognize them as Arabs and therefore they serve in the Israeli army and the Border Police. Historically they have close relations with the Zionists and they played no part in either the Arab rebellion of 1936–9 or the war of 1948. Consequently they have been awarded a special status by the Israelis and they suffer little of the discrimination directed against Muslim and Christian Arabs. Alone of all the Arab communities they are not treated as a minority and their affairs are dealt with by the regular offices of ministries rather than by the special minorities departments.[55] They are also over-represented in parliament: although there are only about 35,000 Druzes in Israel today, they have three of their number in the Knesset including the extreme right-wing member of the government coalition, Amal Nasir al-Din.

The Druzes are a striking example of the Israeli policy of 'divide and rule', but it seems unlikely that the alliance will continue for much longer. The educated Druzes – like the Communist poet and strong anti-Zionist, Samih al-Qasim – know perfectly well that they are Druze by religion and Arab by nationality. Their people are heretics from Islam spread over southern Syria, the Lebanese Chouf region and northern Israel; whatever community characteristics they may have acquired, they are ethnically and linguistically Arabs. As the increasingly influential Druze Initiative Committee proclaims: 'We share the Arab religion and the Arab tradition; our past and our future is Arab.' Israeli Druzes are now also identifying themselves with their co-religionists elsewhere and did so particularly with the Lebanese politician, Kamal Jumblatt, who led the Arab nationalist movement in Lebanon for twenty years until his assassination in 1977. One indication of the influence of this movement is the number of Druzes who have recently deserted from the Israeli army or who have refused to undergo military service on the grounds that they are either religious students or Arabs.

The Israeli method of solving the problem of Arab representation was thus to attach a number of tame Arabs to the main government party. But in order for this policy to succeed, it was necessary to prevent the emergence of genuine Arab parties. The Israelis have managed this with great success: between 1951 and 1965 there were seven attempts at creating an Arab party and every one failed.[56] Even the Arab Workers Congress, the trade union movement which had functioned during the mandate, was snuffed out soon after independence. Since the official union body, the Histadrut, was closed to non-Jews, this effectively prevented Arabs from being members of a labour organization.

The most dangerous movements, from the Israeli point of view, were the Arab Front of 1958 and the al-Ard group of 1964. The Front was a coalition of Arab nationalists and communists who campaigned for an end to land expropriation and the abolition of the military government. It was formed at the high tide of Arab nationalism, when the pro-British Hashemite regime in Iraq had been overthrown and when Gamal Abdel Nasser was president of the United Arab Republic (Egypt and Syria). It caused great enthusiasm among the Arab population and considerable unease to the Israeli authorities. The latter, however, were reluctant to declare it illegal since this would have antagonized the Soviet Union. Instead they decided to make it impossible for the Front to function by banning meetings and imposing travel restrictions on its leaders.[57] Eventually the split between Arab nationalists and communists throughout the Arab world caused it to disintegrate.

Tougher tactics were employed against the al-Ard (the Land) group, established by the Arab nationalist opposition in 1964. In that year it decided to register itself as a political party and sent a statement of its policy to the district governor. Although the group's leader, Mansur Qardush, declared in print that al-Ard believed 'the Jewish people has a right to its own independent state,'[58] the district governor refused to accept it as a political organization. It had been set up, he explained, with the object of 'prejudicing the existence and security of the State of Israel'.[59] Later the Supreme Court upheld the decision and the minister of defence produced the Defence (Emergency) Regulations in order to ban the group altogether. The following year members of al-Ard decided to stand in the Knesset elections and presented a number of candidates calling themselves socialists. They fulfilled all the electoral requirements and, had they been allowed to stand, they would certainly have gained representation. The Israelis reacted by expelling candidates from the Arab areas — Qardush himself was exiled to the Negev desert — and restricting the movements of their supporters. Finally, they simply banned the candidates from taking part in the elections.[60]

In Israel today members of the old al-Ard group are still active in local politics though the name no longer exists. Some of them have joined a movement called the Sons of the Land which is still fighting the same battles as al-Ard. Land confiscation remains the main issue for the Arabs and the cause of the growing radicalism in Galilee. On 1 March 1976 the Israeli government announced plans to expropriate 7,500 acres in the region. More than half of this land was to be confiscated from three neighbouring villages north of Nazareth: Saknin, ʹArraba and Deir Hannā. The Arab response was to set up a Committee for the Defence of the Land which called for a general strike on 30 March. The evening before the strike Israeli soldiers and police raided the three villages, shot three people dead and wounded many others. The following day they repeated the performance and killed three more people. In order to punish the Arabs for peacefully protesting against the theft of their land, Israeli forces killed six people, wounded sixty-nine and arrested another 260. This piece of brutality on what is now known as the 'Day of the Land' has only hardened Arab opinion against the regime and the three villages, with their memorial to the dead, have become a focal point for the Arabs' struggle.

A product of the new mood of determination is the Progressive Nationalist Movement, which co-operates closely with the Sons of the Land. As an organization it is far less effective but it is more openly provocative. In January 1979 it created a huge row in Israel when a handful of its members declared that they 'did not recognize the Zionist entity' and announced their support for the P.L.O. They also denounced the Communist Party because it recognizes the state of Israel and they accused it of 'attempting to usurp the leadership of the Palestinian Arab struggle'. The movement, which consists almost exclusively of students, rejects the idea of a Palestinian state on the West Bank and Gaza and calls for a secular democratic state in all of Palestine. Although its leaders admit that their goal may not be attainable for 'decades' (the number of decades is not specified), they see their immediate duty as the need to 'educate' people and remind them of their Palestinian identity.

The Progressive Nationalist Movement attracts little support outside the student population. Many Arabs find it futile and provocative, 'a group of silly students with slogans'. They believe it is jeopardizing their position and handing the Israelis an excuse for continuing the oppression of their community. The Communists accuse them of being extremist and unrealistic. In characteristic jargon, party members condemn the movement for its 'chauvinistic and petit-bourgeois ideology'. Others complain that the students are obscuring the real problems facing the Arabs. They are behaving like the mufti by insisting on a policy which cannot possibly succeed while they should be concentrating on the difficulties which the Arab minority encounters as an underprivileged section of the Jewish state.

In spite of the opposition of the Progressive Nationalist Movement, the Communist Party, or RAKAH as it is known, is the only political party which represents the Arabs in Israel at a national level and which is prepared to fight for their rights. This is perhaps the result of Israel's refusal to allow an Arab nationalist party to be set up. But it is also a product of the party's consistent opposition to the policies of the Israeli regime since the years immediately following independence. In 1947 the Soviet Union supported the American position and voted in favour of partition. In consequence the Israeli Communist Party was distrusted by the Arab population for some years. It soon became clear, though, that it was the only organization capable of standing up to the government, and when Nasser, who was as popular among the Israeli Arabs as he was in the Arab countries, turned to the Soviet Union in his struggle against the West, the party's standing rose. At a time when Israel was being strongly supported by Britain, France and the United States, the Soviet Union's arms sales to Egypt and its assistance over the High Dam at Aswan were greeted with enthusiasm. The party's fortunes dipped again with the collapse of the Arab Front in 1958 but the failure of the al-Ard group in 1965 left it as the natural party of the intellectuals and nationalists. One of the finest Palestinian poets, Tawfiq Zayyad, is a RAKAH Knesset member, and another, Selim Jubran, is general secretary of the party's Nazareth branch.

Although some of its officials admit that they have never read Marx and prefer decorating their rooms with posters of Nasser rather than Lenin, RAKAH is still far from developing a kind of 'Eurocommunism'. The party's relationship with Moscow is close and its structure is organized on classic Soviet lines. It has a politburo, a central committee and membership which are split almost evenly between Arabs and Jews, although its supporters are overwhelmingly Arab. In the national elections, RAKAH provides over ninety per cent of the voting strength for the Democratic Front for Peace and Equality, which returned five Knesset members (out of 120) in the 1977 elections. Three are RAKAH members, one is a leader of the Black Panthers and the fifth is the president of the Arab Mayors Association. The party's links with the nationalist movement are also emphasized in local elections. RAKAH prefers to work in alliances and the Democratic Front of Nazareth, for example, which is again dominated by RAKAH, also includes independents, the Association of Nazareth Academics, the Trade Union of Merchants and Independents, and the Nazareth Student Union.

In spite of its rigid adherence to the Moscow line, RAKAH is a popular party in a very real sense and its supporters come from all sections of the Arab community except the smaller villages, where deference voting still persists, and the Bedouin. In most of the towns RAKAH now polls between two-thirds and three-quarters of the Arab vote, taking thousands of votes once reserved for Mapai and the National Religious Party. (The strange phenomenon of Arabs voting for a Jewish religious party is easy to explain. The N.R.P. traditionally holds the ministries of education and the interior: teachers and other employees of these ministries are therefore 'encouraged' to vote for it.) It is not that Israeli Arabs are enthusiastic communists – RAKAH supporters out-number Communist Party members by more than 200 to one – but because it is the only party in the country which is prepared to take a stand on the basic, everyday issues of confiscation and discrimination.

The party's practical and realistic approach is typified by Tawfiq Zayyad. Born in 1930 and a member of the party at thir-teen, Zayyad has been imprisoned eight times since 1948; in November 1955 he was beaten up and tortured after making a speech in Tiberias. He was elected to the Knesset in 1973 and became mayor of Nazareth two years later. A poet and a writer, he is a small, shambling figure with early grey hair and a tired smile. Unlike many Marxists, he rarely breaks into 'pamphletese' and his politics are always practical. He is an Arab and a nationalist but he is also a realist. He probably represents the Israeli Arab position as well as anybody, certainly better than the angry students of the Progressive National Movement. With Zayyad there is no breast-beating, no empty talk of unattainable rights. Whether he likes it or not, he is an Israeli citizen and his policy is to work for equality and full national rights for the Arabs within the framework of the Israeli state. It is calm, undramatic stuff but, in view of the other options open to Israeli Arabs and the delicate position they occupy in the Zionist state, there is no sensible alternative.

6

Jerusalem and the Occupied Territories

Jerusalem is the city of the three great monotheistic religions and, for most of its history, Christians, Jews and Muslims have been able to live there. There are important holy places of all three within the walls and, for the most part, each religion has enjoyed the freedom to visit them. But, while Jerusalem belongs to no particular religion, it does belong to a particular people. In character and in composition it is an Arab city and, except for three short periods during the Crusades, it has been so for 1,340 years. It is so today, though several thousand of its Arab inhabitants have been expelled over the last decade and replaced by Jews.

The 1949 armistice line drove through Jerusalem in a north-south direction. The old, walled city and a few areas to the north of it remained in Arab hands; the modern city to the west, with its Arab and Jewish suburbs, became part of Israel. In June 1967 the old city was captured by the Israeli army and three weeks later it was annexed by the government. The Israelis termed their action 'unification' or 'coexistence', but it was nothing of the sort. It was illegal occupation. As one Israeli writer, Amos Elon, says: 'It's the same coexistence as between a rider and his horse. Dayan's [phrase] "living together" means the rule of one people over another.'[1]

A short walk around the city proves Elon right. The great piazza before the Wailing Wall, built on the site of the old Moghrabi quarter, whose 650 inhabitants were expelled at a few moments notice in 1967, is not much of a monument to 'coexistence'. The Israeli soldiers who swagger down the souks past a sullen population fail to indicate the benefits of 'living together'. And nothing demonstrates the Zionist domination better than the view from the Mount of Olives: in the middle distance stand the great walls of the Haram ash-Sharif, the Muslim sanctuary which encloses the mosques of al-Aqsa and the Dome of the Rock; beyond are the domes of the Holy Sepulchre and at dusk the sound of bells from the churches and the calls of the muezzins from the mosques are carried across Gethsemane and the Valley of the Kidron – but the effect of this timeless combination is wrecked by the apparition behind them: the massive vulgarity of the new Israeli hotels which leer insolently over the Old City. And as the observer looks both north and south he will grasp the extent of Israeli dominance. Jerusalem is ringed by Jewish housing estates, built on confiscated Arab land, which are placed strategically on the summits of the surrounding hills, cutting off the city from its Arab hinterland.

Israel's annexation was illegal and was condemned as such by the international community. A week after 'unification', the General Assembly of the United Nations adopted a resolution calling 'upon Israel to rescind all measures already taken and to desist forthwith from taking any action which would alter the status of Jerusalem.'[2] Not a single nation voted against this resolution – except, of course, for Israel – and not a single delegate spoke in support of Israel's annexation. The Israelis replied that Jerusalem must never again be a divided city and insisted that the benefits of 'unification' would be spread evenly over all sections of the population. During the years that followed it was difficult to see much evidence of this. Even the Jewish mayor of the newly 'united' city (the Arab mayor of the Old City was expelled to Jordan) regretted 'the hard and sometimes offensive Israeli attitude' and criticized his government's 'complete lack of consideration towards the way of life and the culture of East [i.e. Arab] Jerusalem'.[3] One example of this 'complete lack of consideration' was in the field of housing: while tens of thousands of new apartments were built for Jewish settlers on the outskirts of Jerusalem, nothing was done for the Arab inhabitants who lived in overcrowded conditions inside the Old City. Not until 1979, twelve years after the start of the occupation, was the first Arab housing built – a collection of two-room houses near Bethany.

A few Arabs optimistically believed that they would benefit from the 'unification'. These were the people who had property in

West Jerusalem but who had ended up on the other side of the 1949 armistice lines. When they were annexed in 1967 and told that they were now Israeli citizens, they expected at least to be allowed their property back. But not at all: since they were 'absentees' in 1948 they were no longer entitled to it. Muhammad Jarallah, the son of a former mufti of Jerusalem, lost his home and land in 1948 and became a refugee.

In 1967 the Israelis captured my second home, annexed our city and told us we were Israeli citizens. So I went to the Israeli government with my title deeds and I said: 'Since I am now an Israeli subject, may I have my land back?' The land was vacant, you understand; there was nobody living in my house. But they said no. They did not explain; they could not. They had no logic. A people who are so logical in everything else do not pretend to be logical when they are dealing with us Palestinians.[4]

In the years following the 1967 war the Israelis expropriated some thirty acres of buildings inside the Old City on the site of the traditional Jewish quarter. Even before 1948 the area was less than twenty per cent Jewish owned but this didn't prevent the Israelis from taking it all and forcing more than 5,000 Arabs from their homes in the process. Outside the walls the confiscations were on a grander scale: during the first five years of the occupation nearly 4,000 acres of Arab land were expropriated in Arab Jerusalem.[5] By the end of 1978 a total of 23,640 acres in the East Jerusalem area had been taken for Jewish building sites and 76,000 settlers were living on Arab lands. The whole process was, as usual, given a legal face and the Israelis were able to carry it out through the Land Acquisition for Public Purposes Ordinance of 1943. Like the other laws designed to facilitate expropriations inside Israel itself, this ordinance was a fig-leaf and its original purpose was something altogether different. As Arnold Spaer, a successful Israeli lawyer, has remarked: 'I fail to see how it can be defined as a public purpose to move out an Arab family and replace it with Jews. . . . They [the Israelis] are creating an *Arabrein* (a place free of Arabs) that is morally no more defensible than the *Judenrein* in Europe before the last war.'[6]

The Jerusalemite Arabs call this process the 'Judaization' of the Holy City. They see their own numbers diminishing as Jewish immigrants from the Soviet Union and elsewhere settle on their land. They see the great fortress-like buildings surrounding their city almost severing their traditional links with the towns of Ramallah and Bethlehem. And they hear of the government's plans for their future: the housing minister reported as saying, 'the master plan is to make Jerusalem more Jewish,' and the immigration minister as proclaiming that the essential thing for Jerusalem is 'a numerous, stable and permanent Jewish majority'.[7] They hear Dayan saying that 'maybe Jerusalem will not be beautiful. The important thing is that it shall be built to stretch from Anata in the north to Bethlehem in the south, from the Judaean hills in the east to Nebi Samwil in the west.'[8] They watch as the whole world condemns Israel's behaviour – from the United Nations to *The Times,* from Arnold Toynbee to Yehudi Menuhin – and they see the Israelis, as usual, paying no attention. Arthur Kutcher, a former planning officer for the Old City, was moved to write a book criticizing his government's mindless barbarism. He wrote:

> The fundamental, commonly shared awareness that Jerusalem's spiritual essence is inextricably bound up with her visual, tangible qualities, an awareness evidenced by four thousand years of building in the city, is now not simply ignored, it is not even recognized. Instead, a new way of thinking about Jerusalem has sprung up: the city is a resource to be exploited, its spiritual and visual qualities are commodities to be bought and sold.[9]

Before the annexation, Jerusalem was the capital of the West Bank, the central hill-country comprising the biblical regions of Judaea and Samaria and the heartland of old Palestine. The Judaean landscape is harsh and arid and its central feature is the line of hill towns that runs northwards from Hebron through Bethlehem and Jerusalem to Ramallah and Bira. Samaria is gentler and more fertile, producing olives and fruit; it is dominated by Nablus, a large Muslim town lying between the historic hills of Ebal and Gerizim. To its north stands the market town of Jenin, on the edge of the Vale of Esdraelon; westwards Qalqiliya and Tulkarm, near the armistice borders of 1949, lie almost on the coastal plain; on the eastern side of the hills, a few miles to the north of the Dead Sea, sits Jericho, 800 feet below sea level and the solitary town of the Jordan valley. Besides Gaza and the small strip of land surrounding it, the West Bank was the only region to escape the Israeli conquest of 1948. It is worth looking at it in some detail because, although it has been occupied by Israel since 1967, and although a large number of its inhabitants are refugees from 1948, the West Bank is the only area anywhere in which Palestinian society still exists in anything approaching its natural surroundings.

The Husseini–Nashashibi rivalry continued during and after the 1948 war. The mufti established a 'government of all Palestine' in Gaza in the autumn of 1948. Raghib al-Nashashibi's ally King Abdullah of Transjordan was recognized as 'king of all Palestine' by a conference of West Bank notables held at Jericho in May 1949. Transjordan was renamed Jordan and formally annexed East Jerusalem and the West Bank in 1950, though the Jordanian parliament's resolution to take this step expressly declared that it was in order to 'preserve all the rights of the Arabs in Palestine' and was 'without prejudice to the final settlement of the just cause' of Palestine. Nashashibi himself was made military governor of the annexed area.

The unification of both banks of the river was, at the time, probably the most sensible course of action. The people of the West Bank were so demoralized that they could never have formed a state on their own. Moreover, Abdullah and the Nashashibis, who had been scheming for this solution ever since the Peel partition plan of 1937, felt they had a better claim to the West Bank than the mufti. It was, after all, only the performance of the Transjordanian soldiers of the Arab Legion that had prevented the Israelis from seizing the whole area.

The problems confronting the West Bank after the 1948 war were enormous. Economically it had always looked westwards and its trade was tied closely with the coast. Now it was forced to turn around and face east. The river and the desert beyond had previously played no part in its existence; now it had to look to them for its survival. Hebron's trading partners had historically been Beersheba and the port of Gaza; Nablus had close social and economic relations with the villages of the Triangle. Both had now to look to the east, towards Amman. It was even worse for the towns of Tulkarm and Qalqiliya, which overlook the Mediterranean. After 1948 they were deprived not only of their traditional outlets to the sea; they also lost most of their lands which lay on the plain itself. Instead of the rich fields they had previously farmed and whose produce they had sold to the coastal towns, the inhabitants of Qalqiliya had to turn to the infertile hills behind their homes and try to sell their new and more meagre crops to poorer markets in the east. Jerusalem had similar difficulties. The natural expansion of the city had always been to the west, along the Jaffa road, and during this century most of the new building — Arab, Jewish and foreign — has been erected west of the Old City. In 1948 the Jerusalem—Jaffa axis was cut and the Arabs of the Old City found themselves denied access to the west. As the main road to Bethlehem in the south was also blocked and expansion eastwards was prevented by the Valley of the Kidron and the Mount of Olives, Arab Jerusalem suffered a major economic reverse after 1948 and became almost wholly dependent on Amman.

The Jordanian regime was anxious to preserve as much continuity as possible in the West Bank. At a senior level it was easy to integrate the remnants of the Nashashibi political following into the administration and until 1967 there were always a number of West Bank notables in senior positions in the cabinet. Ahmed Tuqan, an Oxford graduate from one of the leading Nablus families, served as education minister, foreign minister, minister of defence and prime minister. At one stage during the 1950s he headed four ministries at the same time. At a local level the Jordanians managed to retain traditional sheikhs and other landowners as mayors in the towns and in the villages they carefully preserved the office of mukhtar which they had inherited from the Ottomans and the British mandate authorities.

Under Jordanian rule, the West Bank Palestinians were the best educated community in the Arab world. Their ratio of students to population was higher than in any country in Europe and ten times higher than among the Arabs in Israel.[10] In the villages that were split between the West Bank and Israel by the 1949 armistice line, there were six times as many students per thousand inhabitants on the Jordanian side.[11] Most of the West Bank Palestinians, particularly those studying medicine and engineering, attended universities in Cairo; others went to Syria, often to the Faculty of Law in Damascus, a few to Lebanon and Iraq, and a handful to Europe.[12] On returning to the West Bank to live in the new suburbs of Nablus or Ramallah, these well educated doctors and lawyers became impatient with the conservative administration of the notables and the often uneducated mukhtars. With the introduction of local elections they were able to impose some limitations on the powers of the traditional families. It was not until the elections of 1976, however, which took place under Jordanian law and Israeli supervision, that the pro-Jordanian leaders were finally beaten and the most famous of them all, Sheikh Ja'abari, turned out of the mayor's office in Hebron.

Some economic decline of the West Bank after 1948 was an unavoidable consequence of the war and the creation of Israel: the area had become a backwater, passed over by the new trade routes which ran from the Red Sea to Amman via Aqaba and from the Mediterranean to Amman via Beirut. It possessed no raw materials of its own and little industry above the workshop and artisan level. It was a land of agricultural smallholdings and these formed the basis of its economy. But although there was little economic development, some towns prospered for other reasons. Both Hebron and Ramallah were helped by remittances sent home by migrant workers in the oil-producing countries. Jerusalem always benefited from tourism and in the 1960s began to experience something of a boom in the hotel trade. Bethlehem was also sustained by the growth of tourism and the development of local handicrafts made from olive-wood and mother-of-pearl. And Jericho actually benefited from the new geographical realities, since it was situated just off the Jerusalem–Amman road. Already established as a winter resort where important Jerusalem families like the Cattans and the Alamis had built houses, its growth was aided by an influx of refugees who provided labour and by Musa Alami's discovery of water in the desert nearby.

In general, however, the West Bank economy remained stagnant and the small growth in agriculture was not sufficient to keep pace with the increase in the rural population. Since 1967, under the Israeli occupation, the economy has shown no improvement and compares very badly with the development of the East Bank. Industrial and commercial activity have been the chief sufferers because neither have been allotted much room in the new Israeli order. A good illustration of the West Bank's problems is the town of Nablus, the largest in the West Bank after Jerusalem, with 80,000 inhabitants. Its economic life has always revolved around a handful of small industries and the surrounding farmland. In addition to its famous soap industry and an excellent matches factory, Nablus also manufactured tin cans, vegetable oil and chocolate. Since 1967 it has suffered a disastrous decline. Products from subsidized industries in Israel have swamped the market and caused the closure of some businesses, such as the matches factory, while exports to Jordan have greatly diminished. Nablus businessmen are now having to compete with East Bank Jordanians on very disadvantageous terms. They cannot import raw materials through Israel and only those factories established before 1967 can export goods to Jordan. Besides, costs and taxes are far higher under Israeli occupation than they are in Jordan. The consequences for Nablus are economic inertia and large-scale unemployment.

The lack of job opportunities is one of the major problems facing the West Bank. It drives perhaps a third of the labour force to seek unskilled work inside Israel and it drives most of the educated abroad. Of the West Bank's population of some 700,000, every year some 20,000 are emigrating and most of these are the well educated who are unable to find work in their homeland. Most families in the West Bank have sons or nephews working abroad, either in the Gulf or in the West, and any signs of prosperity in Ramallah or Nablus or Hebron today are usually attributable to remittances from these emigrants. Colonel Salah Jallad is a former police chief in Jaffa who fought at Alamein and served with Glubb in the Arab Legion. He now lives alone in Tulkarm. Three of his children are working in the United States; the other three are in the Gulf. Emigration is an escape not only for the educated but also for the skilled workers. At the Qalandia Vocational Training Centre near Ramallah, boys can choose between courses in welding, plumbing, carpentry, machine tools, electricals, auto-mechanics and construction. A majority of pupils in all courses except carpentry emigrate on graduation.

The extent of emigration from the West Bank can be appreciated from a glance at the statistics for the Christian population of Jerusalem. According to the Anglican Bishop, Faik Haddad, there were 26,000 Christians in Jerusalem in 1948 and, given the natural population growth, there should be some 50,000 today.[13] In 1961 the figure was down to 13,000 in the sector of the city under Arab control. Today, the whole of Jerusalem contains only 9,000 Christians. While some Christians have been deported by Israel, few would dispute that the main cause of the exodus has been the lack of employment opportunities combined with the other depressing effects of the Israeli occupation.

The decline of the West Bank since 1967 has not been unintentional. It is the direct result of the policy of the Israeli government which has chosen to exploit the area (as well as Gaza) for the advancement of its own economy. The relationship between Israel and the Occupied Territories is like that between a colonial power and its colonies. The Israeli lawyer, Felicia Langer, has described this relationship and its development, how the West Bank with Gaza became 'a not-so-small pool of cheap labour, a market for Israel's products; its land a place for settlement, and its wells a source of "black gold".'[14]

Of the several economic advantages which Israel derives from the West Bank, the most important are labour and water. Both are vital to the survival of the Israeli economy. Without the 'not-so-small pool of cheap labour', several sectors, such as the construction industry, would collapse immediately. In the summer of 1978, there were 75,000 registered workers from the Occupied Territories working in Israel,[15] 40,000 of them from the West Bank and the others from Gaza and northern Sinai. But these are only the registered workers. Some Israelis estimate that there are well over 100,000 Arabs from the Occupied Territories commuting daily to Israel. With nearly half its labour force working outside the West Bank, it is hardly surprising that the area should be in economic decline. The shortage of labour has had deleterious effects on olive cultivation and on sheep and goat farming. Once inside Israel the migrants are shunted off to factories, farms or building sites. Most of the menial jobs in Tel Aviv — rubbish collection, dish-washing and so on — are done by Arabs, while the construction industry takes more than half its labour from the Occupied Territories.[16] The great building sites in Jerusalem — where thousands of apartments are being built on Arab land for the exclusive use of Jews — are manned almost entirely by Palestinians.

But the exploitation of the West Bank is more complicated than this. The Israelis have imposed high tariffs on all imports to the Territories from every country except Israel. This is of little use to the local producers, who are unable to compete with Israeli manufacturers, but it does ensure that the Territories take ninety per cent of their imports from Israel. The Israeli government has done much to promote the flow of Israeli goods to the West Bank. Poultry producers, for example, enjoy large government subsidies and are thus able to undercut their Arab competitors. The end result has been to make the economies of the Territories dependent on Israel, and this arrangement works out very much to the Israeli advantage. The West Bank and Gaza are now Israel's second largest export market (after the United States) but their contribution to Israel's imports is an insignificant two per cent. In 1977 Israel's trade surplus with the West Bank alone was 1.7 billion Israeli pounds[17] (about £100 million sterling).

One feature of the occupation which the West Bankers particularly resent is the establishment of Jewish settlements on their land. Israelis justify these colonies either by pointing out that Judaea and Samaria were populated by Jews in the days of David and Solomon or by saying that they are necessary for 'security reasons'. How civilian settlements in 'enemy' territory can be of security value either in war or peace is never explained. But then 'security reasons' are like 'public purposes'. If you are grabbing somebody else's land it sounds much better if you say you are doing it for 'security reasons' rather than admit that you are simply stealing it. Not that world opinion has been deceived by the jargon: no country in the world supports Israel's colonialist policy. Moreover it is forbidden by the Fourth Geneva Convention of 1949 (of which Israel is a signatory) which declares that an occupier 'shall not transfer parts of its own population into the territory that it occupies'.

The great colonization drive began in 1968 when a series of nahals (military settlements) were established along the Jordan valley. Once they had been built and prepared for civilians, they were handed over to settlers from the National Religious Party and other political groups. All these settlements and the ones that followed throughout Gaza and the West Bank were built on land previously owned by the Jordanian government or on land belonging to nearby Arab villages. The Israeli government pretends that only Jordanian state land is used but it is difficult to find a single settlement that has not taken village land. And, indeed, the government doesn't try particularly hard to keep up its pretence. A glance at the pages of the semi-official *Jerusalem Post* is more likely to reveal the government's true attitude. In May 1978 it announced: 'Israel will have to take over large tracts of Arab-owned land in the West Bank if plans for Jewish settlement are to be implemented there.'[18] This seizure of village lands is not a rare phenomenon: it happens all the time. In the first ten days of February 1979 the *Jerusalem Post* carried details of land-grabbing on the 1st, 5th and 9th. One concerned the expansion of the settlement of Kiryat Arba at the expense of the landowners of Hebron; another detailed the protests of the villagers of Nebi Saleh near Ramallah against the construction of the Neve Tzuf settlement on their land; and a third contained the following bland notice:

Some 150 landowners from the villages of Hizma and Jaba, north-east of Jerusalem, have received letters ordering them to present themselves at the offices of the military government as they have been served with 'purchase orders' for their property. The land selected for expropriation is on the border of the Neve Ya'aqov neighbourhood, and the authorities are keen to buy it from the Arab owners to expand the Jewish quarter to the north and east.

In this instance the authorities do not even bother to say it is being done for a 'public purpose' or for 'security reasons'. It is simply a case of taking land away from *Arabs* so that *Jews* can build on it.

The confiscation of village land naturally undermines the local Arab economy. In some cases it destroys it altogether. When the Israelis established the settlement of Mehola at the northern end of the Jordan valley, not only did they take 375 acres of land from the nearby village of Bardala; they also positioned their water tank directly above that of Bardala so that the villagers had no water at all except at the time of the spring rains.[19] Similar behaviour ruined the economic life of the village of Rafidia near Bethlehem. The village lands used to consist of some 800 acres from which more than two-thirds of the labour force earned their living. In 1973 about 700 acres were expropriated and handed on to the settlement of Tekoa, and almost all the villagers lost their livelihood. Today they are part of the thousands who have to commute to Israel in search of work.[20]

By the end of 1978 there were over sixty Israeli settlements in the West Bank. (Another fifty were spread over Gaza, the Syrian Golan Heights and northern Sinai.) They were established on

128 THE NEW DIASPORA

87,000 acres of Arab land and contained 90,000 settlers, most of whom were living in Jerusalem. In the agricultural areas of the West Bank, 14,000 settlers were farming 63,000 acres of land confiscated for the most part from the villages of the Jordan valley and the regions of Bethlehem and Hebron[21] (another 300,000 acres have been taken for 'security reasons'). The Israelis claim that the land is underpopulated and that no harm is being done to anyone. Even leaving aside the villagers who have lost much of their property, this is a ridiculous assertion. In the West Bank today there are more than 300,000 refugees; in Jordan there are more than a million, many of whom are West Bank residents who fled in 1967. Surely, if the West Bank really was underpopulated, then the spare land should be used to accommodate those whose original homes have long been absorbed by Israel? It seems an act of almost incredible selfishness that the Zionists, who had already seized more than three-quarters of the land of Palestine, should now be busily colonizing the meagre remnant still left for the Palestinians.

The West Bank has no minerals and, apart from land, only one major resource: water. The area provides some 620 million cubic metres a year, which would be ample if they were all used inside the West Bank. From drillings in Israel itself, however, 500 millions of this is taken and used in Israel. Even the remaining 120 millions is not left to the Palestinians, since 15 millions is required for the settlements.[22] In other words, the settlements receive more than 1,000 cubic metres per colonist while the Arab inhabitants are each allotted only 150 cubic metres. Moreover, while the Israelis have drilled seventeen wells in the West Bank since 1967 and enjoy the use of others belonging to 'absentees', not one Arab has been allowed to drill a single irrigation well in the last twelve years. As Dr Paul Quiring, who made a study of the subject during three and a half years in Jerusalem as representative of the Mennonite Central Committee, has reported: 'This lack of water resource development, together with the confiscation of wells on "absentee" property, means that there are fewer wells for Palestinian agriculture in the Jordan valley today than were available on the eve of the 1967 war.'[23]

These restrictions have virtually crippled the charitable farm run by Musa Alami's Arab Development Society near Jericho. Musa Alami, who is now in his eighties, is a member of the old Jerusalemite aristocracy. In 1948 he lost most of his property in

Jerusalem and the Galilee and went to live near Jericho where he acquired a concession of 5,000 acres of desert from the Jordanian government. After he discovered water he founded a large farm and a school for refugee children. Both were highly successful until the Israeli invasion of 1967, when two-thirds of the land was laid waste and twenty-six of the twenty-seven wells destroyed. The Israeli army systematically smashed the irrigation system, the buildings and the well-boring machinery. Most of the land quickly reverted to desert.

Perhaps some of this destruction was unavoidable in wartime but what seems utterly callous and outrageous is the way the Israeli authorities have behaved since 1967. A chunk of the land was predictably wired off for 'security reasons' and turned into a military camp. It is now deserted, a mangled collection of barbed wire, broken pipes and derelict houses crouched in the desert where banana plantations and fields of tomatoes once stood. In Jericho, where the rainfall is virtually non-existent, no plants can live without irrigation and, if Musa Alami wanted to keep his farm running, he had to repair his wells. But the Israelis refused to allow him to buy the necessary equipment either to restore the damaged wells or to drill new ones. So he made some manual repairs to four of the least damaged wells and with these he was able to salvage a fraction of the land and keep the farm and the school functioning. But even this was too much for the Israelis. They are now telling him that he has too much water – though he has less than a fifth of what he used to have – and have warned him that they will be fixing a limit on his consumption and will be taking away the surplus for their own 'projects' (i.e. their expanding settlements near Jericho).

Musa Alami has seen the Palestinian tragedy from beginning to end: from the Ottoman defeat and the British occupation to the wars of 1948 and 1967 which brought with them the Zionist colonization of all Palestine. His scepticism is thus understandable. He laughs at President Carter's obsession with human rights because he knows they will never be observed in Palestine. 'Liberty and justice are meaningless words for my people and my country. We have never known either.' He waves towards his farm, a philanthropist's dream that was once brilliantly succesful. 'I gain no pleasure from this place now,' he says, 'I stay here out of duty. I know the Zionists have been wanting to get rid of us for years.

They want me to go and have told me so. They want to build a kibbutz here. But I have a duty to keep going, a duty to my people.'[24]

Israeli colonization also takes place in the Gaza strip, a narrow stretch of coast running for forty miles down to the pre-1967 Egyptian border. Gaza was the only other fragment of Palestine to survive 1948 and it too was taken in 1967. It is wretchedly poor and overcrowded, crammed with more than 350,000 refugees as well as the native population, and yet Israel insists on taking some of its most fertile land and settling its own inhabitants upon it. Even the Zionists find this difficult to justify. Gaza was never a part of the kingdoms of Judah or Israel and its only contact with Jewish history was in 92 B.C., when Alexander Jannaeus captured the city and massacred its inhabitants. Nor can the Israelis use the ubiquitous 'security reasons' quite so readily since they signed a peace treaty with Egypt.

Gaza, which was once a prosperous Greek city, is an ugly sprawl today. The orchards around the town now house an enormous refugee population. Standards of living are low and the camps are some of the worst anywhere. The refugees, who come from Jaffa and Beersheba, live in squalid huts mass-produced by U.N.R.W.A. About 200,000 people live in the vast camps of Jabalia, Rafah, Beach and Khan Younis, most of them without prospects of employment or anything else.

After 1948 Gaza was administered by the Egyptians and its capture by Israel in 1967 cut it off both from Egypt and from the rest of the Arab world. This has made Gaza even more economically dependent on Israel than the West Bank, though its exploitation is managed in much the same way. The Gaza citrus industry, for example, is prevented from competing with Israeli growers. Usually the Gaza farmers sell their fruit to Iran, Eastern Europe and the Gulf States, while the Israelis reserve for themselves the more lucrative markets in the West. In 1979, however, Iran decided not to buy the three and a half million cases of Valencia oranges which Gaza normally exports. So the Israeli Citrus Marketing Board decided to sell the fruit through its own network. This piece of altruism disguised the real purpose behind the action which, according to the deputy director of the Board, was 'to prevent uncontrolled competition with Israeli-grown fruit'.[25] As the Board well understood, the Gaza orange ripens a month earlier than the

Israeli Shamouti, and would compete with it in the West European export market. But the citrus grower in Gaza faces worse problems than this. Like the West Bank farmers who are prevented from drilling wells, the people of Gaza are not allowed to plant fruit trees. From the Israeli point of view they are inconvenient enough as it is, so no more may be planted. Even if it is a case of replacing a single dead tree, the farmer will have to get a permit from the military governor.

Employment opportunities in Gaza are even more limited than on the West Bank and so tens of thousands of refugees leave their camps each day before dawn to assemble at one of the labour markets near the border. It might be Ashqelon Junction or the Erez crossroads. From 4.00 a.m. onwards the Israeli employers arrive – market gardeners and building contractors mostly – and the bargaining opens. The markets are crowded with people of all ages and there are hundreds of children aged twelve and over who are eager for work. Many employers prefer them to the adults because they are cheaper and easier to handle. Child labour is, of course, illegal in Israel and the Youth Employment Law of 1953 stipulates that 'one may not employ a child under sixteen years of age'. But nobody does anything about it. There are no policemen patrolling the labour markets, and no inspectors from the Labour Ministry. Obviously the children have neither insurance nor social security and, since their day's wages are very low, they are considerably cheaper to hire than the adult labourers – and about ten times cheaper than an Israeli worker. For a day's work picking tomatoes a child from Gaza will earn about three dollars.[26]

There are twenty-six Israeli settlements in the Strip and in the Rafah salient to the south, many less than in the West Bank, but the area is so miserable and so overpopulated that they are more obtrusive. During 1980 they were still being established, with the maximum degree of publicity and provocation. A site is chosen, the Israeli army moves in, barbed wire is erected and the flag is flown from the nearest piece of high ground. Over the following months concrete buildings are put up and the land is levelled by army bulldozers. Finally the planting begins and the greenhouses are erected. These colonies, smart and streamlined, inhabited by people who have no right of any sort to the land, make an unpleasant contrast with the wretched refugees in their shacks outside, separated from the colonists by great walls of barbed wire.

John Reddaway, a former deputy commissioner-general of U.N.R.W.A., has written of his disgust

> at the sight of these greedy intruders grabbing large tracts of some of the best land in this small corner of Palestine, where for thirty years past hundreds of thousands of refugees of farming stock have been living without a hope of ever getting even a small plot of land to cultivate for themselves, because what land there was to farm barely sufficed for the local population. In Gaza of all places I do not understand how these Zionist land-grabbers can live with the injustice they are perpetrating every day of their lives to their wretched fellow men whose land they have stolen and fenced off to keep them out.[27]

Edward Hodgkin, then foreign editor of *The Times,* visited the Occupied Territories in 1969 and wrote of 'the intensity with which the Israelis are hated everywhere by all sections of the population'.[28] It is not simply the enmity which any people might show towards an occupying power; it is a vivid loathing of a power that is not only occupying land that does not belong to it, but which is also colonizing that land and throwing out its rightful owners and inhabitants. Fahd Qawasma, the mayor of Hebron, a town of 60,000 people south of Bethlehem, insists on the distinction: 'The Israeli occupation is different from others. When the British went to Egypt they exploited the people and the country but they did not build settlements. They did not take land away from the Egyptians. In our case occupation is a euphemism: settler-colonization is a better term. Our people are being supplanted by another.' Qawasma, like Rashad Shawa, mayor of Gaza, or Karim Khalaf, mayor of Ramallah, does not hide his hatred of the Israelis. He makes no concessions to them and he does everything he can to resist their policies. He admits that he is a supporter of the Palestine Liberation Organization and that he acts as one of its representatives in the West Bank. If questioned about the morality of violent resistance, he says: 'You cannot ask us to do nothing. We have been under enemy occupation for twelve years now. During the Second World War most European countries were occupied and they resisted. We are doing the same thing.'[29]

The oppression to which Israel has resorted in order to extinguish any sort of resistance, civilian or military, has been documented by, among others, the International Red Cross, Amnesty International, *The Sunday Times,* the United States National Lawyers Guild, the Israeli League for Civil and Human Rights and the United Nations Special Committee to Investigate Israeli Practices Affecting the Human Rights of the Population of the Occupied Territories.[30] The conclusions which these organizations arrived at indicate that the Palestinians under occupation possess not even the most elementary democratic rights. As Michael Adams, a former correspondent of the *Guardian* in Beirut, has written:

> Palestinians in the Occupied Territories have enjoyed since 1967 no rights and no representative institutions. There is no authority to which they can appeal, no protection which they can invoke. Their every movement and action is subject to the arbitrary authority of the Israeli military governor. They can be detained, imprisoned, deported, without the intervention of any tribunal. Their houses and property may be destroyed, their lands confiscated, their crops burned and their trees cut down.[31]

Israeli oppression is directed against various targets. Individuals who are considered political obstacles to the occupation are as vulnerable as those suspected of military activities. But it doesn't stop at individuals because the Israeli government is a firm believer in the principle of collective punishment. As practised in the West Bank and Gaza, this means that the inhabitants of houses, villages or even towns can be punished because of the activities of one man over whom they have no control. In 1979 development funds for Nablus were blocked because the town's mayor had held a conference with the mayor of Hebron against the orders of the military governor.

One of the most popular forms of collective punishment is the curfew, which can be imposed without warning on towns, villages or refugee camps. In May 1979 the 4,000 inhabitants of the Jalazoun camp north of Ramallah were subjected to a twelve-day curfew after some youths from the camp were suspected of throwing stones at Israeli military vehicles. The curfew lasted for twenty-two hours a day and in the remaining two hours the residents were

allowed out of their huts to receive flour rations from
U.N.R.W.A. No other food was allowed into the camp.[32] At
about the same time a sixteen-day curfew was imposed on the
small town of Halhul near Hebron. Stone-throwing was again the
pretext, although on this occasion two of the stone-throwers were
shot dead either by soldiers or by Israeli civilians from the settlement of Kiryat Arba. This curfew confined people to their homes
for twenty-three hours a day. Halhul is a predominantly
agricultural town and its farmers were thus prevented from working in their fields. According to the town's mayor, Muhammad
Milhem, forty per cent of their crops were ruined.

A more drastic form of collective punishment is the demolition
of houses. The president of the Israeli League for Civil and
Human Rights has revealed that during the first four years of the
occupation, 16,312 homes were destroyed by Israeli forces for
'security reasons'.[33] The Israelis do not pretend that all these
houses belonged to terrorists. As long as they are owned or rented
by relatives of suspected terrorists, then they can be considered
fair game for the army bulldozers. And invariably the demolition
takes place before the suspect is brought to trial. On 31 January
1979 the *Jerusalem Post* announced that the East Jerusalem house
belonging to an uncle of a certain Muhammad Abu Hillal had been
bulldozed. Abu Hillal was a suspected terrorist who had been arrested shortly beforehand. There was no suggestion that he had
ever lived in the house or that his uncle either knew or approved of
his activities. The fact that they were relations made the uncle's
house a suitable reprisal target. A couple of days later the same
paper reported a similar incident: 'Security forces removed the occupants of two East Jerusalem houses early yesterday morning and
sealed the buildings' doors and windows with cinder blocks and
concrete.' And why had these houses been made uninhabitable?
Because two alleged terrorists '*were said* to have lived *at one time
or another* in the two houses' (my italics).[34]

The logic behind these forms of retribution hardly needs
clarification. The policy is simple and ruthless, clearly designed to
make the Palestinian population realize that it is going to suffer
more than the Israelis if violent resistance continues. The aims of
Israel's other policies are equally clear: the deportation of hundreds of West Bank leaders and interference with the area's education system are methods calculated (wrongly) to prevent the

emergence of an articulate nationalist leadership. To this end, schools, training centres and universities are subjected to regular harassment by the army and many of them are periodically closed down. In March 1979 every educational institution in the West Bank was closed down, some for periods of two months.

Bir Zeit University near Ramallah is the best university in the region and the oldest Arab institution of higher education on either bank of the River Jordan. Yet, although it has high educational standards, it doesn't confine its activities to academic work. It plays a central part in West Bank life, seeing itself as a focal point for Palestinian aspirations, and it takes its community work seriously. It has an illiteracy programme consisting of twelve centres in the West Bank and Gaza and undertakes a large amount of similar work, such as courses for teachers and school-building projects in the refugee camps. The Israeli authorities naturally find Bir Zeit a highly inconvenient institution and regard it as a centre of subversion and terrorism – although not a single faculty member has ever been found guilty of any 'security' offence. Since 1973 the university has been subjected to constant interference. Its teachers course has been permanently closed down, its president deported, its lecturers refused work permits and planning permission for its new buildings rejected. In May 1979 army units stormed the campus, beat up large numbers of students and confiscated several hundred identity cards. The university was then closed down for a period of two months.

Bir Zeit's president, Dr Hanna Nasir, was one of 1,151 Palestinians deported from the West Bank and Gaza between 1967 and 1978.[35] Compared with the mass expulsions during the 1948 and 1967 wars, it is not a high number, yet it includes large numbers of the most prominent Arab leaders in the Territories – teachers, doctors, lawyers, journalists, students and so on. Among the fifty-four deportees from Jerusalem are the mayor, the president of the Islamic Council, a former foreign minister of Jordan, a trade union leader and the director of the Maqasid Islamic charitable hospital. Politicians are among the most favoured candidates for expulsion. Mayors of Ramallah and Bira have been deported and so have the brothers of the current mayors of Hebron and Halhul. Two days before nominations closed for the municipal elections of April 1976, candidates for the mayorship of Hebron and the Bira council were expelled to Lebanon while their appeals to the courts against their deportation were still pending.[36]

In this manner Israel manages to eliminate the Palestinian leadership in the Occupied Territories. Behind this policy stands the same reasoning that advocates collective punishment. If enough people are punished – even if they are completely innocent and have never even been accused of a particular crime – then the others will be discouraged from any kind of criticism of the occupation. The aim was to cripple the leadership and to dampen any feelings of nationalism. As a policy it was a total failure, for nationalism in the West Bank is infinitely stronger today than it was ten years ago. Moreover, some of the deportees are more important national figures now than they were in their homeland: a doctor and a lawyer who were expelled together in 1973 are now senior officials in the Palestine Liberation Organization.

The Israeli authorities never explain why people are deported – if they had committed some sort of crime, they would presumably be charged in court – and usually the deportation is carried out so quickly that there is no means of appealing against it. In December 1967, Judge Antun Atalla, a septuagenarian Christian whose family had lived in Jerusalem since before the Muslim conquest, went to Amman with official Israeli permission. On Boxing Day, shortly before he was due to return, the Israeli Radio announced that he was not being allowed back. No reason was given and the old man was not permitted to see his home again until ten years later, on his eightieth birthday, the Israeli authorities declared that on 'compassionate grounds' he would now be allowed to visit his own house.

Rouhi al-Khatib, the mayor of Jerusalem, has never been allowed back. Mayor of the city since 1957, Khatib and his council were dismissed by the Israelis when Jerusalem was annexed in 1967. After his deposition, which he refused to acknowledge, he remained in the city and continued his work as director of the Arab Hotels Company and the Jerusalem Electrical Company. In March of the following year, he was woken by Israeli policemen at 3.00 a.m. and told he was wanted for interrogation. But instead of being taken to the military governor in Jerusalem he was driven directly to Jericho where he was handed a deportation order alleging that his presence in Jerusalem constituted a danger to the security of Israel. He was then escorted to the border and handed over to the Jordanian authorities. He was not allowed to take anything with him and his family was not told of the expulsion. They learnt of it later from the wireless.

Mr Khatib's wife and his two children decided to stay, hoping that he would be permitted home. A year and a half afterwards, policemen collected Mrs Khatib for interrogation. She was detained for several hours and then sentenced to three months imprisonment. No reason was given. After protests from a number of people, she was released after fifteen days, probably because she was critically ill with suspected cancer. She was then given a permit to visit her husband and to undergo an operation in Beirut. Although her permit was extended once, she was still receiving treatment when it expired for a second time. The Israelis refused her a second renewal and when she tried to return to Jerusalem after her convalescence, she was turned away at the frontier.

During the first two years of the occupation, the deportees were simply taken to one of the bridges across the Jordan and told to walk to the other side. After pressure from the Committee of Expelled Palestinians in Amman, however, the Jordanian government refused to admit any further deportees. The Israelis then opened two other expulsion routes, one in the mountainous region near the Lebanese border and the other in the Wadi 'Araba desert south of the Dead Sea. Dr Walid Qamhawi, a charming, soft-spoken gynaecologist from Nablus, has the honour of being the only person to have been expelled along both routes. In September 1970 twenty soldiers arrived outside his house and took him to the office of the military governor. There he was told he was to be deported. He asked permission to return to his house, say goodbye to his family and collect a few belongings, but it was refused. He was then blindfolded, handcuffed and driven to the Lebanese border with five others. On arrival they were ordered to walk northwards and told that, if they looked back, they would be shot. For some reason, which he has never learnt, Dr Qamhawi was allowed home two months later, but in December 1973, on the anniversary of the Declaration of Human Rights, he was once again dumped in a truck and taken to the Wadi 'Araba. An officer pointed to a Jordanian military post ten miles across the desert and told him and his companions to start walking. Qamhawi, who had never been politically active (though he has become so during his exile), was never given any indication on either occasion of why he was being expelled.

Israeli oppression of the Palestinians of the West Bank and Gaza thus takes many forms. For 'security' or other reasons an Arab can be deported, or arrested and held without trial; his land can be confiscated and his home destroyed. The Israeli government does not deny that these things take place. But there is one method of oppression that it does not admit and that is the practice of torture. Incidents of torture are, of course, difficult to prove since they rarely involve witnesses whose testimony is likely to be accepted. Nevertheless, *The Sunday Times,* Amnesty International, the United States National Lawyers Guild and the International Committee of the Red Cross have all produced evidence indicating that torture is frequently used against the Arabs of the Occupied Territories. As *The Sunday Times* Insight team reported in the summer of 1977: 'Israeli interrogators routinely ill-treat and often torture Arab prisoners. . . . Prisoners are often hooded, blindfolded, or hung by their wrists for long periods. Many are sexually assaulted. Others are given electric shocks.'[37]

There is not enough space here to discuss all the allegations or to comment on the Israeli denials. But it is worth looking at a particular case in which the Israelis were finally forced to admit that torture had taken place. Anyone who saw Ismail Ajweh in London in the summer of 1979 would have guessed that he had been tortured. His eyes were half closed and watery, perhaps permanently damaged. He walked with a terrible limp, the result of atrophy of the left thigh and calf (according to a medical report from a Jerusalem hospital, his left calf was six centimetres thinner than his right). He also had gastritis, a damaged colon and lesions to his vertebrae.

Ismail Ajweh was the acting editor of *al-Fajr* paper in East Jerusalem. At 1.00 a.m. on 16 December 1978, he was taken from his home and thrown into prison, accused of having 'connections' with the P.L.O. For the first eighteen days of his imprisonment he was questioned every day before being taken out to the yard to be beaten. On one occasion he was chained to a pipe for seventy-two hours with a bag over his head and was regularly hit. His chief tormentor was a man known as Uzi who was in charge of the torture sessions. Uzi also used psychological methods to break Ismail. Sometimes he told him that the government had ordered his execution; more frequently he invented stories of how Ismail's wife, who was pregnant, was sleeping with other men. The other policemen pretended to be nicer. They would say to Ismail: 'Confess that you are a terrorist and we won't send you back to Uzi.' When this did not work, they tried to persuade him to emigrate, 'otherwise we will have to make you another appointment with Uzi'.

Ismail did not see his wife or lawyer for thirty days after his capture and then only for five minutes. He was not allowed to see a representative of the Red Cross for three months despite Israel's claim that Palestinian prisoners have 'guaranteed' access to the Red Cross within eighteen days of their arrest. During the four months of his imprisonment, Ismail was neither charged nor brought to a court. He was not allowed to see a doctor and his diet consisted of bread and water and potatoes. He spent a whole winter in Jerusalem in solitary confinement without blankets and with water dripping from the roof.

After his release Ismail revealed the details of his imprisonment. He underwent two lie detector tests (one at a police station) which, according to an Israeli newspaper, 'proved that the interrogator had hit Ajweh on the head, handcuffed him to a pipe and beaten him with his fists. The test also proved that the journalist . . . had been offered his release in exchange for a promise to leave the country.'[38] The Israeli authorities eventually admitted their guilt by reprimanding Uzi and transferring him to another post.

During Ismail's imprisonment, his pregnant wife and two small children lived in complete poverty. They received some assistance from his brother-in-law, who rents his camel to tourists, and also from his father, who from time to time brought them vegetables from his village. When Ismail was released, his family was poorer still because he could not work and he needed hospital treatment. And naturally he received no assistance from the government. Even though they admit that the man was beaten up so badly that he needed several months of medical treatment, the Israelis made no apology, gave no compensation and did not pay for his treatment. But then Ismail is an Arab, an Arab from East Jerusalem which Israel has annexed, and evidently anything that can be done to discourage him from staying there meets the approval of the Israeli government.

After this book went to press, Mayor Qawasma of Hebron and Mayor Milhelm of Halhul were deported by the Israelis.

PART THREE

War and Politics

7

The Structure of the Resistance

In the fifty years that followed the decease of the Ottoman Empire, the dominant ideological force in the Middle East was that of Arab nationalism. It was a muddled concept, not easy to define, but for the most part it expressed little more than a strong feeling that all Arabs, whatever their religion, possessed a common culture and formed a single nation. 'Unity' was the most effective rallying-cry of this period and, in all parts of the Arab world, political parties, some legal and others clandestine, worked towards this ideal. The 1950s was the decade of the Arab nationalists, the only period when it seemed that this romantic and somewhat self-contradictory objective might be attained. The conservative monarchies of Egypt and Iraq were swept away; the Ba´ath (Arab Socialist Renaissance Party) came to power in Syria; and Arab nationalist aspirations throughout the Middle East were symbolized by Gamal Abdel Nasser's defiance at Suez.

The Palestinians embraced Arab nationalism because they believed it would enable them to regain their homeland. Palestine was not merely a Palestinian problem: since it was an integral part of the Arab nation, they expected Arabs everywhere to assist in its liberation. Even in 1948 the pro-Western monarchies and republics had fought, however ineffectually, against the Zionists. With their overthrow, and the establishment of nationalist governments in Cairo, Baghdad and Damascus, it seemed that the Palestine issue would at last be resolved. So the Palestinians joined the nationalist parties in their countries of exile – the Ba´ath, the Nasserist groups, the Communists, the Arab Nationalist Movement – and waited for the war which would liberate their country.

The high point of expectation was 1958 when the union between Syria and Egypt in the United Arab Republic seemed to herald a closer degree of Arab unity. When the union collapsed three years later, the pan-Arab ideal was already receding. By then many Palestinians were disillusioned by the failure of the Arab states to do anything to help them and some began to rethink their ideas on the nature of the Palestine question. Instead of seeing it as an Arab problem, they came to view it more as a matter between the Israelis and themselves. With the Arab states they had achieved nothing, and their frustration was immense. So they decided to work on their own, to set up a popular resistance, and to fight by themselves. They had the example of Algeria before them and Vietnam was just beginning.

The anger and exasperation of the Palestinians were noticed by the Arab states who in 1964 decided to create the Palestine Liberation Organization. At that time the P.L.O. was not in fact designed to do much about liberating Palestine. Its role was to shout a lot about solidarity and so on, but not to do any actual fighting. Its purpose was to contain rather than express Palestinian nationalism, to act as an outlet for Palestinian frustration − not to be an effective military organization which might drag the Arab states into a war with Israel. Moreover, it was to be an official body of the Arab League and therefore easily supervised by the member states.

The more militant Palestinians saw the then P.L.O. for what it was and took little notice of it. They began to form commando groups and to prepare themselves for a guerrilla war. The Palestine National Liberation Movement, known by a reversal of its Arabic initials as Fatah (conquest), emerged in the early sixties and carried out its first operation in 1965. Although it received weapons and training from Algeria, it was at first greatly mistrusted by the other Arab states, which realized that it was likely to be more active and troublesome than the P.L.O. Fatah members were arrested in Egypt, Lebanon and Syria, and the group's future leader, Yasser Arafat, spent seven weeks in a Damascus prison.

The guerrilla movements were of little significance − Fatah had only two or three hundred commandos − before 1967. But the June war, which ended in the defeat of the Egyptian, Syrian and Jordanian armies, demonstrated once more that the Arab states were incapable of liberating Palestine. The post-war demoralization was followed by a new mood of militancy and the feeling that the Palestinians would have to fight for their homeland without the aid or the interference of the Arab states. The commandos therefore stepped up their military activity, and their raids into Israel brought them increased respect and support from the refugees. The skirmish at Karama in March 1968, when commando units, backed by the Jordanian army, inflicted heavy casualties on invading Israeli forces, added impetus to the guerrillas. Reluctantly, the Arab states concluded that Fatah reflected the aspirations of the Palestinians more accurately than the P.L.O. and, in the summer of 1968, President Nasser accorded Arafat official recognition by including him in an Egyptian delegation to Moscow. The P.L.O. also admitted the success of the guerrilla movements by allocating them seats in its National Council. During 1968 Fatah gradually extended its influence over the organization and in February 1969 it established its domination by electing Arafat as chairman of the P.L.O.'s Executive Committee.

Fatah's message was simple: Palestine would only be liberated by Palestinians fighting a popular war. All effort should be concentrated on a nationalist uprising with a solitary goal: the liberation of the homeland. Everything else was secondary. Ideological debate and social revolution have had no place in Fatah's activities. They are to be discussed later, after the liberation. Before that, only the question of recovering Palestine can be admitted. Fatah has thus appealed to all Palestinians, irrespective of class or profession, who support the resistance movement. This pragmatism and lack of dogmatism, this refusal to waste time on recondite ideological quarrels, has contributed to Fatah's supremacy within the P.L.O.

Fatah's beginnings can be traced to seven Palestinians who were working in the Gulf during the fifties. All of them were Sunni Muslims and – apart from the two who were gunned down by an Israeli assassination squad in Beirut – they still form the core of the Fatah leadership. Yasser Arafat comes from a middle-class Jerusalem family. As a youth in the 1948 war, he worked for Abdel Qader Husseini, the mufti's cousin and leading military commander. After the war he went to Gaza and then to Cairo where he became president of the Palestinian Students Federation. In Egypt he made preliminary plans for the establishment of a liberation movement with Salah Khalaf, Khalil Wazir, and Muhammed Najjar. Later he went to Kuwait, where he worked as an engineer, and became friends with three other future leaders of Fatah: Farouk Qaddoumi, Kamal Adwan and Khaled al-Hassan. It was during this time, when the seven were working in the oil-rich states of Saudi Arabia, Qatar and Kuwait, that they acquired the political and financial support from the Palestinian communities in the Gulf which was later to be an important element in Fatah's success.

By its adoption of a simple, nationalist struggle, and its avoidance of ideological dispute, Fatah has managed to gain the support of both conservative and revolutionary regimes in the Arab world. This has given it an enormous advantage over the smaller, left-wing groups, and enabled it to dominate the resistance. But is has also meant that Fatah's survival depends on skilful handling of the Arab regimes. Inter-Arab problems have consumed most of Arafat's time and caused most of Fatah's difficulties. Although the public image he has established is that of a rough, unshaven freedom fighter, Arafat is in fact a diplomat and a practical politician rather than a military man or a revolutionary fanatic. He has had occasion to mediate in a number of disputes between other Arab leaders and also in quarrels between different movements inside the resistance. Perhaps his greatest diplomatic feat was to acquire simultaneous backing from both the Soviet Union and China.

Although Fatah's leadership is relatively homogeneous, it has naturally developed different factions and Arafat has had to work hard to retain a balance between them. A strong leftist faction is led by Salah Khalaf, and its position is often supported by Farouk Qaddoumi. A more moderate group is led by Khaled al-Hassan, who has close relations with the Saudi government and who favours still closer ties with the Arab states. From both these factions, smaller offshoots have appeared and Arafat's task is to keep them together. He is a skilled political manipulator and his achievement in keeping the organization together after fifteen years is considerable. But in order to achieve this he has frequently had to follow political trends rather than direct them and he is charged by his rivals with inconsistency and lack of principle.

Unlike its Algerian allies, Fatah decided not to liquidate the smaller commando organizations but to try to bring them together under the overall leadership of the P.L.O. Khaled al-Hassan describes Fatah's relationship with these groups as like that between 'a mother and her naughty children' but it is often much worse than that and some Fatah leaders clearly regret that they did not take a firmer line with the extremists at the beginning. The Popular Front for the Liberation of Palestine (P.F.L.P.) and its offshoots have repeatedly embarrassed the P.L.O. leadership and sabotaged its diplomatic efforts with their spectacular brand of terrorism.

The P.F.L.P. was formed shortly after the 1967 war following the merger of three small guerrilla groups. It began to split soon afterwards. During 1968, when its leader, George Habash, was in a Syrian prison, two factions left the Front and set up their own organizations, the P.F.L.P.–General Command and the Palestine Arab Organization. The process of fragmentation accelerated some months later when a large group of young P.F.L.P. activists broke away and formed the Popular Democratic Front for the Liberation of Palestine (P.D.F.L.P.). Later still, secessionists from the P.F.L.P. created the Popular Organization for the Liberation of Palestine (P.O.L.P.) and the Popular Revolutionary Front for the Liberation of Palestine (P.R.F.L.P.). More recently, the P.F.L.P.–General Command also split, dividing itself into pro and anti Syrian factions.

The history of disunity in the P.F.L.P. can be ascribed partly to Palestinian individualism and partly to the fact that the Palestinians had been living in so many different places after 1948 that they came under the influence of a number of different regimes and different ideologies. Dr Habash's background was very different from that of the Sunni leaders of Fatah. One of the most brilliant doctors in the Middle East, he is an Orthodox Christian from Haifa who studied at the American University of Beirut. Many of his supporters are also Christians who have grown up, not in Egypt or the Gulf like Fatah's leaders, but in Syria, Jordan and Lebanon. Habash's second in command, the late Dr Wadi Haddad, and the leader of the breakaway P.D.F.L.P., Nayif Hawatmeh, were also Greek Orthodox. By 1970, the Marxist P.F.L.P. contained so many Orthodox commandos that it recruited a chaplain, Hanna Sakkab.

Habash and Hawatmeh belong to an entirely different ideological tradition from the Muslim Palestinian nationalists of

Fatah. They are the spiritual descendants of the Christian Arab nationalists of the nineteenth century who believed that in Greater Syria (i.e. what later became Syria, Lebanon, Jordan and Palestine) there existed a national identity which should be expressed in a single state. This state, they maintained, should be based not on the religious solidarity of Islam, but on the idea of Greater Syria as a distinct, historical, cultural, and geographical unity – as in fact it is – which had been suppressed for centuries by the Ottoman occupation. When Habash formed the Arab Nationalist Movement in Jordan in 1953, he was aiming for the same objectives as the nationalists of the Turkish era and for the next fourteen years he believed that the Palestine issue would be solved by Arab nationalist action led by Nasser.

Habash saw the problem in much wider terms than Arafat and his friends and considered it part of the struggle for Arab freedom which had been blocked successively by the Turks, the colonial powers, and the Zionists. To Habash, Palestine was an Arab responsibility, and it would be liberated by the joint efforts of all the Arab people and not by guerrilla warfare conducted by the Palestinians. When the Arab regimes revealed their feebleness in 1967, Habash reacted very differently from Arafat. While Fatah insisted that the regimes should now be ignored, Habash argued that they should be overthrown. If the Arab world as it stood was too impotent to regain Palestine, then it would have to be changed. But Habash also concluded that Nasser and Arab nationalism were not sufficient to unite the Arabs and defeat Israel. A revolutionary creed was also needed 'to mobilize the masses' and this explains Habash's late conversion to Marxism. As he once explained:

'The war of 1967 and the new defeat brought a full revolution in our thought. We decided to adopt the Vietnamese model: a strong political party, complete mobilization of the people, the principle of not depending on any regime or government. The situation was now clear. The true revolutionary forces began to emerge. We are now preparing for twenty or more years of war against Israel and its backers.'[1]

Habash's analysis of the situation was in many ways more clear-sighted than Arafat's. He realized that the Palestinians would never defeat Israel if they had to fight on their own or with pro-Western regimes such as those in Jordan and Lebanon. Their enemies, he argued, were not only the Zionists but also 'imperialism', by which he meant the United States and any other country which gave military or financial support to Israel, and the Arab 'puppet regimes' which, he claimed, were only kept in power by the West. As a first step, therefore, the Hashemite monarchy in Jordan, alternately referred to in P.F.L.P. bulletins as the 'puppet' or 'hireling' regime, was to be overthrown. The Lebanese 'fascist' government, the 'arch-reactionaries' of Saudi Arabia and the 'capitulationist regime' of Egypt were to follow. Only when Palestine is surrounded by united Marxist states will it be liberated. When that happens, according to the P.F.L.P., 'not only will Palestine be free from Zionism, but Lebanon and Jordan will be free from reaction, and Syria and Iraq from the *petite bourgeoisie*. They will be transformed in a truly socialist sense and united. Palestine will be part of a Marxist-Leninist Arabia.'[2]

The P.F.L.P.'s adoption of Marxism was in part prompted by tactical considerations. The old nationalist slogan of 'unity' had lost its appeal. It had to be reinforced by a revolutionary doctrine, involving social work and propaganda. Thus, much of the Front's time has been taken up by 'ideological training' in the camps and in the countryside. Before 1970 even Jordanian Bedouin were being given Marxist lessons in their tents.[3] The Front's acceptance of Marxism has also brought an international flavour to its propaganda. Foreign precedents are frequently cited and the P.F.L.P. bulletin is fond of quoting stuff like the last words of Salvador Allende or a poem dedicated to Amilcar Cabral. Fraternal messages are regularly sent to countries like Cuba, North Korea and South Yemen and one commando who was killed in the Occupied Territories was known as 'Gaza's Guevara'.

Nayif Hawatmeh, the leader of the P.D.F.L.P., belonged to the left-wing faction of the Arab Nationalist Movement and became a Marxist long before George Habash. Early in 1969 he took his supporters out of the P.F.L.P. and, after Fatah had intervened to prevent a major gun-fight between his men and the Front, he set up his own organization. Hawatmeh had been quarrelling with Habash for some years, his principal complaint being that the P.F.L.P. leader was not revolutionary enough. The issue that caused many of the arguments, first in the Arab Nationalist Move-

ment and later in the committees of the Front, was the role the
'petit bourgeois' were to play in the Palestine revolution. Neither
Habash nor Hawatmeh liked the 'petit bourgeois' (both of them
seemed to ignore the fact that they and their supporters were 'petit
bourgeois' themselves) but while Habash believed that they should
co-operate with them in the early stages of the revolution,
Hawatmeh refused to have anything to do with them. Habash,
who knows his revolutionary history and realizes that even Marxists have to compromise – one example he likes to give is Mao's
alliance with the Kuomintang against the Japanese – calls
Hawatmeh's attitude 'infantile leftism'. Certainly the P.D.F.L.P.
approach lengthens the list of Arab regimes which have to be overthrown before its commandos can get on with the business of
liberating Palestine. Only the government of South Yemen, whose
political programme was partly drawn up by Hawatmeh himself in
1968, receives the approval of the P.D.F.L.P.

The quarrel over the 'petit bourgeois' and other, similarly
recondite subjects, such as the relationship between military
struggle and social revolution, brought about the first split in the
P.F.L.P. Ahmed Jibril, a former Palestinian officer in the Syrian
army, had formed the Palestinian Liberation Front a few years
before the 1967 war. Later he brought it into the coalition that
produced the P.F.L.P. But he was so disgusted by the time-
wasting ideological disputes in which the Front specialized that he
took it out again less than a year later and renamed it the
P.F.L.P. – General Command. Jibril maintained that the duty of
the resistance was to fight and not to talk about the 'petit
bourgeois'. His own organization, though small, soon established
itself as the most militarily effective of the lesser commando
groups.

Fatah and the splinter groups of the P.F.L.P. are the only independent organizations of the resistance. The others owe their existence to particular Arab governments which finance and support
them and expect them to follow government policy in return. The
Arab Liberation Front (A.L.F.), for example, is Iraq's way of
expressing interest in the resistance. Yet it has no independent
identity. It does what it is told by Baghdad and it is consequently
ineffective as an instrument of the resistance. Its establishment
owed little to any spontaneous manifestation of Palestinian political aspirations: it was set up simply to counteract the influence

which Iraq's main rival, Syria, was seen to have over the resistance through its own organization, Saiqa.

Wherever its ultimate loyalties lie, Saiqa is at least a serious military force and numerically it is second only to Fatah. It was set up after the 1967 war by the ruling Syrian Ba'ath party, which, for various reasons, decided not to support either Fatah or the P.F.L.P. It was trained by Syrian officers and it received Syrian funds and Syrian arms. Its active membership consisted largely of Palestinian members of the pro-Syrian (as opposed to the pro-Iraqi) faction of the Ba'ath Party who were living in Syria, Jordan or Kuwait. Until his assassination in 1979, Saiqa was led by Zuheir Mohsen, the head of the P.L.O.'s military department. While it adheres to the complicated ideology of the Ba'ath – a compound of socialism and Arab nationalism – Saiqa normally sides with Arafat in the major debates inside the P.L.O.

The guerrilla organizations not only disagree about the strategy they should follow in order to achieve their goal; they disagree about the goal itself. In the early years of the resistance, when it was clear that the struggle would last for several decades, there was no need to specify the ultimate objective. 'Liberation' was a vague enough term that satisfied everyone. In October 1968 the Fatah leader, Salah Khalaf, defined what later became the official P.L.O. objective: Palestine was to form a single, secular, democratic state for the Palestinian people. The state would automatically cease to be a Zionist one but all Jews who were established there and who wished to remain would be able to do so. As the P.D.F.L.P. explained to the Palestine National Council the following year: '[In the secular, democratic state] both Arabs and Jews shall live without discrimination, and will be granted the right to develop and promote their respective national culture.' In addition, the new Palestine would 'include Arabs and Jews enjoying equal national rights and duties'.[4]

The secular, democratic state, then, was the aim, but there was no pretence that the Palestinians were anywhere near achieving it. According to Habash it would take at least twenty years. With such a prospect there was no need to start thinking about compromises; the guerrillas could live with their dream.

Political attitudes in the Middle East were shaken by the war of October 1973 when the armies of Syria and Egypt recovered some of the prestige they had forfeited in 1967. The war and the oil embargo that followed finally made the rest of the world wake up and start thinking about a possible settlement to the endemic conflict in the Middle East. As the participants prepared for the peace conference in Geneva, the Palestinians also had to stir themselves, to define their position and to formulate their demands. Fatah and the other organizations which had official contacts with the Arab world had to take into account the positions of the relevant Arab states; the Front and its offshoots, which considered all the countries of the Middle East as their enemies, except Iraq, South Yemen and possibly Algeria, could afford to be less diplomatic. It was clear, for example, that Egypt, Syria and Jordan were prepared to accept a settlement if Israel evacuated the areas occupied in 1967, but that they were not going to demand the rest of Palestine conquered in 1948. The Palestinians, therefore, had to decide whether to go along with the Arab consensus or to reject it. They had to decide whether or not they were prepared to abandon their vision of total liberation and accept a lesser but more tangible thing – Palestinian rule in those small areas of their homeland, the West Bank and Gaza, which stood a chance of being restored to them by diplomatic means.

It was a difficult decision but many Palestinians made it. Fawaz Turki wrote of how he was 'lured by the agony of wanting, *now*, in my own lifetime, the chance to know what it feels like, how the experience would sense in my brain, to be, for the first time since I was a child, the citizen of a country, a native of a land that is my own, all my own, with hills and mountains, and children in brick houses, where I could sit with my people, no longer menaced, no longer destitute.'[5] A compromise solution was implicitly accepted by Fatah, Saiqa, most of the Palestinian community in the diaspora and the Palestine National Council which, in June 1974, declared its willingness to set up an 'independent national authority in any part of the Palestinian land that is liberated'.[6] No Palestinians accepted this as an ideal settlement but they believed that it was the only practicable way of bringing a sort of justice to their people. Besides, once Zionism had been pinned back behind its old borders, they argued, it would be destroyed as an expansionist force. This would inevitably lead to better relations between Israel and the Arabs and might open up the way to the eventual return of the refugees to their homeland. In any case, as Saiqa's leader, Zuheir Mohsen, said shortly before his death: 'It is nonsense to talk about a secular state when we do not possess a single inch of our territory. The time has come to be practical and realistic.'⁷

To the arguments of the moderates, the newly labelled 'rejectionists' replied with unanswerable logic and without any concession to the realities of the situation. They pointed out that most of the refugees came from Jaffa, Haifa and Galilee, and that a 'ministate' in the West Bank and Gaza would solve none of their problems. They reminded their opponents that the Zionists had bought only six per cent of the land of Palestine and that the rest was stolen. And if criticized for their failure to compromise, they replied that colonialism was inevitably doomed and that the Zionist settler state could not last. After April 1975 they were able to point to Vietnam and Cambodia as countries that had refused to compromise with 'imperialists' and had defeated them in the end.

Palestinian rejectionism, the refusal to make concessions, the insistence on going on fighting when there is no chance of victory, has a long ancestry. It was present in 1917, in 1922, and at other moments during the mandate. The Palestinian leaders who refused to take part in the legislative elections or talk to the royal commissions were rejectionists. The mufti was a rejectionist. So were many of the leaders in the 1948 war. Abdullah of Transjordan, who was emphatically not a rejectionist, found them incomprehensible. He once said to Sir John Glubb:

'If I were to drive into the desert and accost the first goatherd I saw, and consult him whether to make war on my enemies or not, he would say to me, "How many have you got and how many have they?" Yet here are these learned politicians [the Arab leaders], all of them with university degrees, and when I say to them, "The Jews are too strong – it is a mistake to make war," they cannot understand the point. They make long speeches about rights.'⁸

Rejectionism, by its nature, is romantic and irresponsible. It is not aimed at achieving anything, it is concerned with preventing something. It has no answers to give, no alternative to suggest. It is convinced of nothing but the absolute truth of its cause. That is not to say that the rejectionists do not have a case – they obviously do: if you are a Galilean you should be allowed to go to Galilee not the West Bank – but they are refusing to examine anyone else's.

And while, in a negative sense, they have the power to decide their people's future (i.e. by wrecking a settlement), they refuse to accept the responsibility of providing an alternative. 'Twenty years or more of war' may satisfy Dr Habash's philosophy – not that he will live through it as he is a sick man with heart and kidney troubles – but it will not do much for the barefoot children selling bubblegum in the streets of Beirut. As Fawaz Turki has written: 'If you give twenty years of your life in a refugee camp, you have paid a high price. If you are asked to sacrifice another twenty, the price becomes intolerable. If you are asked to make your yet unborn child take on your burden, you are committing an injustice.'[9]

Zuheir Mohsen, who was one of the leading moderates before his assassination, once explained the background to rejectionism:

> Before the last war our thoughts about the struggle against Zionism were romantic. We never specified what we wanted. This was both logical and natural, because for twenty-five years we have suffered successive defeats. We wanted war for its own sake, to instil in us the spirit of fighting rather than to seek crystal-clear goals by stages. Feelings of impotence dominated all our actions and thinking.[10]

Those feelings of impotence still dominate the Rejection Front. When Ahmed Jibril launches his guerrillas of the P.F.L.P. – General Command on suicide missions inside Israel, he has two objectives: to wreck any chance of a peace settlement and to invite Israeli reprisal raids which will drive moderate Palestinians into the Rejection Front. With Jibril stand Habash's P.F.L.P., the Iraqi-backed A.L.F., and a dissident pro-Iraqi faction of Fatah led by Abu Nidal. It is this last group which was largely responsible for the internecine warfare which broke out between Palestinians over the 'mini-state' controversy. Prominent Fatah moderates – including the P.L.O. representatives in London and Paris, Said Hammami and Ezzedine Khallak – were assassinated because they were outspoken advocates of a peace settlement involving compromise and acceptance of Israel as an established fact. While Fatah claims that its men were killed by Israeli agents who had infiltrated this pro-Iraqi group, few people doubt that the ultimate responsibility for the murders lies with Abu Nidal and his Baghdad protectors.

One group which is, rather surprisingly, *not* in the Rejection Front is Hawatmeh's P.D.F.L.P. Capable of a degree of self-criticism unusual among revolutionary movements, the P.D.F.L.P. reversed its attitude after the 1973 war, allied itself closer to Fatah and proclaimed itself in favour of a state in the West Bank and Gaza which it saw not as an end in itself but as a step towards the eventual establishment of a united, secular and socialist Palestine. Hawatmeh's change of policy predictably resulted in a macabre renewal of the rivalry between his group and Habash's P.F.L.P. In May 1974, when P.D.F.L.P. guerrillas led a suicide mission against the Israeli town of Ma'alot, they left behind a document calling for the establishment of a 'national authority on any territory wrested from the Zionist enemy' (i.e. a state on a part, not the whole, of Palestine), which was to be read out at a meeting of the Palestine National Council. The following year the P.F.L.P. retaliated. When three of Habash's commandos died at Kibbutz Kefar Jal'ad, they left behind a message for Hawatmeh's men, urging them 'to put pressure on your leadership to take a clear position of rejection since it has become clear that any settlement can only be an imperialistic one'.[11]

So the moderates and the rejectionists battled for the hearts of the Palestinians. But there was not really much doubt about the result. The moderates were bound to win because they included Arafat and the top Fatah men and also because they offered at least some hope to their people. Thus, in the years after 1973 the P.L.O. began to move towards acceptance of a Palestinian state in the West Bank and Gaza.

Israel and its apologists often claim that the Palestinians' offer to accept such a state is insincere, and point to the Palestine National Charter, drawn up in 1964, which calls for 'the total liberation of Palestine'. They thus wilfully ignore the political programme of the Palestinian movement (as represented by the Palestine National Council) and concentrate on a document which has the same sort of symbolic meaning for the Palestinians as the Basle programme has for the Zionists or clause 4 for the British Labour Party. The charter is a proclamation of historic rights, a symbol of national pride; it is not a statement of intention.

The aims of the Palestinian movement are to be found not in the charter but in the resolutions of the Palestine National Council and in the statements of its leaders. Apart from the crucial resolution of June 1974, which remains official P.L.O. policy, there have been numerous statements by Arafat and others indicating willingness to accept Israel's existence in exchange for a Palestinian state in the West Bank and Gaza. In May 1978 Arafat told the *New York Times* that 'the only possible solution was the coexistence of Israel and a Palestinian state'[12] and at the Baghdad conference later in the year the P.L.O. confirmed its acceptance of Israel's pre-1967 borders when it committed itself to a 'just peace based on the total Israeli withdrawal from Arab territories occupied in 1967'.[13]

The principal body of the P.L.O. is the Palestine National Council (P.N.C.), which is the nearest thing the Palestinians have to a parliament. The P.N.C. meets once a year, nowadays in Damascus, where it lays down the principles of P.L.O. policy, elects the Executive Committee and approves the budget. While it is obviously not strictly democratic — it is not practicable to organize elections for a community so widely dispersed as the Palestinians — the Palestinians themselves feel that the P.N.C. is as representative as it can be in the circumstances. The delegates come from all over the world, in numbers roughly corresponding to the strength of the communities in different countries. Forty come from Jordan and eighteen from Kuwait while the United States provides eight, Brazil two and the rest of Latin America four. Of the 301 delegates, a hundred of them are from the resistance groups (thirty-five are Fatah members) who are selected at the annual conferences of the respective organizations. Fifty-seven are members of various syndicates, such as the Labour Syndicate, the Student Movement, the Teachers' Syndicate and the Women's Organization, and a smaller number are chosen as representatives of the refugee camps. The remainder are independents chosen for their ability to contribute in one way or another to the cause. A significant number of P.N.C. members are writers and historians who have written about Palestine, and businessmen who have made large contributions to the Palestine National Fund.

Although it possesses less than twelve per cent of the seats, Fatah is the dominant force in the P.N.C. — as it is in all the bodies of the P.L.O. The independents receive a sympathetic hearing but they have no power base of their own. Most of them are linked in some way to one or other of the guerrilla organizations, and the majority, for obvious reasons, choose Fatah. A Palestinian businessman living in Saudi Arabia, for example, is more likely to be attracted by Arafat than by Habash or Hawatmeh. The syndicates are also behind Fatah: thirteen of the fifteen P.N.C. members of the Labour Syndicate support Arafat and so do ninety per cent of the students.

The P.L.O.'s finances are controlled by the Palestine National Fund which levies a tax on Palestinians working in the public sector in Arab countries. 'Liberation tax' is small, three per cent on low incomes, five per cent on higher, and it is deducted at source by the host governments. Palestinians working in private business are expected to make voluntary contributions of a similar size. The fund's other source of income is the Arab countries. Until 1979 particular states would choose the guerrilla organizations they wanted to back and finance them directly without going through the P.L.O. Iraq could thus finance Habash, Jibril, the A.L.F. and Abu Nidal without backing Fatah. But it also meant that Habash and the others would have to follow Iraqi policy if they wanted to stay on the payroll. This state of affairs was plainly intolerable and steps were recently taken to reduce the guerrillas' dependence on particular states. At the Baghdad summit meeting of March 1979 it was decided to raise 250 million dollars for the P.L.O. to be distributed to the various organizations not by the Arab governments but by the Palestine National Fund.

It is often overlooked in the West that, beside its military function, the P.L.O. runs a whole series of welfare and other services for the communities of the exile. In Kuwait it has its own educational system; in Lebanon it operates some thirty factories through the S.A.M.E.D. organization. The most important of the P.L.O.'s services is its health programme, run by the Palestine Red Crescent Society, which was set up by Fatah in 1969 and is headed by Dr Fateh Arafat, brother of the P.L.O. chairman. The Red Crescent operates thirty-five hospitals and more than a hundred clinics throughout the Arab world. There are Red Crescent societies in the United States, Britain, France, Switzerland and Sweden. In Beirut the P.L.O. has also established its own news agency, research centre, radio station, magazine and film centre.

Political power in the P.L.O. resides in the Executive Committee which meets two or three times a month and consists of representatives from all the guerrilla organizations (except the P.F.L.P. which periodically refuses to take part) and a small number of independents who are mostly supporters of Arafat. But while political activity is usually co-ordinated by the Executive Committee, military action is decided by the organizations themselves independently of the P.L.O. This situation is a source of frequent embarrassment to Arafat and the mainstream leadership but they are unable to change it. Although they have made several attempts to unite all the different factions under one command, this only happens during an emergency. Jibril and Hawatmeh insist on their military independence and would refuse to belong to the P.L.O. if they found it endangered.

Arafat and the P.L.O. thus have full control only over Fatah and the Palestine Liberation Army (P.L.A.), a regular force of three infantry brigades which are traditionally stationed in Egypt, Syria and Iraq. The smaller groups insist on their freedom to pursue their own tactics without interference. They have their headquarters in dingy offices in Beirut, most of them in the slum quarter of Sabra. The district is overcrowded, full of guns and mutilated people – boys without legs, children with repulsive scars, women with their arms and legs in plaster. It is a regular target of Israeli bombing raids.

Since 1971, when they were ejected from Jordan (see Chapter 8), the leading guerrilla groups have been based in Lebanon and Syria. Fatah and Saiqa have regular training camps in both countries; they also have cells in Jordan, the West Bank – some of which were set up personally by Yasser Arafat in the early years of Fatah – and in Gaza. The P.F.L.P. and its offshoots also have cells in the Occupied Territories and in the early seventies Habash's men operated effectively against the Israeli army in Gaza. Most of these groups have bases in Lebanon and also in Syria if they are tolerated by the Damascus government. The P.D.F.L.P. and the P.F.L.P.–General Command have at times enjoyed Syrian support, but the Iraqi-backed A.L.F. and the P.F.L.P., which has also received assistance from Baghdad, stick to Lebanon. Even there they are not safe: George Habash never spends two nights in the same place and neither his wife nor his friends usually know where he is.

In the years that followed the 1967 war, the P.L.O. guerrillas were registering considerable successes against the Israeli army which, in the summer of 1970, was suffering some fifty casualties a month. Soon after, however, their effectiveness declined as the Israelis tightened up their control of the new frontiers and wiped out the cells in Gaza. The guerrillas found their movements increasingly restricted by the harshness of the Israeli military rule in the Occupied Territories and also by the surrounding Arab governments who were anxious not to attract the usual Israeli retaliation against their territory. Many of the guerrilla leaders came to realize that the conditions of the Palestine conflict made a conventional guerrilla war impossible. It was all very well to take the Algerian war as guide and inspiration but Algeria was eighty times larger than Palestine and, like China, an ideal place for guerrilla warfare. In the West Bank there was no Yen-an to which Arafat or Habash could retreat and consolidate their positions. Even from the Nablus mountains, where the Palestinians had achieved a limited success against the British in 1938, they could be flushed out by the Israelis within a day. Nor was it very productive to encourage the population of the Occupied Territories to follow the Algerian precedent since it merely gave the Israelis a pretext to enlarge the Palestinian diaspora by expelling more villagers from their homes.

Since the guerrillas were unable to establish bases in Palestine, they had to set them up in the neighbouring Arab states, and from these they launched their raids into Israel. The Israelis replied with massive retaliatory attacks aimed not only at the guerrilla bases and the refugee camps but also at targets belonging to the countries which were sheltering the commandos. The consequences of these attacks and the crises they provoked between the Palestinians and the Arab countries will be discussed in the following chapters. In effect, they prevented the commandos from fighting the Algerian-type guerrilla war they had intended and forced them to adopt the terrorist tactics their enemies had used in Palestine twenty-five years earlier.

Palestinians think that Western perspectives of terrorism are absurdly distorted. They believe that the West judges the issue with much emotiveness but with little understanding of its context. Moreover, its view is almost entirely one-sided. A guerrilla with a gun is more 'newsworthy' than an air-force pilot spraying napalm over a refugee camp, but is he more of a terrorist? The eleven Israeli athletes who were killed at the Munich Olympics are remembered all over the world, but how many people recall the four hundred refugees who were killed in the Israeli vengeance raid three days later?

No people are naturally terrorists, least of all the Palestinians who have no military traditions of their own, and it is futile to condemn them without examining what has led them to use violence. As any Palestinian will say, the propulsion comes from a combination of frustration and desperation. Sami al-Karami, a Palestinian living in Canada, has explained: 'the non-violent methods are very beautiful and very easy, and we wish we could win with these methods. Our people don't carry machine-guns and bombs because they enjoy killing. It is for us the last resort. For twenty-two years we waited for the United Nations and the United States, for liberty, freedom, and democracy. There was no result. So this is our last resort. This is the only way to get back to Palestine.'[14] This insistence on the failure of the international community is widespread among Palestinians. They point out that since 1947 the U.N. has ostensibly been in favour of an Arab state in Palestine and that since 1948 it has voted annually for the repatriation of the refugees. In both cases it has failed to implement its own resolutions and the Palestinians feel that as the international community has ignored them, they have no special obligations to the international community. Why should they obey international rules when those rules are not applied to them? Fawaz Turki has written:

> Outcasts, shunned by a world that refused to recognize our existence, denied forever the right to participate in people's spontaneous and well ordered reality, yet we are called upon to respect laws that we did not frame, principles that were never applied to us, rules of a game that we were not invited to play, and borders that we did not know. We are to respect international society, its morality and its 'free institutions', when international society rejected the notion that we be included in it. For me as a Palestinian, *respect* for and adherence to the law, the law that oppresses me and perpetuates my sense of degradation, is meaningless and absurd.[15]

Many people in the resistance have disapproved of terrorism from the beginning. They are disgusted and embarrassed by it and they believe that it has damaged their reputation and made it more difficult for the P.L.O. to secure international recognition. This was the view of the moderate men of Fatah such as Said Hammami and Khaled Al-Hassan who were realistic enough to see that the military struggle was less important than the diplomatic. Yet, in a sense, the terrorist campaign of the early seventies *did* help the Palestinians; it did bring them recognition of a kind. While they were merely refugees the world could afford to disregard them; it was only when they began killing people that Western politicians began talking about a solution to their problem. As George Habash himself pointed out: 'When we hijack a plane it has more effect than if we killed a hundred Israelis in battle. For decades world public opinion has been neither for nor against the Palestinians. It simply ignored us. At least the world is talking about us now.'[16]

A large majority of the terrorist actions were committed by two extremist groups, Habash's P.F.L.P. and the Black September Organization, an anonymous group of Fatah dissidents and others who began their operations with the assassination of the Jordanian prime minister, Wasfi Tal, in 1971. Nearly all of the most spectacular acts – the hijackings, the attacks at airports and Israeli airline offices, the seizure of embassies and so on – were the work of these two organizations. Their aims were various. Sometimes they seem to have had no objective at all other than to remind the world of their existence. More generally, they took hostages and tried to exchange them for commandos in Israeli prisons. Occasionally, as with the murder of Wasfi Tal, terrorism was carried out as an act of revenge. After the war of October 1973 acts of terrorism were committed by both the P.F.L.P. and the P.F.L.P. – General Command specifically in order to frustrate any chance of an agreement between Israel and the Arab states.

It was not surprising that the proponents of terrorism were the commandos of the P.F.L.P. It was more evidence of their irresponsibility and their romanticism; it was also evidence of their defeatism. The P.F.L.P. is the most pessimistic of all the organizations. It knows it is fighting a lost cause and yet it often seems relieved that the cause is lost. Certainly the P.F.L.P. will never do anything to retrieve it if, in the process, it is asked to compromise. Because it believes, above all, in the sanctity of its mission – in the liberation of all the homeland and the return of all the refugees.

The mission must never be sullied by half-measures, by the liberation of some of the homeland, by the return of some of the refugees. Politics and diplomacy must not be allowed to interfere in a process that is both mystical and sacrificial.

The P.F.L.P. commandos would not behave as they do if they believed they could win. Consciously or not, they aspire to martyrdom. There are more chances of survival in a game of Russian roulette than in a hijacking operation. Yet the beautiful Palestinian girl, Leila Khaled, underwent three plastic surgery operations after her first hijacking so that she could attempt another against a heavily armed Israeli aeroplane. In other operations P.F.L.P. commandos have followed the example of their allies in the Japanese Red Army and deliberately thrown away any chance of escape. By 1973 they were setting off on expeditions from which it was taken for granted they would not return. They were suicide missions and everyone knew it. The selected commandos would be taken to southern Lebanon and given their instructions. They would leave messages for their families and their comrades and then they would be photographed repeatedly, fists clenched and guns brandished. Eventually they would cross the border and not be seen again, except by their victims and their killers. It was the martyrdom which they expected and which they wanted. The only question left was: how many people would they be able to take with them? The world had rejected them and turned them into Samsons, determined to destroy even though they themselves perished in the act. Their only aim was vengeance against the world and their only hope was that as many as possible of their enemies would die beside them.

8

The P.L.O. and the Arab World

Palestine has been an Arab cause for 1,300 years. It stands geographically near the centre of the Arab world and it has always had a significance to the Arabs which other regions, except the Hejaz, have lacked. No other part of the Arab homeland has been considered so important, and no other part has been so vigorously defended against invading armies. The Third Crusade, the Mongols and Napoleon were all defeated in Palestine by Arab or Ottoman armies composed only partly of Palestinians.

Palestine has remained an Arab cause during this century. When Arnold Toynbee visited Baghdad and Aleppo shortly after the 1929 riots in Hebron and elsewhere, he encountered a 'tense atmosphere' and found the inhabitants much concerned about events in Palestine.[1] In 1936 the Iraqi government, 'actuated by racial ties which bind them with the Arabs of Palestine', decided to mediate between Britain and the Palestinians,[2] and, during the revolt itself, the rebels received considerable financial aid from Syria, Iraq and Egypt. When the Arab Higher Committee, dominated by the mufti's supporters, foolishly rejected the British government white paper in 1939, all the Arab countries except Transjordan dutifully, but rather reluctantly, followed suit.

Since the establishment of the State of Israel, Arab identification with the Palestinians and their cause has become still more intense. Egypt has fought four wars on behalf of the Palestinians, and Syria, Jordan and Lebanon have also made considerable sacrifices. Arab countries try to outbid each other in their support for the Palestinians and no regime can afford to alienate popular opinion by ignoring them. Saudi Arabia's Crown Prince Fahd has called the Palestine issue 'the fulcrum of Saudi Arabia's diplomacy, the target of its efforts and its primary and greatest preoccupation'.[3] This is an exaggerated claim as anyone who glances at Saudi Arabia's foreign policy can see, yet Arab popular support for the Palestinians is so strong that Arab leaders are forced to make that sort of statement. Similarly, when Major Atta began his ill-fated three-day rule in the Sudan in 1971, almost the first thing he did was talk about his devotion to the Palestinian cause: 'We emphasize that the Sudan will give all its resources for the liquidation of the Zionist-imperialist aggression on Arab land,' he announced. 'The Sudan will give everything that the Palestinian revolution will demand for the restoration of its land and building of its democratic state. The Sudan shall reject any solution that is unacceptable to the people of Palestine represented by its democratic commando organizations.'[4]

Some Arab governments do not go as far as this because, although they loudly proclaim their allegiance to the Palestinian cause whenever they have the opportunity, they fear and dislike the P.L.O. itself. Conservative monarchies like Saudi Arabia and Morocco understandably feel uncomfortable with a man like Habash, while the Omanis hate the P.F.L.P. leader because it was a section of his Arab Nationalist Movement which came to power in Aden and another which began the rebellion in their western region of Dhofar. Nevertheless, even the Saudis and Moroccans genuinely support Palestinian aspirations even if they do not particularly like the Palestinian leaders. Nearly all Arabs believe not only that the cause is just but also that it is to a large extent their own. King Feisal of Saudi Arabia felt so strongly about the Israeli annexation of Jerusalem not simply because it is a Palestinian city but also because it is a holy city sacred to all Arabs.

While the sincerity of Arab passion for Palestine is unquestionable, the Arab commitment to the struggle for Palestine is uneven and takes second place to internal or national considerations. If there is a clash of interests between a particular country and the P.L.O., that country usually follows its own interests. When Jordan or Lebanon had to choose between restricting the movements of the guerrillas on their territory or being subjected to reprisal bombing raids by Israel, they predictably chose the former. Equally predictably, the Arab countries which did not have to face this problem protested loudly against interfering with the activities of the resistance.

Algeria, aided by a distance which gives the country immunity from Israel, has been perhaps the most stable of the P.L.O.'s friends, yet even here there is little hesitation about putting Algeria first if the national interest so demands. Algeria was the first Arab country to back Fatah, long before anyone else had heard of Arafat, in 1962. But two years later, when the Arab League established the P.L.O. in an attempt to curb Palestinian restiveness, the Algerians decided to protect their own position inside the Arab League by abandoning Fatah and closing down its offices in Algiers. Like most of the Arab states, Algeria was a strong supporter of Fatah a few years later when it came to dominate the P.L.O. In 1970 and 1971 it was a vociferous backer of the P.L.O.'s struggle against the Jordanians and it even broke off relations with King Hussein's regime. Had they been consistent, the Algerians would have severed diplomatic ties with Damascus in 1976 when the Syrian army entered Lebanon and defeated the P.L.O. But, to the astonishment of some of the resistance leaders, the Algerians remained completely silent. It was not difficult to see the reason. Algeria was in the middle of an angry dispute with Morocco over the future of the former Spanish Sahara, and Syria was one of its few supporters. Once again, rather than antagonize important allies, Algeria abandoned the Palestinians.

Most Palestinians understand that the loudest-mouthed of their supporters are seldom the most reliable. Iraq and Libya are so uncompromising on the Palestine issue because they can afford to be: they have no Palestinian refugee problem to cause them trouble and they are too far from the scene of conflict to tempt the Israelis. They can therefore adopt moral postures which countries with more responsibility, such as Jordan and Syria, cannot do. They can also indulge their habit of criticizing other states for not being sufficiently pro-Palestinian. Colonel Qadafi has always been very free with advice for the Arab countries, constantly urging them to allow the guerrillas to operate from their territory and insisting that no one should seek a peace settlement with Israel, even if the Zionists were to return to the 1967 borders. Iraq is equally prone to taking nations to task if it considers them to be softening on the issue. In November 1967, when Egypt accepted the U.N. Security Council resolution 242, and in 1970, when Nasser agreed to a ceasefire along the Suez Canal and accepted peace proposals put forward by the American secretary of state, the Iraqis were the first to make a fuss. President Nasser, however, was brusquely dismissive. At a speech to the National Assembly in Cairo on 24 November 1967, he declared: 'We are not prepared to listen to those who advocate immediate war. These people have never been in a war in their lives, and they have no intention of being in one.'

The Arabs have made a number of sacrifices for the Palestinians. Apart from the costly wars they have fought on their behalf, they have helped the refugees in numerous ways: Jordan gave them citizenship, Syria found them employment, Egypt took thousands of them to Cairo and gave them places in its universities. Nevertheless, the Palestinians have also suffered greatly at the hands of their fellow Arabs, particularly in the countries with large refugee populations bordering on Israel: Syria, Jordan and Lebanon. This is not because any of these countries are unsympathetic to the Palestinian cause but because there is, and always has been, a fundamental contradiction between the needs of these states and the needs of the resistance. A Syrian, for example, will say that he wholeheartedly supports the Palestinian cause and he will point, as evidence, to the high price that his country has paid for that support. But he will also say that there is a limit to the amount of sacrifices he is prepared to make. In 1976 the world was astonished by the sight of two former allies, Syria and the P.L.O., fighting each other in Lebanon. Moreover, the Syrians were actually supporting a right-wing Lebanese movement whose closest friends were Israel and the Americans, and they intervened in order to save this movement from military defeat and to prevent its replacement by a government dominated by left-wing Lebanese Arab nationalists and the P.L.O. Taken in isolation, the Syrians would obviously have preferred a Palestinian and Arab nationalist regime in Lebanon, with which they would have had close ideological links, to a pro-Western, right-wing one, with which they had been at odds for half a century. But they couldn't afford to view the matter in isolation. They had to look at it in the context of regional politics and, when they had done this, they concluded that a P.L.O. and Arab nationalist victory, however desirable in theory, would be a disaster for Syria and for the area as a whole.

The Syrians argued that if the P.L.O. was in charge in Beirut, an Israeli invasion of Lebanon would follow and they would be dragged into a full-scale war which they would be bound to lose. So they went into Lebanon and stopped the P.L.O.

A country which has even closer ties with the Palestinians, but whose interests are still more opposed to those of the P.L.O., is Jordan. After King Abdullah's annexation of the West Bank following the 1948 war, the Kingdom of Jordan found itself with a population containing a majority of Palestinians. In addition to the half million Transjordanians, the country now housed more than 850,000 Palestinians, of whom about half were refugees from conquered areas of Palestine, and the others were residents of the West Bank.[5] The refugees came from Lydda and Ramle, from West Jerusalem, from Jaffa and the coastal strip, from the Beersheba region and from the eastern Galilee. Most of them settled in refugee camps around Nablus, Ramallah and Jericho, but more than 100,000 crossed the Jordan river and moved into the miserable camps near Amman and Zarqa.

At the beginning the refugees were demoralized and without organization. They were grateful to the Jordanians for providing them with a refuge and most of them accepted Abdullah's annexation of Jerusalem and the West Bank as the only practicable option. But in the years after 1948, as the United Nations did nothing for them beyond passing well meaning resolutions, they became embittered and frustrated. Some of them began going back to their homes at night, risking Israeli border patrols to collect valuables or harvest their fruit. Many were shot by Israeli soldiers and others were prevented from infiltrating by the Jordanians. Tension along the armistice lines increased when Israel began reprisal raids on West Bank villages. In October 1953, after three Israeli civilians had been killed by a bomb, the Israeli army took revenge on the village of Qibya. In the middle of the night it destroyed the whole village, blowing up the houses with their inhabitants still inside them and killing sixty-six people. It was obvious that the inhabitants of Qibya had had nothing to do with the earlier outrage, which had been committed by desperate infiltrators rather than by peaceful villagers. The Israelis knew this but they went ahead regardless. They were not interested in finding the real assailants – the commander of the Jordanian army, General Glubb, had offered to co-operate with the Israelis to prevent infiltration even to the point of inviting them over the border with bloodhounds to track the killers – they were interested in establishing what has since become the standard Israeli method of dealing with Palestinian infiltrators: the use of indiscriminate terrorism against the inhabitants of neighbouring Arab countries so as to force the governments of those countries to defend Israel against the Palestinians by policing the borders and preventing infiltration. This tactic is far removed from accepted notions of self-defence, such as the right of 'hot pursuit'. Nor is it truly a resort to the more old-fashioned idea of a 'right' of reprisal, since the people who are attacked and made to suffer are not those who inflicted the damage on Israel. Having refused to remedy the justified grievances which are the cause of Palestinian violence, Israel then refuses to accept the consequence of having to defend itself, without help from its neighbours, against Palestinian infiltrators. Instead, it seeks to bully those neighbours into sharing with it the onus of curbing Palestinian resentment and violence against Israel. The dilemma which Israel thus imposes on the Arab host governments is a truly cruel one; they can only resolve it at the expense of either their own citizens or their support for the Palestinian cause. No one can really blame them if they put their own people first.

Glubb and Abdullah were realists. They knew they had lost the war and they were prepared to admit it and to start building the peace. But neither the Palestinians nor the Israelis were willing to co-operate. Few Palestinians were prepared to give up their homeland and they resented Jordanian attempts to make them do so. During the 1950s they became increasingly critical of the Jordanian regime which they believed had capitulated to the Zionists. They also disliked the regime itself, which they saw as a feudal anachronism, protected by British 'imperialists', and an enemy of Arab nationalism. The Palestinians were frustrated by their new position. They believed that they belonged to a more sophisticated society than the Transjordanians, whom they rather despised and referred to as 'Bedouin' – though even in 1948 the nomadic population of Transjordan was less than a tenth of the whole. It was galling for a people who had been ruled from Jerusalem to have to submit to Amman and the Palestinians resented it. They were better educated than the Transjordanians, there were many more of them, and they felt they should have a government which was more sympathetic to them and their aspirations.

The Transjordanians were naturally uneasy about the Palestinian influx. Although the East Bank had had a settled agricultural population in the regions of the Salt and Irbid for a long time, it was a very different society from that existing in Palestine. Bedouin influence was far greater than on the West Bank and it became more so when Abdullah was made Emir of Transjordan by the British. Abdullah was a Hejazi, a son of the sharif of Mecca, and when he came to Amman he brought with him a large number of his dark-skinned Bedouin followers. These later formed the basis of his British-officered Arab Legion, commanded by Glubb. Ethnically and culturally they differed appreciably from the Arabs of Palestine and from the beginning there was mistrust between them. Like many Englishmen who have lived for years with the Bedouin, Glubb was suspicious of the urban Arabs. He found them untrustworthy and doubted whether they would remain loyal to the Jordanian royal family. In the 1948 war he had seen his Bedouin troops defeat the Israelis when all the other Arabs had been humiliated, and he was convinced that the core of the Arab Legion should remain Bedouin. Few Palestinians joined it and those who did were used mainly as technicians and mechanics.

The Jordan of the fifties was thus a dangerously divided country. On the one side stood the traditional society of Transjordan, the Bedouin followers of the Hashemites, the Arab Legion, and a number of the more conservative Palestinian notables who during the mandate had supported the pro-Abdullah Nashashibi faction. Opposed to them were the refugees, the intellectuals and the politicians who still supported the mufti in his Cairo exile and who refused to accept Abdullah's annexation of the West Bank. Enthusiasts for Nasser and Arab nationalism, they detested what they perceived as the regime's defeatism over Palestine and accused it of collaborating with the Israelis. In their criticism of the Jordanian government they received strong vocal backing from Egypt, Syria and most of the Arab world.

The present king, Hussein (Abdullah's grandson), formally took power on his eighteenth birthday in 1953. Initially he tried to reconcile the two factions. But as one side made little attempt to conceal its dislike for him, while the other remained unhesitatingly loyal, it was not long before he turned to the coalition that had been put together by his grandfather. Throughout Hussein's reign, Jordan has been split between two camps and on several occasions the survival of his throne has been in doubt. In 1958, when his cousin, King Feisal II of Iraq, was murdered in Baghdad, and Arab nationalism was riding triumphantly across the Middle East, Hussein called in British troops to protect his regime. During the following years he was the target of a series of attempts to assassinate or overthrow him. But it was not until after the 1967 war that he had to face his most difficult crisis.

The new challenge came from the Palestinian guerrillas who had achieved great popular support in the aftermath of the June war. They attracted large numbers of recruits from the refugee population and in a few months the camps on the East Bank had become centres for commando raids into Israel and the Occupied Territories. Hussein disliked the resistance organizations because they provoked the Israelis into retaliating against Jordan and because they constituted a direct challenge to his authority. Large numbers of well armed commandos on his territory – many of them Marxists who were looking forward to the monarchy's overthrow – were in themselves dangerous. Even worse, from Hussein's point of view, was their claim that they were the true representatives of the Palestinian people. This was something that the king could not be expected to accept. To have admitted that the guerrillas were the rightful leaders of two-thirds of his subjects (including those now under Israeli rule in the West Bank) would have destroyed the entire basis of his regime. To Hussein at this time, the Palestinians on both the East and the West Banks were Jordanian citizens and he was their sovereign.

Many Jordanians watched the emergence of the guerrillas with dismay. They saw them as a potential threat which would become more dangerous unless they were brought quickly under control. From the beginning Hussein's advisers, his army commanders and even his brother, Crown Prince Hassan, urged the king to limit the guerrillas' presence and the scope of their activities. The Americans were also keen to disrupt them and the Jordanian secret service (the Mokhabarat) was chosen as the instrument to do so. From the end of 1967 the Americans encouraged Jordan to send its army officers to the United States for counter-insurgency training. Most of them went to Fort Bragg in North Carolina while others received similar training in Taiwan. Meanwhile, members of the Mokhabarat were able to infiltrate most of the guerrilla organizations, in particular a group called the Ketayeb al-Nasr. This process was facilitated by the battle of Karama in November 1968 which won the guerrillas their reputation and encouraged thousands of volunteers to apply for membership. The resistance accepted them without being able to vet the majority, and officers from the Mokhabarat were able to join without difficulty.

The chief role of the Mokhabarat seems to have been to provoke the Jordanian army into a confrontation with the guerrillas which would result in a defeat for the resistance and the loss of its power and prestige. Accordingly, the Mokhabarat elements which had infiltrated the Ketayeb al-Nasr were able to draw both sides into a clash in November 1968. The Jordanian army was ordered in to deal with the Ketayeb, but it also took the opportunity to crack down on the other organizations. Only when the government saw that the resistance was too strong did it call for a ceasefire. Both sides made a few concessions and then settled down to wait for the next round. Fighting began again in February 1970 and, as the crisis worsened, Hussein once more came under pressure to move against the guerrillas, now grouped together in the Fatah-dominated P.L.O. In fact Hussein was more cautious and more moderate than his advisers and he hoped to come to some sort of accommodation with Arafat. But, while the king was having difficulty in restraining his more impulsive supporters, the P.L.O. leader was having problems with Habash and Hawatmeh. The P.F.L.P. had been urging a showdown with the regime for some time and believed, probably rightly, that in the first half of 1970 the resistance could have defeated the Jordanians. But Arafat the diplomat refused to take on the government and insisted on trying to reach an agreement with it. He believed that even if the guerrillas defeated Hussein, the Israelis, supported by the Americans, would intervene against them. Habash reacted by precipitating another crisis in June 1970 when his men seized eighty guests at the Intercontinental hotel in Amman and kept them hostage. But the P.L.O. leader still refused to move; so in early September the P.F.L.P. made civil war virtually certain by successfully hijacking four international airliners and blowing three of them up at a small airfield in northern Jordan.

Arafat was furious and suspended the P.F.L.P. from the Central Committee of the P.L.O. Hussein was both furious and humiliated that such outrages had taken place on his territory and that he had been unable to prevent them. With his army com-

manders determined to fight, the king realized that a confrontation was now unavoidable. Besides, he was now stronger and more
confident. Arafat's diplomacy and constant willingness to
negotiate had given Hussein time to consolidate his position. He
had been able to dismiss the pro-Palestinian officers in the army
and the excesses of the P.F.L.P. had turned many people against
the resistance. Public opinion had moved more behind the king
and in September he was in a far more powerful position than he
had been in the spring.

On 17 September Hussein let his army loose on the refugee
camps of Amman and the war began. In the north the guerrillas
made some early gains and Hawatmeh's P.D.F.L.P. took over the
town of Irbid, which they called 'the first Arab soviet', and installed a 'politburo' to run it. Two days later a large Syrian tank force
invaded the country to support the resistance. Many Jordanians,
including the king, felt that they would be beaten, and Israel and
the United States started making contingency plans for an attack
against the P.L.O. and its Syrian allies. Unexpectedly, though, the
guerrillas began to lose the initiative soon afterwards, principally
because their Arab supporters were not prepared to help them.
From the beginning of the crisis almost the whole Arab world had
pledged itself to support the guerrillas. In Egypt, the government
radio regularly denounced Hussein while President Nasser ordered
him to fly to Cairo and explain his behaviour. Iraq, which had
been equally vociferous, had a fine opportunity to influence the
fighting, since 12,000 Iraqi troops were stationed on Jordanian territory ostensibly to help the guerrillas against Israel. Arafat, who
had been assured of their support on a recent visit to Baghdad,
pleaded with them to join the battle, but the Iraqi government,
which was prepared to encourage anyone to fight Hussein though
it was not prepared to do so itself, tamely withdrew its forces and
sent them back home.

A further disappointment was the behaviour of the Syrians.
Had the Syrian regime wholeheartedly backed the guerrillas, there
is little doubt that Hussein would have been overthrown. But the
Damascus government was divided and uncertain what to do. The
tank force was not ordered into Jordan on the instructions of the
government: it was sent in by one of the rival factions led by
Major-General Salah Jadid, and this was done without the approval of the defence minister, General Hafez al-Assad. Assad,

later to become president, opposed the incursion because he believed it was bound to provoke Israeli intervention and perhaps a large-scale war. Although he could not prevent the tanks going into Jordan, he was able to stop the Syrian air force from giving them cover. The Jordanian army, which was badly outnumbered in the north, was thus able to hold off the invaders until Hussein's own air force reached the battlefield and knocked out most of the Syrian tanks. When the remains of the invasion force returned to Syria the war was all but over and Hussein's sole remaining task was to mop up the guerrilla bases in the rest of the country – a process his forces finally completed, with brutal thoroughness, the following July. By the autumn of 1971, there were no guerrillas left in Jordan.

The Jordanian civil war showed the Palestinians that, in the final analysis, they could rely on none of their friends in the Arab world. Egypt, Iraq and the others had stood by, cheering from the sidelines but not daring to intervene, while Syria's help had been worthless. Many Palestinians at last realized that a conventional guerrilla war on the Algerian model was not possible because no Arab country was prepared to give them a base and accept the consequences from Israel. So some of them went underground and opted for a different campaign of secret terror. A group known as Black September, named after the month of the Jordanian war, began its own vendetta against anyone it considered an enemy of the Palestine revolution. In November 1971 it struck for the first time and there were few Palestinians who regretted that its first victim was Wasfi Tal, the Jordanian prime minister who had directed the war.

In 1970–1 the P.L.O. suffered its heaviest military defeat, and yet it was able to survive as an organization and even to increase its stature in the coming years. Perhaps it is inherent in the circumstances that the Arab world will always prevent the resistance from becoming a serious military power while allowing it to remain a major political factor in the region. In the spring of 1972, less than a year after his last decisive victory over the guerrillas, a renewed attempt by Hussein to press his claims to the West Bank was rejected by the Arab world. His plan for a United Arab Kingdom on a federal basis, with two regional capitals in Jerusalem and Amman, was almost unanimously rejected. The P.L.O., despite the near annihilation of its forces in the field, still retained the loyalty of the Arab countries and in 1974, at the Rabat summit conference, even Hussein was forced to admit the Palestinians' political victory and acknowledge, along with the rest of the Arab League, the P.L.O.'s claim to be the 'sole, legitimate representative' of the Palestinian people.

Jordan was only the first of the Arab countries to embark on a full-scale military confrontation with the P.L.O. Lebanon and Syria were to follow and their conflicts will be described in the following chapters. But for many Palestinians the greatest 'betrayal' of all came from Egypt which was the first Arab country to give up the fight for Palestine and make a peace with Israel.

Although President Sadat of Egypt did not sign the Egypt–Israel treaty until 1979, it was the culmination of many years of diplomacy. Arguably the process was begun in 1967 by his predecessor, Gamal Abdel Nasser, when Egypt accepted U.N. Security Council resolution 242, and thus, by implication, accorded Israel recognition conditional upon a peace treaty – although it is improbable that Nasser would ever have gone so far as to make a separate peace with Israel. Since the 1950s the Palestinian refugees had looked to Nasser for the liberation of their land but it is unlikely that Nasser ever seriously contemplated the conquest of Israel. After 1967 it was clear that he was only interested in the recovery of the territories lost in the June war and in justice for the refugees – his acceptance of American peace proposals in 1970 indicated that he had no designs on Israel itself. He wanted peace with the Israelis based on the pre-1967 borders and this remained the basic aim of Anwar Sadat when he took over the presidency on Nasser's death. As early as 1971 the assistant secretary of state in Washington, Joseph Sisco, told the Israelis: 'He [Sadat] wants an agreement with Israel, but one that he can defend and justify vis-à-vis the Arabs.'[6]

In October 1973 Egypt and its Syrian allies attacked Israeli forces in Sinai and the Golan Heights. But it was a political as much as a military war and it was fought with strictly limited objectives. Sadat's aim was to regain the Occupied Territories either through battle or through post-war negotiations between all parties as well as the Soviet Union and the United States. And, even though he was unsuccessful, he insisted that there would be 'no more wars' and that the Arab–Israeli dispute could be settled through diplomacy. He believed that if the Russian-backed Arab states went on fighting an American-backed Israel, no progress could be made. The vital thing was for the Arabs to win American friendship since the United States was the only country in the world capable of putting pressure on Israel to relinquish Arab territory.

Egypt's preparedness to run ahead of the other Arab states in compromising on the Palestine issue was largely the result of internal considerations. Throughout the nineteenth century and for much of the twentieth, Egypt had been one of the most prosperous countries in the Middle East. By 1970 it was the poorest after North and South Yemen. Cairo of the 1970s was one of the most poverty-stricken cities of the world and nearly as overcrowded as Calcutta. Most of its 9 million population lived in appalling squalor without enough to eat, and in 1977 there were bread riots in which a considerable number of people died. While Egypt's poverty was mainly ascribable to large increases in population which the limited area of the Nile valley was unable to support, the enormous standing army which was needed to fight Israel was clearly a considerable drain on the country's resources. The capture of the Sinai by Israel, the loss of revenue caused by the closure of the Suez Canal, and Israel's massive bombing raids in 1970, which destroyed the towns of the Canal Zone as well as towns and villages of the Delta, added to Egypt's impoverishment.

The commercial classes, which saw the return to prosperity prevented by the heavy military commitment and by the firm alliance with the Soviet Union (which had 25,000 'advisers' stationed in Egypt before 1972), were the first to press for withdrawal from the Arab–Israeli conflict and for closer relations with the Americans. But there was also a widespread feeling throughout Egypt that the country had done enough for the Palestinians and should now look after itself. People complained that the well-being of 40 million Egyptians was being sacrificed for 2 million refugees, many of whom were living more comfortably than the Egyptians themselves. They felt that it was time for Egypt to concentrate on its own problems. The country had led the Arab world, had taken part in great pan-Arab ventures like the war for Palestine, the union with Syria, and the defence of the Yemeni revolution – and all it had succeeded in doing was to ruin its own economy. Egypt, it was claimed, had made great sacrifices for the Arab world, including the Palestinians, and had received little in return. Even the oil-rich states had proved strangely parsimonious in helping the Egyptians out of their economic difficulties.

When Sadat made his visit to Jerusalem at the end of 1977 a large majority of his countrymen supported him. They believed that their country had no option but to make peace and they backed their leader's attempt to achieve it. As the playwright, Yousef Idriss, wrote: 'I support Sadat's Egyptian, popular and peaceful initiative, a stand which may not be understood by our Arab brethren. . . . We in Egypt do not have the means of rejection or war. Rejection requires a strong economy which would enable you to say no without dying of hunger, or prostituting your women and daughters for a handful of bread.'[7]

The 'Arab brethren' reacted very badly indeed to the initiative, accusing Sadat of selling out to the Israelis and of selfishly attempting to regain his own territory at the expense of the other Arabs. They were outraged still further by the Camp David agreements of September 1978 and the Egyptian–Israeli peace treaty six months later. For the Palestinians these were the great betrayals. That the largest Arab country, once the proponent of the pan-Arab ideal, should make peace with Israel while every inch of Palestine remained in Zionist hands, was to them an act of treachery and a final blow to the Arab nationalist cause. In a sense it was a worse setback for the Palestinians than the Jordanian and Lebanese defeats earlier in the decade. For while President Assad was battering away at the P.L.O. in 1976, he remained in agreement with its basic political position. He disagreed with Arafat over Palestinian policy in Lebanon but he supported Arafat's policy for Palestine itself: Israeli withdrawal from the territories conquered in 1967, including East Jerusalem, and self-determination for the Palestinians.

President Sadat seemed to the Palestinians to have abandoned them altogether. When he made his speech to the Israeli Knesset he did not mention the P.L.O., and the documents which he signed at Camp David and in Washington allocated no role to the organization he had previously accepted at Rabat as being the 'sole, legitimate representative' of the Palestinian people. Sadat's signatures gave the Palestinians nothing except an Israeli commitment to grant autonomy to the inhabitants of the West Bank and Gaza – a commitment which Israel later reneged on. Furthermore, most of the crucial issues – such as the question of repatriation for the 1948 refugees and the future of Jerusalem – were virtually ignored.

The Palestinians watched Sadat signing away their rights with disgust but also with astonishment. Palestine had always been an Arab cause and suddenly the Palestinians were being made to witness the leading Arab nation voluntarily washing its hands of their homeland. For refugees all over the Middle East it was the most demoralizing blow of all. People who hadn't seen Palestine for thirty years had still believed that one day, 'if not the next war, the one after or the one after that', the Arabs would win and they would finally be allowed home. But as Sadat signed the treaty in Washington, sitting contentedly on the White House lawn beside President Carter and the Israeli prime minister, that last hope, at least for the older generation of Palestinians, was finally extinguished.

9

Lebanon and the Palestinians

Lebanon, like Palestine, was still a part of the Ottoman Empire in 1917 and was regarded as part of the region known as Greater Syria. Like Palestine it was also coveted by an outside power and at the end of the First World War the futures of the two regions were debated in much the same way. In both cases there were large numbers of Arab nationalists who wanted their region to remain independent and Arab; and in both cases there was a Western power anxious to exercise control both for its own benefit and for that of a particular protégé. In Palestine, Britain was pledged to build a Jewish national home for the Zionists; in Lebanon, France was determined to set up a pro-French state which would be dominated by its long-standing ally, the Maronite Catholic community.

Until the beginning of the twentieth century, the most important religious community in the area was the Sunni. From the same sect as their Ottoman rulers, and forming a majority in Greater Syria, the Sunnis were naturally the most powerful and privileged of the communities. Those from the region later to be known as Lebanon always regarded themselves as being part of a large cultural and political area, and their links were much closer with Damascus and the Syrian hinterland than with the nearer but often hostile region of Mount Lebanon, the homeland of the Maronite and Druze peoples. Predictably, they have been among the most enthusiastic supporters of the Arab nationalist ideal since the declining years of the Ottoman Empire.

One community which had never displayed either loyalty to the Ottoman Empire or enthusiasm for the Arab nationalists was the

Maronite Catholic. Firmly based in Mount Lebanon, it was unwilling to lose the semi-autonomous position it had enjoyed under the Ottomans. Although the Maronites certainly wished to be rid of the Turks, they did not want to be swallowed up by Greater Syria and absorbed by an Arab and predominantly Muslim empire.

The Maronites, who are a mountain community and form only a small proportion of the coastal population, are traditionally the most independent of all the peoples of the Levant: certainly they have little cultural or historical affinity with the smaller, urban-based Christian sects of the littoral. According to Istfan al-Duwaihy, a Maronite patriarch of the seventeenth century, 'the Maronite community's history is a continuous struggle to maintain a national identity in a dominant Muslim environment.'[1] The remark is true today, though it must be added that the Maronite methods of safeguarding this identity have often been provocative. It is a community very conscious of its history and it remembers the repeated attempts of Byzantines, Mamelukes and Ottomans to control it. Religious and historical symbolism thus play a vital role within the community. Its civil war militias, for example, had strange religious titles, evocative of the Crusades: the Knights of the Virgin, the Wood of the Cross, the Youth of St Maron and so on. Many of them went into battle wearing large crosses over their uniforms.

Because of their local isolation, the Maronites had to look for allies elsewhere and they chose Europe, and in particular France. French interest in the area went back to Charlemagne, and in 1250 Louis XI had written: 'Nous sommes persuadés que cette nation que nous trouvons établie sous le nom de St Maroun [sic] est une partie de le nation française.' Although it is not clear on what exactly he based this claim, the French took it very seriously and Lamartine summed up the feelings of many of his countrymen when he described Lebanon as 'an admirable French colony, waiting for France'. Certainly from the sixteenth century, when a treaty was signed by Francis I and his ally, Suleiman the Magnificent, the Maronites have regarded France as their protector, referring to her as *umm al hannoune,* 'the nourishing mother'.

The French relished the role and from 1655 their consul in Beirut was often a Maronite sheikh. During the eighteenth and nineteenth centuries the Maronites began to rely more and more on the French, who in 1860 landed a military expedition to restore order after widespread fighting between the Maronites and the Druzes. So close was the relationship that in 1915 the Maronite patriarch openly proclaimed his country's gratitude to France, despite the fact that Lebanon, as part of the Ottoman Empire, was actually at war with the French Republic. And when the French occupied the region in 1918, their chargé d'affaires declared in public that the principal reason for the French presence was the protection of their friends the Maronites.

The Maronite outlook, then, has been conditioned by two factors: a turbulent history and the friendship with France. This combination has produced the Maronite creed, or *libanisme,* a word and an idea difficult to translate into English. Its ingredients include an emphasis on individualism and self-sufficiency, rejection of Islam and the Arab world, identification with the West and some Western values, and insistence on the survival of Lebanon as a Christian and democratic heartland in the Middle East.

The demise of the Ottoman Empire left the two principal religious communities in the Levant in a state of widening ideological antagonism. The Sunni concept of nationalism, in its broad pan-Arab context, was so far removed from the Maronite aim of a pro-Western, Christian-dominated little state that compromise was out of the question. The King—Crane commission, sent out by President Wilson after the First World War, inclined strongly towards the Arab nationalist view, recommending the preservation of the unity of Syria and a degree of autonomy for the Maronites and Druzes within a Syrian national state. Unfortunately the victorious Western powers paid no attention to the report, even ignoring the commissioners' declaration that the last thing the majority of people wished for was to be placed under any sort of French control. Meanwhile, the Maronites had sent off delegations to the peace conference at Versailles to press for a French mandate over Lebanon. They realized that they needed the French as much as the French needed them: they would thus be preserved from the ambitions of the Arab nationalists, and in turn would provide support for France to fall back on once it had alienated the rest of the population by opposing Arab nationalism. At Versailles, and later at San Remo, the French—Maronite alliance won the day, and in April 1920 France was offered the mandate for Syria and Lebanon.

The establishment of 'Greater Lebanon' was the first and most important of the French actions. It was a disastrous decision, for the borders drawn up by the French were completely artificial and had no basis in history. Nor were cultural or economic factors taken into account in the delimitation of the frontiers. It was an entirely political decision, taken exclusively in the interests of the French and the Maronites, and as such it made civil conflict virtually certain.

In the demands they had presented to the Western powers, the Maronites had claimed, in addition to Mount Lebanon, the other areas of modern Lebanon including al-Beqa´a valley, the Akkar region in the north, Tyre and Sidon in the south, and the two most important Syrian ports, Beirut and Tripoli. Their aim was to create a viable, independent state dominated by the Christian communities. Yet the addition of these territories in fact ensured that in the long run the Christians became a minority. For while they were a majority in Mount Lebanon itself, the Maronites comprised less than a third of the population of Greater Lebanon – because the new areas, which they had insisted on, contained large Muslim majorities. This enlargement made sense economically, for Mount Lebanon would hardly have been self-sufficient by itself. But by other standards it was shortsighted, as the Arab nationalists deeply resented it and clamoured for federation with truncated Syria.

The resentment of the Arab nationalists – and among their ranks large numbers of the Greek Orthodox and other Christian communities as well as the Sunnis and the non-orthodox Muslims must be included – and their frustration at finding themselves in a westernized country with which they have been unable to identify, has been the elemental factor of Lebanese politics since 1920 and the root cause of all civil strife, including the war that broke out in 1975.

Throughout the mandate, French policy seemed bent on completing the division between those Lebanese who looked towards the West and those whose culture and outlook remained Arab. The Sunnis continued to deny the legality of the new borders and few of them could be persuaded to play any role in the administration of the state. They repeatedly demanded that the Muslim areas be transferred to Syria, and on several occasions, notably in 1936, there was violence in Tripoli and Beirut between their supporters and the Maronite groups now calling themselves Lebanese nationalists.

After a British and Free French force gained control of Lebanon from its Vichy administration in 1941, implementation of a pre-war agreement for independence from France might have led to an immediate conflict had not the folly of French policy alienated even some of their Maronite friends. De Gaulle's reluctance to concede independence and his imprisonment of the Lebanese cabinet which had declared it, convinced many that the French had now exhausted their usefulness and forged a unity among the Lebanese factions that was never to be repeated. Lebanon was also fortunate in possessing two leaders capable of producing an acceptable basis for coexistence, Bishara al-Khoury, the new Maronite president, and Riad Solh, the Sunni prime minister.

The new leaders understood that co-operation between the communities was the only way to prevent Lebanon from falling apart. No single community must be allowed to antagonize the others, especially over foreign policy. The Maronites should not go all out for alliance with the West, and the Sunnis should exercise restraint in their enthusiasm for pan-Arabism. This was the basis of the unwritten national pact between the communities.

The method which was adopted to ensure that each sect did not receive more than its fair share was to create positions in the administration which could only be filled by members of a particular sect. The president was to be a Maronite, for example, the prime minister a Sunni, and the speaker of the Chamber of Deputies a Shiite. In Bishara al-Khoury's first government all the major communities were represented, and this pattern has been repeated ever since. Al-Khoury also managed to make the distribution of offices between Christians and Muslims fairer, and so did much to defuse Sunni discontent. The system was by no means perfect, but it was probably the only one possible at the time. It did give the Christian sects, in particular the Maronites, a predominance which perhaps their numbers and political sophistication then justified. It accorded them a six-to-five advantage in parliamentary representation and gave the Maronites, in addition to the presidency, the command of the army and the office of director-general of public security.

This policy was followed from 1943 until the civil war, and thus 'confessionalism' became the basic principle in Lebanese life. Yet it failed to solve Lebanon's problem; at best it merely diluted it. The dilemma the French mandate had imposed still remained:

should Lebanon look East or West? Notwithstanding the conciliatory government of Bishara al-Khoury, the Maronites and the Arab nationalists remained deeply mistrustful of each other. The Maronites had lost their protectors, and in spite of the way they had ruled, many already regretted the departure of the French. On the other side, the nationalists, though more or less reconciled to the 1920 enlargement of the Lebanese frontiers, had achieved few of their objectives. The country remained dominated by the Maronites, politically aligned with the West, and little interested in the affairs of the other Arab states. Furthermore, their hopes that the Arab League, founded at the end of the Second World War, would be able to induce at least a degree of Arab unity soon proved illusory.

While a succession of new factors has complicated Lebanese politics over the past twenty-five years, the struggle between the Arab nationalists and the Maronites, which the national pact contained but did not resolve, has been, and still is, at the heart of the country's problems. Yet on only one occasion before 1975 did the confessional system break down completely and the country polarize behind the Maronite and Sunni establishments. This was in 1958 when the then President, Camille Chamoun, accepted the Eisenhower doctrine and tried to push Lebanon into an alliance with the West. This was, of course, a negation of the first principle of the national pact, and as such a slap in the face of the Arab nationalists. The latter were then further antagonized by the government's rigging of the 1957 elections, which excluded most of the nationalist leaders from parliament, and by Chamoun's clear intention of altering the constitution in order to allow himself a second term as president. At the high tide of pan-Arab ferment in 1958 it was difficult to remain indifferent and predictably the nationalists revolted. Nasser was their hero, and the Lebanese Sunni leaders, Sa'eb Salam and Rashid Karame, freely echoed the pan-Arab pronouncements of the Egyptian president. But they understood they could not go the whole way with Nasser, as Lebanon's peculiar circumstances required that everything must be decided by compromise. When the revolt was brought to an end by the judicious statesmanship of the new president, General Chehab, Lebanon returned to its previous policy of friendship but not alliance with the West and alliance but not union with the Arab countries.

The Sunni establishment might respect the special nature of

Lebanon, but there were many who increasingly did not. The social situation was partly responsible — while the wealth of the country was rapidly growing, the living standards of many had not moved. Little of this prosperity found its way. to the underdeveloped regions and the absence of any welfare system left the increasing numbers of urban dwellers — most of them immigrants from the countryside — without homes or basic facilities. With the inspiration of Nasser before them, the new generation of nationalists began to demand a fairer share of political and economic power. Why, they asked, did the Christians retain a majority of seats in parliament, when everybody knew they were now a minority in the country? Why were the most important posts filled by Maronites? Why were the overwhelming majority of army officers Christians?

Allied to the social problem was the question of the Palestinians, and on many points their interests and those of the nationalists converged. The Israeli victory in 1967 was a humiliation for all Arabs and ended in the Zionist occupation of parts of Syria, Jordan and Egypt as well as all of Palestine. Henceforth the Palestinian struggle came to be for the Arab nationalists what Nasser's struggle against the West had been for the previous generation. Inside Lebanon itself the position of the Palestinians was not very different from that of the poorer Muslims. Around the capital both lived in disgusting slums and in the south of the country both suffered from Israeli raids.

By the late 1960s many of the old Sunni leaders had become so identified with the regime that they had lost much of their credability with this new, more radical generation of Arab nationalists. The leadership of the movement — 'ideological tradition' is perhaps a better description since there was never much organization — was taken up by the Druze chieftain, Kamal Jumblatt, who formed the National Movement around his own party, the Progressive Socialists. This amorphous and ill-disciplined coalition had taken shape in 1969 when the radicals realized that the traditional nationalist leaders were no longer able to meet their demands. It included several Nasserist and other Arab nationalist groups, the communist parties, the Lebanese branches of the Syrian and Iraqi Ba'ath, and several others.

It was to be expected that the Maronites would view these developments with anxiety. Indeed, they seem to have regarded the designs of the nationalists and their Palestinian allies as a familiar repetition of history. As before with the Byzantines and Mamelukes, they believed themselves threatened and reacted in the way they always had – by refusing to compromise. Their stance was heavily influenced by the political situation inside their own community where the moderate, conciliatory politicians, the followers of Bishara al-Khoury and General Chehab, had lost the leadership and had been replaced by the hard-liners. Maronite policy was increasingly determined by former president Chamoun, and also by Pierre Gemayel's Phalangist Party, a breast-beating, paramilitary organization whose creation was inspired by its leader's visit to Nazi Germany in 1936.

The issue that reopened the conflict between the Maronites and the Arab nationalists was the question of the Palestinians. Lebanon's Palestinian population consists mainly of Sunni Muslims who fled from the Galilee in 1948, coming over the hills of northern Palestine or escaping by boat from Haifa. Smaller migrations also took place in 1967 after the June war and also in 1970, when many Palestinians were forced to leave Jordan. By 1975 the original 140,000 refugees had increased to over 300,000, a third of whom were living in refugee camps distributed around the country. But it was not the number of Palestinians which so upset the Maronites: it was the fact that Beirut had become the head-quarters of the Palestine resistance movement.

By 1971 Lebanon was the one remaining country from which the guerrillas could attack Israel. In the 1967 war they had lost their few bases in Egyptian-controlled territory; in 1970 and 1971 they were driven out of Jordan; and in Syria their freedom of movement was almost entirely restricted. But in Lebanon, where the government was too weak to suppress it, the resistance was allowed to do what it liked. Initially, when the Palestine Liberation Army was formed as the military arm of the P.L.O. in 1964, the Lebanese government had stipulated that it would not be permitted to have bases in Lebanon. Nevertheless, a limited amount of commando training did take place on Lebanese territory and for a time it was tolerated by the authorities. Raids into Israel from south Lebanon, however, were not. After the 1967 war all this changed. Because of the immense popular support the guerrillas then enjoyed throughout the Arab world, the Lebanese government found it difficult to exercise control over the resistance without incurring strong criticism both from other Arab states and from its supporters inside Lebanon. 1968 saw a rapid growth in guerrilla activity in the south of the country and by October of that year skirmishes between the commandos and Israeli forces were taking place several times a day.

The anxiety the Lebanese felt was understandable. At one level was the fear of Israeli retaliation. It was a widespread belief in Arab circles that Israel had long coveted the area in south Lebanon known as the Lītāni basin – a fear reinforced by General Dayan's remark after the 1967 war that all Israel's borders were now ideal with the exception of that with Lebanon. This in itself was one reason why the Lebanese were anxious not to give Israel an excuse to invade the country. As it happened the Israelis decided at that time not to annex the area but contented themselves with hitting back at carefully selected targets in Lebanon. The most spectacular operation took place at the end of 1968 when troops landed by helicopter at Beirut International Airport and blew up thirteen civilian airliners.

At a different level the Lebanese authorities were rightly worried that the activity of the resistance, and the retaliation it provoked from the Israelis, was widening the gap between the Maronites and the Arab nationalists. The latter's natural reaction was to fight back against Israel and accept the consequences. Palestine was their cause and they demanded the removal of all restrictions on the movements of the commandos. The Maronite establishment, for its part, claimed that Lebanon had traditionally avoided taking part in Arab struggles and argued that since the Israelis were by far the strongest force in the region, it was suicidal to go on provoking them. Unfortunately, the leaders of the country ostentatiously began to adopt positions on one side or the other. The Sunni prime minister of the day, Abdallah al-Yafi, even went so far as to say in public that the guerrillas should be allowed total freedom to conduct any operations they liked. He should have understood that this remark, and the reactions it would bring from the other side, could only harm the delicate confessional balance on which the country relied for its survival.

The position of the Lebanese army was an example of just how delicate this balance was. It had never been a strong force and its 14,000 men were used for internal security rather than as part of the Arab front against Israel. But it was the only national institution that had come through the 1958 crisis unsullied and unscathed. Its commander, General Chehab, had at that time maintained a strictly neutral position and had refused to obey the president's orders to use it on the side of the Maronite establishment. In the army, as in everything else in Lebanon, the different religious communities were represented. While most of the officers were Christians, and usually Maronites, a majority of the other ranks were from Muslim sects. With such a composition, the army could only survive if it was used inside the country with rigorous impartiality. Chehab knew this and so refused to commit his troops to a government which had come to represent only the Maronite viewpoint.

The position in which the government found itself over the Palestinian resistance was even more difficult. By 1969 the guerrillas had established a great many bases in the Arqoub, a hilly region in the south-east of the country, which subsequently became known as 'Fatahland'. In this area, the Maronites claimed, Lebanon was now unable to exercise its rightful sovereignty. Such a situation was intolerable to the Maronite leaders, many of whom paid only lip-service to the Palestinian cause, and who privately found much to admire in the Israeli state. They demanded the restoration of Lebanese control over the Arqoub and an end to the guerrillas' skirmishes with the Israelis. As Pierre Gemayel argued with some justification at a Phalangist Party conference:

'If the resistance was capable of protecting the frontiers and protecting itself, or if we, along with the resistance, or even along with all the Arab forces, were capable of protecting them, we might perhaps be willing to surrender this area to the resistance. But the fact that the resistance should insist on the right to dispose of our frontiers, when all of us together are incapable of protecting them, is something very strange indeed.'[2]

The Maronites wanted the resistance tightly controlled by the army. But they did not see that the enforcement of such a policy was bound to have disastrous repercussions. If the army attacked the commandos there were only three possible consequences, all equally catastrophic: in the first place it might be beaten, though this was the least likely; secondly it might split, the Muslim junior officers and soldiers refusing to fight against a cause with which they themselves identified; but even if neither of these events took place, there was the certainty that the Arab nationalist elements in the country would protest, and that a revolt along the lines of the 1958 confrontation would follow.

It was therefore impossible, in 1969, for the government to take decisive action against the commandos in the way that King Hussein was to do the following year. Yet if it did nothing at all, Israel would not hesitate to step up its retaliatory operations against Lebanon. In the event the government muddled its way through the dilemma, ordering the army to take limited action against the commandos. This was followed immediately by uproar in the country and demonstrations by radicals and Arab nationalists in support of the resistance. The behaviour of the army then became tactless, and in putting down an illegal demonstration in Sidon, a number of people were killed. Clashes between the army and the commandos spread to Beirut and Tripoli and continued intermittently from April 1969 to November. Meanwhile the Lebanese government was paralysed and without a prime minister for most of the year, because Rashid Karame resigned in April, refusing to participate in an anti-Palestinian policy.

In the midst of these troubles the government was flooded with a lot of unhelpful criticism from the Arab states, which denounced all attempts at hindering the commandos. There was much hypocrisy in this: the Arab governments which urged Lebanon to give the resistance a free hand would never have entertained a similar idea in their own countries. The Syrians, who protested loudest, refused to allow any guerrilla activity from their territory and had placed their local commandos firmly under the orders of the army. Egypt too, since it had lost most of its own guerrilla population in 1967, felt free to criticize any move against the resistance. One sanctimonious message emanating from the Egyptian National Assembly during a later round of fighting stressed 'that protection of commando action is a sacred duty required of every Arab citizen of every Arab country, and that in fighting the battle for Palestine the Palestinian commandos are in fact also fighting the battle for Lebanon'.[3]

The only way out of the problem was to look for a compromise and in November 1969 the Lebanese army commander and the P.L.O. chairman signed what became later known as the Cairo agreement. In actual fact it was less a compromise than a complete surrender to the Palestinian position. Although the agreement declared that 'the Lebanese civil and military authorities will continue to exercise their full rights in all Lebanese regions in all circumstances,' this was rendered meaningless by the other clauses. On three major issues the Lebanese government climbed down from its previous position: it allowed any Palestinian in Lebanon to 'participate in the Palestinian revolution through armed struggle'; it gave the commandos total autonomy in the refugee camps over which they promptly hoisted their own flags; strangest of all, it actually agreed to help the resistance mount its operations from Fatahland. In return the P.L.O. leaders promised to control the Palestinian extremists, a promise they knew would be difficult to keep. The other concessions required of them were minor.

Many of the Maronite leaders considered the Cairo agreement as a sell-out. To them the Palestinian resistance was invading their independence as others had done before and they were determined not to accept it. If the authorities were unable to keep order, then the Maronites believed they should help them. In the meantime they decided to arm themselves for the conflict which many of them already regarded as inevitable.

The first clash between the Palestinians and the Maronites took place in March 1970 with a direct confrontation between the Phalangist Party militia and the guerrillas on the outskirts of Beirut. With Karame and Jumblatt as prime minister and minister of the interior, and both of them refusing to commit the army against the Palestinians, the Phalangist militia appointed itself the guardian of Lebanese sovereignty. But after more fighting in 1973, the Maronite leadership realized it would have to strengthen its forces enormously if it hoped to contain the Palestinians. In the following months, therefore, large consignments of weapons were landed at the port of Beirut with the full approval of the Maronite president, Suleiman Frangieh. Another route, via the Jounié Yacht Club, was organized by a retired colonel of the American air force, a C.I.A. agent posing as a journalist in Beirut. In both cases the destinations were the same: the Phalangist Party and its ally, Camille Chamoun's National Liberal Party.

Some of the Maronite objections to the resistance were valid. The commandos could be extremely arrogant and used to swagger around Beirut waving their rifles. They would stop motor cars quite arbitrarily and check identity cards. They also took part in Beirut's notorious gang warfare.

More serious were the problems that the commandos' activities were bringing to southern Lebanon. In order to encourage the government into taking the same action against the resistance as Hussein had done in 1970, Israel began a systematic campaign of terror against the Lebanese villages in the south. Air raids against the refugee camps were followed by frequent assaults on any villages suspected of harbouring Palestinians. On each occasion the Israelis blew up houses and bridges, destroyed roads and crops, and often seized the villagers themselves and carried them back to Israel for interrogation.

When the commandos began to conduct their operations from outside the Arab countries, the Israeli reprisal raids against Lebanon increased. After the terrorist attack on Israel's Lydda airport in May 1972, the Lebanese suffered the consequences, though the President pertinently asked: 'How can Lebanon be held responsible for an act by foreigners who were transported to Israel on a foreign airline from a foreign capital?'[4] Lydda was followed by Munich and again a great many people were killed through Israel's eye-for-an-eye policy – though in fact these vengeance missions usually caused casualty figures at the ratio of about ten or twenty eyes for one eye. Four hundred people were killed in the post-Munich air raids. Even when the Palestinians agreed to stop their operations along the border in 1974, the retaliatory policy continued. Israel's plan was to create an upheaval in Lebanon and it succeeded. The measure of its success can be judged by one incident in April 1973. On the 9th of that month an Israeli terror squad arrived in Beirut by boat and murdered three Fatah leaders (including the poet, Kamal Nasser) as well as a number of other people. The Israelis controlled an area of Beirut for several hours and even directed the traffic. Yet the Lebanese army did not fire a shot, nor in fact do anything at all, though they were ordered into action by the prime minister, Sa'eb Salam. Huge demonstrations were immediately held to protest against the army's ineptitude. Salam himself demanded the dismissal of the Maronite army commander, Iskandar Ghanem. But Ghanem was a friend of Frangieh and the president refused to sack him. Salam then resigned and a major political crisis followed. Three weeks later, fighting broke out between the commandos and the Lebanese army for the first time since the signing of the Cairo agreement.

As the Israeli reprisals continued, the depopulation of the border villages began and a stream of refugees, mainly Shiite Muslims, made their way to Beirut. The Maronite groups complained bitterly that Lebanese citizens should be made homeless on account of a conflict that did not concern them. 'We welcomed the Palestinian refugees and gave them homes,' wrote one Maronite, Jean-Pierre Haddad. 'Then, having allowed the commandos to do what they please, we have to welcome our own refugees, chased from their lands because of Palestinian aggressions against Israel.'[5] But Maronite compassion for the new refugees wasn't convincing. Had they really been concerned about the fate of the Shiites, they might have done something for them when they arrived destitute in Beirut. The fact that the refugees remained homeless and unemployed, living in wretched poverty in the shanty towns around the capital, indicated that the Maronite protests were prompted by political considerations rather than by any new-found spirit of altriusm.

Perhaps the principal Maronite objection to the resistance was that it provided a bandwagon for all the radical Lebanese parties to jump on to. This is exactly what did happen. Radical strength was then dispersed among a considerable number of small parties, some communist, some Arab nationalist or Nasserist, others supporting the Syrian or Iraqi wings of the Ba'ath Party. By themselves they were inconsequential, their supporters few and their parliamentary power non-existent. Allied in some form or other to the resistance, or to Kamal Jumblatt's National Movement, which wholeheartedly supported the resistance, the radicals became more conspicuous and began to demand a series of reforms from the government. These were not very radical and most of them would have been accepted without hesitation by any Western government. But the Maronites acted with their usual stubborness and refused to accept anything from the Left. One issue was parliamentary representation. The ratio of six Christians to every five Muslims had been fixed at independence on the assumption that the Christians were a small majority in the country. This may or may not have been true but no census was taken to find out. During the next thirty years, however, the very high birth rate of the Muslims, particularly the Shiites, and the emigration of many Maronites, decisively altered the balance. By the 1970s it was obvious that about sixty per cent of the population were Muslims. Nor was this seriously disputed even by the Maronites. Yet they refused dogmatically to consider altering the ratio or even to hold a population census to find out what the true figures were.

Among other things, the radicals and Arab nationalists sought also to abolish the confessional nature of the state, a reform the Phalangist Party had suggested many years before. But to this and any other proposal the Maronite establishment replied unequivocally in the negative. Politically on the defensive, aware that their numbers less and less justified their privileges, the Maronites were unable to understand where their real interests lay. They adopted, quite needlessly, a 'backs against the wall' position and came to see the alliance of radicals, Arab nationalists and Palestinians as a plot of the international Left. Furthermore, by their refusal to make any concessions at all, they forced many of the moderate Sunnis into the radical camp.

The hard-line Maronite leaders had long been preparing for a showdown. The Chamoun family and its National Liberal Party, for example, had, privately, never accepted the Cairo agreement and were not interested in making it last. Camille Chamoun had no sympathies for the refugees. He disliked the Palestinians and later referred to them as 'the assassins of Lebanon'.[6] His son Dory, the secretary-general of the party, held similar views. In private he referred to the Palestinians as a race of cowards whose refugee existence was no more than they deserved.[7] They were hated by all the Lebanese, he claimed, and the sooner they were kicked out the better. 'If it's necessary, we will chuck the Palestinians into the sea. They will pollute it, but that's too bad.'

By 1975 large numbers of the Maronite community had managed to convince themselves that the resistance seriously intended to take over the country. According to Jean-Pierre Haddad, the Palestinian aim was 'the physical and political liquidation of the Lebanese resistance, and the setting up of a popular republic dominated by the Palestinians of al-Fatah and their Marxist allies.'[8] Nothing could have been further from the truth. The last thing the Palestinians wanted to do was to fight inside Lebanon, and Arafat's diplomacy during the war was proof of this. All they wanted was to retain their one remaining base for operations against Israel. They did not wish to provoke the Lebanese into adopting the same policy as King Hussein. Nor did they want to risk losing their current prestige, which, following Arafat's speech at the U.N. in November 1974, was at its highest point, not only in the Arab countries but throughout the world.

Nevertheless the Maronites believed, or at least pretended to believe, that the existence of their country was at stake. They argued that if Lebanon was to survive, the resistance must be crushed and the Palestinians ejected. Lebanon, they pointed out, was the smallest and most densely populated country in the Arab world. Why should it have to house such enormous numbers of refugees? Why could they not be redistributed around the Middle East? In the course of the war President Frangieh publicly supported this view, declaring that the Palestinians should be 'dispersed among all the Arab countries according to the possibilities of each'.[9] Others went even further. One Maronite group, which called itself the Guardians of the Cedars, retained as its slogan: 'Not one Palestinian left in Lebanon.'

The central Maronite objective thus gradually became clear: the suppression of the Palestinian resistance in Lebanon and, as a subsidiary, the removal of at least some of the refugees. According to the Maronite thesis, this would solve the two greatest problems confronting the country. The elimination of the guerrillas and the restoration of Lebanese control over the Arqoub and the refugee camps would terminate the Palestinian 'state within a state' to which the Maronites objected. It would also presumably bring an end to the Israeli reprisal raids. Secondly, the power of the radical and Arab nationalist groups, which demanded political reform and an end to the special Maronite privileges, would be considerably reduced once the Palestinians had gone.

Yet the Maronites knew that they could not do the job by themselves. They had neither the strength nor the inclination to do so. A straightforward Maronite–Palestinian clash would be disastrous, and not only from the military angle. If they were to succeed, the Maronites had to present their struggle as one between the Palestinians and the Lebanese. Once this had been established, they believed they could force the army to intervene on their side and crush the guerrillas.

Thus the Maronites and their apologists went to work and propounded the myth that the Lebanese crisis had nothing to do with inter-Lebanese problems. The traditional enmity between Maronites and Arab nationalists, the political struggles between

Left and Right, the problems with Muslim—Christian relations, the flagrant social injustice — all these were dismissed as mirages. The issue, they claimed, was simply one between the Lebanese and the Palestinians, who had abused the hospitality of their hosts and were bent on the destruction of 'the only true democracy' in the Arab world. To this challenge the Maronites had risen. According to Lady Cochrane,* the Phalangist Party formed 'the nucleus of the Lebanese resistance against foreign occupation and aggression'.[10] As for Camille Chamoun, who had himself provoked the purely Lebanese confronation of 1958, he apparently expected to be taken seriously when he said that 'in spite of foreign interference which promotes the conflict, nothing can prevent the entente between the Lebanese'.[11]

This thesis was so transparently absurd that it deceived nobody. For the Maronites were totally unable to explain away one obvious fact. Why, if the Palestinians were the enemy of Lebanon, did at least three-fifths of the population actually prefer them to the Maronites? Of course there was no answer. In an unsuccessful attempt to explain why the Palestinians and the Lebanese Muslims had become allies, Lady Cochrane blamed 'Left-wing propaganda which identified the Palestinian cause with that of Islam'.[12] Others claimed that some of the Muslims were communists without loyalty to Lebanon and whose first duty was to revolution — Kamal Jumblatt was represented as the tool of anti-Lebanese factions. Thus they resorted to the palpable untruth that they were only fighting foreigners (i.e. Palestinians) and extremists (i.e. communists) backed by foreign powers (i.e. Russia). In time, a conflict precipitated by the Maronites in order to suppress the resistance could be represented by Gemayel as a 'communist offensive'[13] and by Dory Chamoun as 'a plot of the international Left under orders from Moscow'.

Thus the Lebanese war was launched. To remove an irritant — and the Palestinian presence could certainly be irritating — the Maronites gave the country a civil war. For they badly miscalculated. Nobody was taken in by their propaganda, least of all the other Lebanese, most of whom joined the enemy. Nor was their reliance

* Lady Cochrane was a Lebanese who married an Irishman. A member of the old Sursock family, she was one of the richest people in Lebanon and a passionate supporter of the Maronite position.

on the army justified: it did split and in the event its more effective elements took the field against them. The Maronites were thus left fighting it out by themselves; and they lost. Only the intervention of a foreign army prevented their total defeat.

10

The Lebanese Civil War

To the British poet, James Elroy Flecker, the Italian bombardment of Beirut in 1912 was a memorable sight: 'unforgettable the thunder of the guns shaking the golden blue of sky and sea while not a breath stirred the palm trees, not a cloud moved on the swanlike snows of Lebanon'. The bombardments of 1975 and 1976 were less poetical. The palm trees had gone, their places taken by lines of new tower blocks, once white and arrogant, now smirched and pock-marked. Great clouds of smoke drifted over the city, concealing the 'swanlike snows' of Lebanon. There was no thunder of the guns but continuous bomb explosions and the sharp, insistent cracks of Russian and American rifles.

No precise date can be given to the beginning of the Lebanese war. Even the year is in question, some maintaining that the crisis of 1975 was merely a continuation of those of 1969 and 1973. Perhaps the civil war had no real beginning just as it appears to have no end. It was certainly not preceded by ultimata and grandiose declarations. It simply grew, from small, isolated incidents, which steadily became larger and less isolated, until eventually they followed each other so closely that it was impossible to separate them.

Probably the first shots were fired during a dispute that was quite unconnected with the Palestinians or any of the other major issues affecting the country. In February 1975 there was trouble in Sidon over fishing rights. The local fishermen believed they were being threatened by the establishment of a fishing group called the

Protein Company, a joint Lebanese—Kuwaiti concern presided over by Camille Chamoun. Encouraged by some radical groups, they protested vigorously and organized a large demonstration in Sidon on 26 February. A small army unit tried to prevent the demonstration taking place but only succeeded in causing a riot. In the confusion Maarouf Saad, the mayor of Sidon and a supporter of the fishermen, was mortally wounded.

It was a local incident and could have remained so. Unfortunately both the Maronites and the radicals thought they could score political points by turning it into a major issue. The radicals moved first, demonstrating in Beirut on the 28th; cars were burnt and streets blocked by barricades of burning tyres. On 1 March they organized a further protest in Sidon and cut the coast road to Tyre. As the army moved in to take control, it was ambushed by gunmen and forced to retreat. Reinforcements were quickly brought up but these encountered only fiercer resistance from the radicals, who were being supported by members of the Palestinian Rejection Front. Rather than risk further casualties, the Maronite army commander, General Ghanem, made the amazing decision to bombard Sidon itself. Eventually a cease-fire was arranged, with the help of the Palestinians, on condition the army withdrew from the city.

In the capital the loudest-lunged were just loosening up. Denunciations of the army and its behaviour were followed by demands for the resignation of the government. Even the Muslim Higher Council, a conservative body representing the Sunnis, clamoured for the reorganization of the army command and in the cabinet itself there was talk of resignations unless Ghanem was removed. The death of Maarouf Saad after a week in hospital made matters worse, and his funeral, during which the Palestinian flag was ostentatiously draped over his coffin, merely gave the Maronites a further opportunity of denouncing the unholiness of the Palestinian—radical alliance.

Although the actions of the fishermen and radicals in Sidon had obviously been provocative, the response of the government and the army was unnecessarily heavy-handed. The handling of the crisis was from the beginning tactless and insensitive. It was therefore unfortunate that the Phalangist Party and other Maronite groups should have picked this moment to make a passionate declaration of support for the army. They organized demonstrations and made loud assertions of solidarity. The Maronites of East Beirut marched across the capital, proclaiming their total confidence in the armed forces and shouting anti-Palestinian slogans. It was a crude and ultimately self-defeating political exercise.

The Maronites' objective was obvious. They were making a blatant attempt at identifying the Lebanese state with their own community, presenting themselves as the upholders of the nation at a time when 'communists' and 'foreigners' were undermining its authority. Frequently attacked as a selfish and privileged minority, they were anxious to seize any opportunity of putting themselves forward as the true defenders of Lebanon. In the event, however, these extravagant gestures of solidarity actually reduced the effectiveness of the army, for the Muslims and the Arab nationalists came to regard it as a close ally of the Phalangist Party. To the Muslims, the message was clear — the Maronites and the army were on the same side. Even the conservative Sunnis, the older, traditional Arab nationalists like Sa'eb Salam and the mufti, Hassan Khaled, could not accept that. They demanded the reform of the army for they understood — as surely anybody should have understood — that it would never again be of any use in inter-Lebanese disputes if the Muslims believed it to be merely the protector of the Maronite community. It was not as if the Muslim demands were particularly revolutionary. All they asked for was equal representation in the army command, to which their numbers, if nothing else, clearly entitled them. Yet both Gemayel and Chamoun, the leaders of the two main Maronite parties, refused to consider such a plan.

The majority of the Lebanese were not seriously worried by the Sidon incidents. A few talked of the possibility of a replay along the lines of the 1958 confrontation, but the general mood was not pessimistic. Demonstrations and political instability had become endemic to Lebanon yet the wealth of the country was still increasing. People had faith that a compromise could, as usual, be worked out, and this optimism continued until the late summer. Naturally there was a lot of resentment and recrimination, directed particularly at the Palestinians. Because of the role the resistance had played in setting up the cease-fire, the Maronites complained that it had become more powerful than the state itself. Consequently, anti-Palestinian feeling ran very high that spring and the guerrillas became the scapegoats for everything that went wrong in Lebanon. To the Maronites, every incident, every problem, every evil, could be traced ultimately back to the resistance. It was not difficult to see what they regarded as the ideal solution to the problem – King Hussein's name was one often quoted with approval in Maronite circles.

On Sunday 13 April 1975 fighting broke out again when Phalangist gunmen ambushed a busload of Palestinians in the Christian suburb of Ain al-Roumaneh and killed twenty-seven of them. The next morning the battles began in Beirut. Phalangist militia went into action against commandos of the P.F.L.P. and its splinter groups, shelling the Tal Zaatar refugee camp from its positions in Ashrafiyeh. Commandos from Borj al-Barajneh retaliated by invading the Christian quarter of Chiah. There was also shooting in some of the other suburbs and in Tripoli and Sidon. For most of the following week the fighting continued and, although the official death toll reached 150, everyone knew they had to multiply the number several times before they got the true figure.

The Ain al-Roumaneh affair naturally became the central issue of Lebanese politics. The radicals claimed it was part of an international conspiracy to liquidate the Palestine resistance. While some blamed the C.I.A. and others the Zionists, a few declared that the massacre had been planned with the connivance of President Frangieh. The Phalangists, for their part, maintained that the Palestinians had deliberately provoked the battle by bringing their commandos into a Maronite stronghold – though this argument was not entirely convincing since the bus had also contained a large number of women and children. Gemayel pointed out that if he paraded his troops in full battledress through the Palestinian quarter of Sabra he would expect trouble. He also declared that the massacre had not been an isolated episode, but had been provoked by two Palestinian attacks on his men that same morning, also in Ain al-Roumaneh. In the second incident a Peugeot with covered number-plates had been driven at great speed towards the entrance of a church in which Gemayel himself and other Phalangist leaders were attending a consecration ceremony. Gunmen inside the car had sprayed the entrance with bullets and got away. Four people were killed, including two officials of the Phalangist Party. Gemayel remarked that in this context the arrival of a busload of commandos in the same area could only be regarded as provocative. Nevertheless, the very efficiency with which the operation was carried out, and the fact that so many commandos had been killed, convinced many people that it had been planned beforehand.

On the evening of the 16th a cease-fire was announced, but despite a heavy thunderstorm everyone could hear that the guns were still firing. The following day the tension was kept alive by unidentified gunmen operating from rooftops in downtown Beirut. While the government blamed the shooting on a third party, it soon became obvious that the snipers had at least the tacit support of the president and the Maronite parties. Most of the gunfire was coming from the Christian quarters; moreover, the government was refusing to reveal the identity of the snipers, although the security forces had shot or captured several of them. This only reinforced the feeling among Muslims and radicals that the Maronites had no interest in stopping the fighting. If the crisis continued, they believed the Maronites would be able to force the army into action alongside the Phalangist militia and break the Palestinians.

Ain al-Roumaneh placed the Phalangist Party politically on the defensive. On the evening of the massacre the leaders of the National Movement gathered at Kamal Jumblatt's house and demanded the dismissal of the two Phalangist ministers in the government. A fortnight later Jumblatt declared that his parliamentary bloc would vote against any government which included members of the Phalangist Party. This piece of intransigence was badly timed, and even the Palestinians, who were after all the victims of Ain al-Roumaneh, were apprehensive of its consequences. Confident of the support of the other Christian parties, with the exception of the moderate National bloc, and aware that many Sunni politicians were dismayed by Jumblatt's move, Gemayel decided to turn up the pressure. His men resigned on 7 May and with them went three ministers of Camille Chamoun's National Liberal Party (N.L.P.) and Emir Majid Arslan, an elderly Druze chieftain whose political life revolved around almost blanket opposition to any proposal of Jumblatt's. A week later the prime minister, Rashid Solh, resigned. In the ensuing negotiations over the formation of a new government, the Phalangists and the N.L.P. made it clear that they would not, under any circumstances, accept Jumblatt's veto on the inclusion of Phalangists in the government.

Meanwhile there was a nearly total breakdown of law and order throughout the country. Almost daily there were bomb explosions, murders and kidnapping, much of it the work of ordinary gangsters taking advantage of the situation. But on 18 May serious fighting broke out again, mainly in the northern suburbs of the capital. It was never clear why these clashes broke out, or who exactly was fighting against whom. In the quarter of Dekwaneh the position was relatively straightforward: Phalangist militiamen clashed with commandos of the Rejection Front from the nearby refugee camps. On other fronts the Phalangists and their allies, including Camille Chamoun's 'Tiger militia', fought against assorted groups of Nasserists, Kurdish slum-dwellers and Shiites backed by the communists and other radical parties.

With the formation of a new cabinet, the situation deteriorated. Jumblatt's insistence on the exclusion of the Phalangist Party from the government, and Gemayel's refusal to accept this, had placed President Frangieh in an almost impossible position. In order to extricate himself, he abandoned all precedent and formed a government headed by a retired brigadier and consisting entirely of military officers – except for his relation, Lucien Dahdah, who became minister of finance and foreign affairs. Given the close Maronite identification with the army, and considering that General Ghanem was to become minister of defence, it cannot have surprised anybody that there was hardly a Lebanese Muslim or a Palestinian willing to support the plan. The enthusiastic reception it received in Beirut's Christian suburbs, where the news was greeted with volleys of gunfire, and its acceptance by Gemayel and Chamoun, made its fate still more certain.

The Sunni establishment, the Shiites, the Palestinians, the radicals and the Arab nationalists were in complete agreement on the matter. There could be no question of co-operating with the military government. Backed by liberal Christians and by the National bloc, they had at least two-thirds of the country behind them and could afford to take a strong stand. Within three days the new cabinet had resigned and Frangieh had called upon Rashid Karame to form a government. Negotiations concerning the new cabinet took over a month, and in the meantime order began to break down throughout the country. But on 30 June a government was at last formed and a few days later the shooting died down, brought to an end by the statesmanship of the new prime minister. Karame had solved the political impasse by excluding members of both the Phalangist Party and Jumblatt's Progressive Socialist Party from the new cabinet. The Druze leader was unable to complain because Gemayel's men had been kept out and the Phalangists were satisfied by the appointment of their ally, Camille Chamoun, as minister of the interior. Karame had thus managed to resolve the principal problem, and the country had a government again. Nevertheless, the members of his six-man cabinet were mainly old and conservative – three of them had been cabinet ministers in 1943 – and were unlikely to put through any of the reforms that the country then needed. In addition, only two of them, Chamoun and Karame, had any real authority in the country.

Karame's success, remarkable though it was in the circumstances, was ephemeral. Even during July and August, when the government was still technically in control, plans were going ahead for what Kamal Jumblatt already referred to as the 'fourth round'. Consignments of weapons were arriving from half a dozen countries. Men of all religions were being recruited and trained. In the hills, strange, half-secret terrorist groups were being formed with medieval sounding names like the Knights of Ali (Shiite) and the Guardians of the Cedars (Maronite).

The fourth round began in early September with fighting around the Maronite town of Zahle on the edge of al-Beqa'a valley. Within a few days it had spread to Tripoli in the north of the country where skirmishing broke out between the Maronites of Frangieh's home town Zghorta, and the radical Muslim groups in Tripoli itself. In a vain attempt to police a cease-fire between the two sides, Karame sent in the army with strict orders to remain impartial. In fact it sided on more than one occasion with the Maronite militias against the Muslims. Thirteen commandos of the radical forces were shot dead by regular troops on the coast at Shakka, but no corresponding move was made to check the Maronite violations of the cease-fire. Over-reacting to the army intervention, Kamal Jumblatt called for a general strike in Beirut, which he then cancelled at the last moment. Nevertheless, the fighting spread within days to the capital and on 17 September the Phalangists at last brought the war into the centre of the city. They drew up their artillery on the eastern edge of the Place des Martyrs and began a fierce bombardment of the souks on the other side of the square. For four days the barrage continued until nothing at all was left of the one remaining traditional quarter of the city. The Damascus fire brigade arrived to help but there was nothing it could do: no one could get near the area without being shot at by the Phalangists.

The complete destruction of this area was fully intended. It was the Maronite answer to the demands put forward by the coalition of radicals, Palestinians and Arab nationalists. It was a reaction typical of a community whose instinctive response to external threats has always been the same — bloody, intransigent, unreasoning. In this case the Maronites were telling their enemies that they were prepared to destroy Lebanon altogether rather than compromise with the Palestinians or anyone else. They were also making a deliberate attempt to escalate the crisis to such a level that the army would be forced to intervene on their side.

As usual they miscalculated. The destruction of the souks was followed by a full-scale attack on the Phalangist positions in West Beirut by the commandos of Ahmed Jibril's P.F.L.P. – General Command aided by a Lebanese Nasserist group called the Mourabitoun. In two phases, at the end of October and again in December, Jibril's forces attacked the Phalangists and beat them. Driven back into East Beirut, the foremost Maronite militia only just managed to save its own headquarters from capture. The continued Maronite attempts to bring the army into the fighting were equally counter-productive. On minor occasions it did intervene on the Maronite side, but never very effectively, and the obvious bias of the military commanders eventually drove large sections of the army into open revolt.

1975 closed with the Maronites a long way from their objectives. They had received setbacks in Beirut and had achieved few of their military targets on other fronts. Moreover, they had been unable to win even though the main body of the resistance had taken no part in the fighting. It was the commandos of the P.F.L.P. and its splinter groups that had been involved with the Lebanese radicals. Fatah and Saiqa had deliberately dissociated themselves from the war and had managed to remain aloof. Indeed, Arafat and other Palestinians, such as the distinguished academic Walid Khalidi, had been acting as mediators between the Lebanese factions and had been partly responsible for the relative calm of July and August.

By the new year the Maronite leaders had abandoned their aim of suppressing the Palestinian guerrillas and their allies. In its place they were concentrating on a smaller objective: the partition of Lebanon. If they were unable to rule the whole of the country as they wished, they were determined to preside over their historic territory – Mount Lebanon and the coastal areas between Beirut and Tripoli. Thus they drew a rectangle between Zghorta and the Cedars in the north, and Zahle and East Beirut in the south, and decided to expel all Muslims and 'foreigners' (i.e. Palestinians) living in their 'heartland'. Throughout the old provinces of the Mountain the Muslim villages were cleared and their inhabitants forced out. The Palestinian refugee camps north and east of Beirut were attacked or blockaded. In the capital itself, the Phalangists began a determined assault on the slum quarters of Qarantina and Maslakh.

Within their rectangle, the Maronites enjoyed some degree of success. They captured the Palestinian refugee camp at Dbayyeh at the beginning of January. The larger camp at Tal Zaatar was surrounded by Camille Chamoun's 'Tiger militia', and a relief column of Palestinians from the south was successfully repulsed. On 18 January Qarantina and Maslakh fell; while the inhabitants were shot or deported, bulldozers were ordered in to flatten their hovels and tenement buildings.

Outside their rectangle, however, things were not going so well for the Maronites. Their towns and villages in al-Beqa'a valley were under siege and their units in the north were losing ground against the radical Tripoli forces. More importantly, they had at last provoked the main body of the Palestinians into joining the war. With the blockade of the Palestinian camps in the north, Fatah finally entered the conflict – nearly a year after the beginning of a war which the Phalangists claimed was begun by the resistance. Only in January 1976 did Arafat order his forces on to the offensive: in order to relieve the pressure on Tal Zaatar, a mixed Palestinian–Lebanese force attacked the Maronite coastal districts between Beirut and Sidon and before the end of the month had captured them.

By the middle of January, any remaining authority that the administration still possessed was fast evaporating. Local government had ceased to exist and affairs were being managed by whichever forces happened to be in control. Time and again the cease-fires, laboriously arranged with representatives of all sides, had broken down amidst mutual recrimination. There seemed, indeed, no prospect of peace without the capitulation of one side or the other. It was at this stage that President Assad of Syria decided to intervene. Committed to the struggle against Israel, and intent on recovering the lands conquered by the Israelis in 1967, Assad could not afford to let Lebanon degenerate into complete anarchy. Though allied to the Palestinians, he could not afford a total victory for the Jumblatt—P.L.O. front which would almost certainly lead to an Israeli invasion and which might also have repercussions on the stability of his own regime within Syria itself. Nor could he allow the Maronites to set up a state which might ally itself with Israel. His only option, therefore, was to arrange a compromise and impose it on the Lebanese. This solution, which guaranteed the continuation of the Lebanese 'system', at the same time introducing some measure of political reform, was probably the best attempt made by anyone at tackling the basic problem. Yet as it was instantly condemned by the Maronites as too radical and by the radicals as too conservative, it could only possibly succeed if it was forced upon the country.

Assad's method of imposing his compromise was firm but tactful. He sent a brigade of the Palestine Liberation Army (P.L.A.) across the Lebanese border on 19 January. Its object was not to ally itself with the P.L.O. – it had Syrian officers and remained under Syrian orders – but to restore order in those areas of the country (some three-quarters of the whole) not under the control of the Maronite militias. The following day the Syrian foreign minister, the chief of staff and the air force commander arrived at Frangieh's palace for 'consultations'. A cease-fire was arranged which the P.L.A. patrolled with impartiality, and, with the single exception of Chamoun, all the Lebanese and Palestinian leaders accepted the Syrian mediation. Frangieh went to Damascus at the beginning of February and was told by Assad what the Syrians wanted. A week later the Lebanese president announced the 'new Lebanese national covenant', in fact drafted by the Syrians.

This declaration was conservative in tone and reaffirmed the right of the Maronite community to supply the country's presidents. It also provided for the demilitarization of the Palestinian camps near Beirut and the re-enforcement of the Cairo agreement. Compensation for the opposition forces was limited. Apart from a vague commitment to 'secure general social justice through fiscal, economic and social reform', and a proposal to extend educational facilities, Kamal Jumblatt's solitary gain was the proposal of equal parliamentary representation for Christians and Muslims.

As with several previous cease-fires, this one was followed by a general explosion of optimism, and people on all sides declared that the war was now definitely over. But the men with the weapons decided that it was not. The Maronites, reluctant to remain part of a Lebanon in which their role would inevitably be reduced, were preparing for partition. They established their 'capital' at Jounié, a small town north of Beirut, created a police force and even built their own airport. On the other side, neither the ragged coalition which regarded Jumblatt as its spokesman, nor the Palestinians under Arafat, were prepared to accept Assad's plan. They had fought well, clearly held the upper hand, and were determined that their sacrifices should be rewarded with a more extensive programme of reform. They knew also that if the P.L.O. guerrillas were given a free hand, they could clean up the Maronite militias in a matter of days. Threatened by a settlement that gave more to the losers than the winners, Jumblatt and his allies were understandably anxious to press on.

By the end of February it was becoming clear that the Syrian intervention had not been a great success. The P.L.A. had not been able to keep order, as Assad had hoped, and it had proved powerless to prevent the dissolution of the country into anarchy. Perhaps the most important feature in this process was the disintegration of the armed forces, a development for which the senior Maronite officers were largely responsible. Although General Ghanem had been replaced, his successor, Hanna Said, soon proved equally partisan. While theoretically supposed to take his orders from the prime minister (who was also minister of defence), in practice General Said chose to ignore Karame altogether. His decisions were made instead in consultation with either Frangieh or Chamoun. This attitude, which led to the deployment of both the army and the air force on the side of the Chamounist 'Tigers' at Damour — where they were defeated — merely resulted in a large-scale military revolt. Whole garrisons mutinied and threw out their Christian officers. The rebellious units, under the command of Lieutenant Ahmed Khatib, then formed themselves into the Lebanese Arab Army and took up positions alongside Jumblatt's men and the P.L.O.

With the final breakdown of law and order in the country, and the determination of the opposing forces to go on fighting, the Syrian-backed cease-fire soon went the way of all the others. The immediate aim of Jumblatt and his allies was to force the resignation of President Frangieh, whom they regarded as the first obstacle to a satisfactory settlement. Contingents of the Lebanese Arab Army therefore moved towards Ba'abda and bombarded his palace. But though Frangieh left in a hurry, he refused to resign, even when a large majority of the deputies demanded that he did so, and after they had elected Elias Sarkis as his successor. In the mountains above Beirut, Jumblatt's Druze forces, supported by Fatah, launched an offensive into Maronite territory and drove back the Phalangist defenders. In the capital itself, Palestinians and Mourabitoun attacked along the sea front and captured the Holiday Inn, the chief Phalangist outpost. By April, the Maronite militias, now unreservedly backed by those army units which had not joined Khatib's Lebanese Arab Army, seemed on the verge of defeat.

The Syrian attitude, however, had not changed. Assad was determined to end the fighting and prevent a total victory for Jumblatt and the Palestinians. Having failed to achieve this through political pressure, he saw no alternative but to intervene militarily. On 1 June regular units of the Syrian army entered the country, one column advancing towards Beirut, another towards Sidon. Relying on their supporters in the Palestine Liberation Army and their commando organization, Saiqa, the Syrians evidently did not expect a very tough battle. But Arafat and the P.L.O. had made their preparations and were waiting for them. When the second column reached Sidon it was ambushed by the commandos of Fatah and the Rejection Front and forced to retreat. A second assault also ended in failure.

On the military front the Sidon reverse was hardly catastrophic for the Syrians. Had they been prepared to accept casualties, they could have pressed forward and would eventually have won through. But internationally their position was disastrous. The sight of Syria, of all countries, apparently trying to eliminate the resistance, brought almost unanimous criticism from the other Arab states. The foreign ministers of the Arab League met in

Cairo and called for the removal of the Syrian troops and their substitution by a mixed Arab force. On Syria's eastern border Iraq was making threatening noises and mobilizing its forces. Even in his own country, Assad realized that there was considerable hostility to his sudden alliance with the Maronites. Judging by the slogans splashed across the walls of Damascus, Pierre Gemayel was about as popular with the Syrians as Prime Minister Rabin of Israel and the C.I.A. Had Assad pushed forward regardless, he would probably have been successful. But he hesitated and the international clamour increased. Realizing that he had lost his chance of quickly occupying Beirut and Sidon, he withdrew his troops to positions overlooking the coast and waited.

The Syrian invasion did not end the war in the way Assad had wanted. Nevertheless it did end it, eventually, and with Assad still in control. Syrian pressure on the Palestinians forced them to divert troops away from the traditional fronts and so allowed the Phalangists to regain some of their territory. Syrian blockades interrupted the flow of fuel and weapons to the commando organizations. And Syrian political pressure forced the leaders of the Shiite community to forsake their former allies. The most dramatic result of the Syrian intervention was the fall of Tal Zaatar. The vast Palestinian refugee camp on the outskirts of East Beirut had been under siege for over seven months. Conditions inside were desperate, as Chamoun's militiamen had prevented the passage of either food or medical supplies to the 30,000 or so inhabitants. By the beginning of August, thousands of people had already died. Yet the Syrian presence effectively prevented other Palestinian forces from going to its relief. Diversionary attacks in other parts of the country failed to relieve the pressure. Tal Zaatar was doomed, and everyone knew it. With the limitless arms provided them by their Israeli allies, Chamoun's 'Tigers' could sit comfortably outside the camp and bombard it day after day. But even after seven months, and in spite of incessant attacks, the Palestinian commandos refused to surrender. On 12 August the camp was finally overrun. Over a thousand people were killed in the final assault; another thousand were lined up and shot immediately afterwards. Chamoun's men killed anyone they could find: doctors, nurses, children, religious leaders – anyone whom they suspected of being Palestinian. They didn't even pretend to be taking prisoners.

Tal Zaatar was the last battle, though the war dragged on until November. In the end the issue was decided in Saudi Arabia at a meeting of half a dozen heads of state and the P.L.O. leader. The Syrian position was by and large accepted by the countries that mattered – Egypt, Kuwait and Saudi Arabia. Arafat knew he was beaten and had to accept what was dictated to him. Lebanon was to be resurrected under the moderate hand of the new president, Elias Sarkis, and its development controlled by Assad. On 15 November, when the Syrians finally entered Beirut without opposition, the war was declared over. But even then the fighting did not stop. Three years after its official close, the Palestinians and their allies were still fighting it out in the south of the country against Maronite troops armed and supported by the Israelis.

Palestinian casualties in Lebanon were even greater than in Jordan – about 20,000 dead, the vast majority of them civilian inhabitants of the refugee camps. The military defeat in Lebanon was less overwhelming yet in one sense it was more serious. After the Jordanian débâcle, the survivors were able to go to Lebanon and operate from there. After the Lebanese civil war they were left without a proper base anywhere, except for the small band of territory in south Lebanon between the Syrian army and the forces of the rebel Maronite leader, Saad Haddad.

Politically, Arafat managed as usual to avoid a complete disaster and soon afterwards he succeeded in coming to an arrangement with the Syrians. The P.L.O. administrative offices remained in Damascus and the military headquarters stayed in Beirut. In the south of Lebanon the guerrillas, though depleted, remained strong enough to fight well against the Israeli invasion of March 1978. Through careful diplomacy Arafat was also able to improve his personal position. By 1979 his standing with the Arab regimes was so high that at the Tunis summit conference in November none dared oppose him during his quarrel with the Lebanese president over the stationing of P.L.O. forces in southern Lebanon.

11

Palestine and the International Community

The condition of the Palestinian people altered little during the third decade of their exile. A number of them raised their standard of living by emigrating to the Gulf and elsewhere but the majority saw only marginal improvements in their existence. Yet if by the end of the seventies the material conditions of the Palestinians were not much better than they had been at the beginning, the decade had also witnessed a spectacular advancement in their political fortunes. Before 1970 the United Nations General Assembly had habitually voted in favour of the refugees' return to their homes but it clearly had no intention of ensuring that they did return. At the same time the P.L.O., while beginning to earn itself a measure of notoriety, received support from the Arab states but from few others. Ten years later this had all changed. The Palestinians' cause had been adopted by the Third World and the international Left. To the countries of Asia and Africa theirs had become the first among liberation movements. Outside America and Western Europe support for the Palestinians had become so strong that Israel now vied with South Africa as the world's most unpopular nation.

From the early sixties the Palestinians saw themselves as a nationalist movement struggling against a colonialist oppressor in the manner of Algeria or Vietnam. But although Israel was indeed an essentially colonialist power, it was not a traditional, imperialist one like France or Britain and it took some time for the rest of the world to see the Palestinian fight against Israel as an anti-colonialist struggle and to accept the resistance as a genuine liberation movement. Over questions like Algeria or Rhodesia the issues were clear-cut and people took sides accordingly. But the Palestinian–Israeli problem was full of contradictions. Zionism was a settler movement, encouraged by an imperialist power, and was easily identifiable as such. Yet, in the aftermath of Hitler's genocide, it commanded support not only in the West but also from the Soviet Union and even, during the early fifties, from China. In the wake of the 1948 war, the Soviet leadership preferred to support Israel against the Arab Middle East, most of which was dominated by Great Britain. Many years passed before the Russians and their supporters in the rest of the world accepted the Palestinian version of the conflict.

The non-ideological character of the Palestine revolution deterred potential supporters from left-wing movements in other parts of the world. Arafat and the Fatah leadership, conducting their battle in a conservative region, realized that the help of Cuban or Vietnamese revolutionaries would be counter-productive and so concentrated on finding support from the Middle East and North Africa. In Algeria they secured their first political and military bases and among the Palestinian communities of the Gulf they found dependable economic backing. From the rest of the Arab world Fatah also received support, though, as this book has shown, it was not always consistent. As far as Fatah was concerned, therefore, the Arab world was its constituency, and support from other areas of the globe, though never shunned, was of secondary importance. Arafat's main diplomatic objective is to retain and increase support firstly from his own people, secondly from Saudi Arabia and the states bordering Israel, and thirdly from the rest of the Arab world. Palestinian supporters in the West often say that if Arafat shaved more often, wore a tie, and occasionally took off his keffiyeh, he would be more successful in attracting the support of Western public opinion. But, rightly or wrongly, Arafat is more interested in Arab and Palestinian public opinion; he is an Arab and he prefers to dress like one.

As Arafat's stature increased after he became leader of the P.L.O., he began to make more international contacts. But there is little evidence that either Fatah or the P.L.O. have fought on behalf of revolutionary movements in other parts of the world. Certainly they have given military training to groups such as the Eritrean Liberation Front, but they have never fought in Eritrea.

Other recipients of Fatah training were the Iranian guerrillas of the Ayatollah Khomeini who played a crucial role in the overthrow of the Shah in 1979. Commandos from Eritrea and Iran have also been trained by the Saiqa organization, whose aid is naturally restricted to the revolutionary movements supported at any particular moment by the Syrian government. These have included the Polisario Front in the Western Sahara, guerrilla organizations in Dhofar, Djibouti, Mozambique and Rhodesia, and opposition groups in Egypt and Turkey.

The P.F.L.P. and its offshoots have much closer links with international revolutionary movements than Fatah or Saiqa but they still suffer from the Soviet Union's ambiguity over the Palestine question and also from Russian disapproval of terrorism. Since the P.F.L.P. recommends revolution in most of the Arab world, its support in the area is limited. Iraq and Libya are its only backers and both of them are unreliable. The Front's one consistent ally is South Yemen, whose present rulers were once a part of Habash's Arab Nationalist Movement. Among revolutionary groups in the Arab world, the P.F.L.P. enjoys close ties with the Popular Front for the Liberation of Oman and the Arabian Gulf but with few others. Faced with a general reluctance among the Arab countries to support his concept of a people's war, Habash has therefore turned to other regions of the world for support. From North Korea he receives political and military backing and from the Japanese Red Army he has found active military support. Since 1972, when members of the organization attacked Lydda airport on behalf of the P.F.L.P. and killed a large number of airline passengers, the Red Army has wanted to extend its operations in the Middle East. During 1974 and 1975 it offered to assist Saiqa in any hijacking operations it might be considering – an offer that Zuheir Mohsen politely refused – and in 1979 it was again discussing possible operations with the P.F.L.P.

'Official' communist support for the resistance has been complicated by the Soviet Union's ambivalent approach to the Palestine problem. In 1947 the U.S.S.R. voted in favour of the partition of Palestine and during the war of the following year it provided the state of Israel with large quantities of arms from Czechoslovakia. The Russians thus became committed to the existence of Israel and they did not complain when the Zionists emerged in 1949 with much wider borders than they had been allotted by the U.N. During the fifties, as Israel's relations with the West became closer, the Soviet Union began backing the nationalist Arab regimes against Britain and the United States. It also started to criticize Israel for ill-treating its Arab minority. This criticism became more strident during the sixties and, after the 1967 war, the Russians broke off diplomatic relations. But, despite the opposition of the Arab world, they remained supporters of Israel's right to exist as a Zionist state. It was this fundamental disagreement over the objectives of the Palestinian struggle which in the early years prevented the Soviet Union from supporting the resistance.

Throughout the fifties the Russians treated the Palestinian issue as a refugee problem without a political dimension. It was not until 1964 that Khrushchev first talked about the 'the inalienable and lawful rights of the Palestinian Arabs.'[1] The Soviet Union was sceptical and reserved about the P.L.O. from its establishment, and, when the first delegation went to Moscow in 1970, it was met not by government officials but by the Soviet Afro-Asian Solidarity Committee. The Russians were worried by the P.L.O.'s lack of unity and by the incessant squabbling between the factions. They were also distressed and embarrassed by its use of terrorism and they disagreed with its ultimate aim. For the Soviet Union, committed to Israel's survival, to give full support to the P.L.O., which at that time called for a reunified Palestine, would have been nonsensical. It thus began to cultivate the moderates in the Palestinian leadership and to encourage them to accept a return to the pre-1967 borders. Avoiding Habash and Jibril, it began to give limited aid to Arafat and Fatah, to Saiqa's Zuheir Mohsen when Russian–Syrian relations were good, and also to Nayif Hawatmeh who, while an extremist on most issues, supported the idea of a Palestinian state in the West Bank and Gaza. But the Russians found all these groups rather unsatisfactory because none of them were prepared to follow the Soviet line or even to listen carefully to Soviet advice. But when, as a reaction, they set up their own guerrilla group, Ansar, both Habash and Arafat refused to allow it into the P.L.O. on the grounds that it was merely a Soviet instrument.

The Soviet Union's ambivalence over the P.L.O. is confirmed by Eastern European attitudes towards the resistance. Normally all six countries behind the Iron Curtain, except for Romania, follow the Soviet line on foreign affairs. But over the question of the P.L.O. there are two clear blocs. During the period of Arafat's great diplomatic gains in the early seventies, which culminated in his invitation to address the U.N. General Assembly in 1974, two distinct attitudes emerged within the Warsaw Pact countries. Hungary, Czechoslovakia and Poland continued to have reservations about the resistance and were even, on occasion, sharply critical of both its tactics and its ideology. These countries, which maintained little personal contact with Palestinian representatives, were perhaps even more hesitant and reserved than the Soviet Union itself. Bulgaria and East Germany, however, were unrestrained in their enthusiasm for the P.L.O. Both countries gave strong backing to the resistance and sent quantities of medical aid. They also encouraged frequent visits from P.L.O. delegations and there were several meetings between Arafat and the East German leader, Erich Honecker. In 1974 Honecker sent Arafat a telegram in which he declared that 'the Socialist Unity Party again stresses its limitless support for the P.L.O. in its struggle to attain the legitimate rights of the Palestinian Arab people.'[2]

These contrasting attitudes towards the P.L.O. may well have been part of a plan by which the Russians were able to keep their options open. The bulk of the Warsaw Pact countries, including the Soviet Union, kept their distance from the resistance partly in case it collapsed and partly because they did not wish to be associated too closely with P.L.O. tactics and objectives; meanwhile, Bulgaria and East Germany were ordered to give the P.L.O. 'limitless support' both in order to promote the Soviet Union's image in the Third World and to prevent China from establishing itself as the principal supporter of the Arab revolutionary movements.

China became a supporter of the Palestinian cause long before the Soviet Union, a fact that the Chinese leadership enjoys pointing out. In 1964 it accepted the idea of 'a Palestinian nation' and the following year it became the first major power to recognize the P.L.O. The Chinese understood that the Palestinian issue was a political question as well as a refugee problem and they liked to compare the Zionist state to Chiang Kai-Shek's regime in Taiwan. In 1965 Mao Tse-Tung told a Palestinian delegation: 'Imperialism is afraid of China and of the Arabs. Israel and Formosa are bases of imperialism in Asia. You are the front gate of the great continent, and we are the rear. They created Israel for you, and Formosa for us. Their goal is the same. . . . Asia is the biggest continent in the world, and the West wants to continue exploiting it.'[3]

This was the sort of talk which appealed to George Habash who later said: 'Our best friend is China. China wants Israel erased from the map because, as long as Israel exists, there will remain an aggressive imperialist outpost on Arab soil.'[4] But although Habash's own ideology was much closer to Maoism than Arafat's, the Chinese made it clear that the bulk of their support would go to Fatah. They took a realistic view of the P.L.O.'s potential and strongly urged the guerrilla organizations to unite. Suspecting Hawatmeh of being too pro-Soviet, and disagreeing with Habash's use of terrorism, they concentrated on providing weapons and instructions for Fatah. These were provided absolutely free and long before supplies were sent by the Soviet Union or its allies. In addition, the Chinese, unlike the Russians, made no stipulations about the politics or the policies (except over terrorism) which they wanted the Palestinians to follow. It was not surprising therefore that Arafat should later claim that China was 'the biggest influence in supporting our revolution and strengthening its perseverance.'[5]

In no area of the world have the Palestinians made so much diplomatic progress during the last decade as in black Africa. Until 1967 the continent south of the Sahara showed little interest in the affairs of the Middle East. Most African countries were just emerging from colonial rule and were too concerned with their own problems to take a stand on the Arab—Israeli conflict. Nor were the Arab countries much interested in African affairs. In fact the Middle Eastern country most active in black Africa from the period of Ghana's independence in 1957 to the June war ten years later was undoubtedly Israel. Rebuffed in Asia, the Israelis needed diplomatic support in the developing world and they concentrated their efforts on Africa and Latin America. In both continents they made allies through expensive programmes of military and technical aid but in Africa they made a number of potential enemies by siding with right-wing countries or movements backed by the colonial powers. They supported France in the Algerian war of independence and Tshombe in the Katanga uprising. They also backed Biafra against Nigeria and their other allies in Africa in-

cluded Houphouët-Boigny of the Ivory Coast, Haile Selassie of
Ethiopia and Hastings Banda of Malawi.[6]

Left-wing African leaders like Julius Nyerere of Tanzania,
Sekou Touré of Guinea and Kwame Nkrumah of Ghana were
strongly critical of Zionism but it was not until after 1967 that they
came to regard Israel as an expansionist and colonialist state. During the early seventies, as Israel showed no signs of withdrawing
from the territory of an African state (Egypt) and, worse, proved
itself to be a friend of South Africa, black African countries began
to reconsider their positions on the Middle East. This was accompanied by an Arab diplomatic offensive led by Algeria and Libya.
At a meeting of the heads of state of the Organization of African
Unity in May 1973, President Boumedienne of Algeria declared:
'Africa cannot adopt one attitude towards colonialism in Southern
Africa and a completely different one towards Zionist colonization in North Africa.'[7] However, even before that date, African
countries had begun breaking off diplomatic relations with Israel.
During 1972 and 1973 – before people in the West began to rethink
their attitudes on the Middle East in the light of the October war
and the oil embargo – Uganda, Chad, Congo, Niger, Mali, Burun-
di, Togo and Zaïre all severed diplomatic ties with Israel. And at
the meeting in May 1973 the O.A.U. adopted a resolution declaring that respect for the inalienable rights of the Palestinian people
was essential for any just and equitable solution of the problem of
the Middle East.

By the end of the seventies the Palestinians could count on win-
ning victories over the Zionists in almost any international forum.
They had the Islamic world, stretching from Mauritania to
Pakistan, behind them, most of the rest of Asia, black Africa and
the communist countries. They were also receiving increased sup-
port in the West, from European nations such as France, Austria,
Spain and Portugal, and from a growing number of Latin
American countries: Argentina, Brazil, Cuba, Grenada, Guyana,
Mexico, and Trinidad and Tobago. By December 1979 Arafat had
been officially received by the prime ministers or heads of state of
Spain, Portugal and Austria while the P.L.O. foreign affairs
spokesman, Farouk Qaddoumi, had met the foreign ministers of
Italy and Belgium. By contrast with this diplomatic success, Israel
could only rely on a handful of supporters: Chile, South Africa,
Haiti, Honduras, Costa Rica and the United States. Even

Nicaragua changed its position after the fall of the dictator, General Somoza.

So the circle has been completed. As early as 1919 the League of Nations had accepted, in principle, the Palestinians' right to nationhood and in 1947 the United Nations had committed itself to the establishment of an Arab state in Palestine. But in the quarter century that followed the establishment of Israel, the political rights of the Palestinians were ignored by the international community. It was not until 1974 that the U.N. woke up and acknowledged that they still had those rights. In September of that year the U.N. General Assembly described these as follows: 'The right to self-determination without external interference; the right to national independence and sovereignty . . . [and] the inalienable rights of the Palestinians to return to their homes.' The Assembly also recognized 'that the Palestinian people is a principal party in the establishment of a just and lasting peace in the Middle East' and 'the right of the Palestinian people to regain its rights by all means in accordance with the purposes and principles of the Charter of the United Nations.'[8]

By 1974, therefore, the United Nations had at last recognized the justice of the Palestinians' struggle for their rights of national self-determination and sovereignty. Even countries which opposed or abstained on the resolution have since accepted the need for Palestinian self-determination. At a press conference in Cairo on 28 December 1977 Chancellor Schmidt of West Germany declared: 'We Germans feel that the Palestinian people are entitled to self-determination as much as any other people in the world, as much as we Germans.' Even the United States, whose indiscriminate support for Israel has obstructed a settlement for so long, has been converted to the view that the Palestinians must have some sort of a homeland. President Carter's statements on the Middle East have often been inconsistent and contradictory but he has accepted the notion in principle. 'There has to be a homeland provided for the Palestinian refugees who have suffered for many, many years,' he told an audience in Massachusetts on 17 March 1977. On 4 January 1978 at Aswan, he declared: 'There must be a resolution to the Palestinian problem in all its aspects. The problem must recognize the legitimate rights of the Palestinian people and enable the Palestinians to participate in the determination of their own future.' The Andrew Young incident in the summer of 1979 in-

dicated how much American public opinion was changing on the
Palestine issue. Young's resignation from his post as American
representative at the U.N., which was demanded by Israeli supporters merely because he had had a conversation with the P.L.O.
representative, created an uproar throughout the United States.

More than thirty years after their dispersal, the world has at last
agreed that the injustice done to the Arabs of Palestine must be
rectified. It has finally accepted that the Palestinians constitute a
separate people and should have their own home – not a Bantustan
patrolled by the Israeli army but a proper home. They must have a
state, not one that displaces Israel but one that can live alongside
it. Such a solution will necessarily involve sacrifices, not from
Israel and the Zionists, but from the Palestinians themselves.
Seventy-seven per cent of historic Palestine is Israel and the remaining twenty-three per cent, which includes the Old City of Jerusalem,
is under Israeli occupation. But the Palestinians now accept Israel's
1948 conquests and annexations – unjust though they were – and
have made it clear that they are prepared to accept an independent
state in that small fragment of their land occupied in 1967.

And even if some Palestinians do still dream of the eventual
peaceful reunification of their country, so that Jews and Arabs can
live there together in peace, is that not a worthy dream, something
to hope for in the next century? They know that it is not possible
now, because the Zionist ideology is too intolerant to accommodate them, but they believe that the successors of Begin and
Dayan must one day recognize that the legal inhabitants of a country should enjoy the right to live in it. For the present, and for the
foreseeable future, the Palestinians – or at any rate the vast
majority of them – are prepared to forget their dream and accept a
compromise and the partition of their country.

The creation of a state in the West Bank and Gaza is the least
that the world can now do for the Palestinians. It cannot represent
full justice and it will not undo the harm done to them over so
many years. But it will restore to them their nationhood – they will
be able to feel that they do belong somewhere, that they can function as a nation in their own land like other peoples.

Sixty years ago their right to all of Palestine was recognized.
Thirty years ago they were offered half of it. Now, when they are
prepared to settle for less than a quarter, surely their case is
unanswerable.

Epilogue:
Beirut '82

It is more than two years since I wrote those last words on the previous page. Nothing that has happened in the intervening period has made that conclusion any less relevant. Indeed, the events of those years have only underlined the need to find a genuine solution to the Palestine question, a solution that is necessary not only to end the nightmare sufferings of the Palestinian people but also to bring peace to an area where continuous warfare is threatening the stability of the whole world.

The main development of the last two years has been the escalation of Israel's vendetta against the Palestinians. This has been pursued with such single-minded ferocity that even Israel's remaining friends in the West have been astonished by it. Many of them find it difficult to understand how the 'liberal, democratic' state they had supported for so long could have become the monster which in a single year (June 1981 – June 1982) attacked Baghdad, annexed Golan, devastated Lebanon and shot students in the West Bank. But it was the scale and not the direction of Israel's behaviour which had changed. It was not as if the state had suddenly produced a new and ruthless brand of leadership, because most of its leading figures have violent backgrounds that go back thirty or forty years. Begin and his foreign minister, Yitzhak Shamir, are old terrorists of the 1940s with dozens of British as well as Arab lives to their credit, while Ariel Sharon, the defence minister, used to command the notorious Unit 101, responsible, among other atrocities, for the massacre of the villagers of Qibya in 1953.

During the last two years Israel's war against the Palestinians has been directed against both the inhabitants of the Occupied Territories and the refugee population of Lebanon. The long process of colonization has been accelerated and Jewish settlements can now be found in almost every district of the West Bank. Forty per cent of the area, which, excluding Jerusalem, houses some 700,000 Arabs and 25,000 Jewish settlers, has been expropriated by Israel. At the same time Sharon has tried to destroy the Arab leadership of the West Bank by dismissing the most prominent Palestinian mayors. After the expulsion of the mayors of Hebron and Halhul in 1980, three other mayors were removed in the spring of 1982. Two of them, Bassam Shaka'a of Nablus and Karim Khalaf of Ramallah, were the crippled survivors of car-bomb attacks by Jewish extremists in the summer of 1980.[1]

Neither Begin nor Sharon took much trouble to conceal the motives behind this policy. The continuous grabbing of Arab land and the dismissal of Palestinian leaders were simply designed to facilitate the eventual annexation of the Occupied Territories. To this end Israel has also tried, with scant success, to establish an 'alternative' leadership on the West Bank of Arab quislings. It was no doubt partly because the great majority of Palestinians paid no attention to this handful of collaborators and remained loyal to the PLO that the Israeli government set out to destroy the guerrilla organisation in Lebanon. Begin and Sharon realised that the elimination of the Palestinians' political leadership in Beirut would make it easier to absorb the Arabs of the Occupied Territories into a Greater Israel or, if the opportunity arose, to expel them altogether.

Israel's murderous assault on Lebanon at the beginning of June 1982 was not the first piece of Zionist aggression against the Lebanese people, nor was Menachem Begin the first prime minister to contemplate an invasion of the country. Anyone who has read the biography of David Ben Gurion will see the invasion less as an act of vengeance against the PLO than as the realisation of a long-held ambition. In 1948 Ben Gurion wrote in his diary that the Lebanese government should be overthrown: 'a Christian state ought to be set us there, with its southern frontier on the Litani'.[1] Eight years later he went into more detail, emphasising that Israel would extend its border to the Litani river.[2] The diaries of Moshe Sharett, Israel's foreign minister between 1948 and 1956, reveal that Ben Gurion, like his chief of staff Moshe Dayan, was obsessed by the idea of intervening in Lebanon. In 1955 Sharett described one of their proposals: 'According to Dayan the only thing that's necessary is to find a Lebanese officer, even a major will do. We should either win his heart or buy him with money to get him to agree to declare himself the saviour of the Maronite population. Then the Israeli army will enter Lebanon, occupy the necessary territory and create a Christian regime which will ally itself with Israel. The territory from the Litani southward will be totally annexed to Israel. [Dayan] recommends this be done immediately, tomorrow. . .'[3]

This extract is worth quoting at length because the policy put forward in 1955 was so faithfully carried out twenty-seven years later. Ben Gurion is dead and so is Dayan but the policy remains, even if it has finally been carried out in a manner more barbarous than even they would have contemplated. 'Even a major will do,' Dayan had said and he was right. In 1978, when the Israeli army withdrew after its first invasion, Saad Haddad, a rebel Lebanese major, was installed as an Israeli puppet in southern Lebanon.

Israeli military action against Lebanon began after the 1967 war and has continued ever since. To begin with, it was on a relatively small scale: troops were landed at Beirut airport to blow up Lebanon's civilian airliners, assassination squads were sent to kill PLO leaders and Skyhawks were repeatedly ordered in to bomb the refugee camps (see pp. 186, 190). Then, in 1977, Begin became prime minister and shortly afterwards he ordered a full-scale invasion of Lebanon. As the Israeli army rampaged around the south of the country in the spring of 1978, scores of villages were destroyed, thousands of civilians killed, and a quarter of a million people made homeless. No country could have been expected to survive such pressure with its society and institutions unharmed — least of all a country trying to recover from a terrible civil war.

Israel's behaviour towards Lebanon during the seventies is not difficult to explain. At the beginning of the decade it followed the policy already successfully carried out in Jordan: to create such turmoil and instability in the country that the government would eventually order its armed forces to put down the PLO. When this policy failed, Israel decided to arm the Phalangists and other Maronite militias in order to encourage them to do the job. Although the Phalangists relished the opportunity, they were in practice unable to defeat either the PLO or their Lebanese allies and were only saved from complete disaster by the intervention of the Syrian army in 1976 (see pp. 204–8). It was in view of the failure or reluctance of the Lebanese to crush the Palestinians that Begin decided to do it himself. The first attempt was made in 1978 and the second in 1982.

It is only against this background of aggression that the attack on Beirut can be understood. Without it the invasion would seem not only criminal but crazy as well. Israel termed its aggression 'Operation Peace for Galilee' and claimed that it was ensuring the security of its northern settlements. But Galilee was at peace and its security not in question. There had been a ceasefire on the Lebanese border from July 1981 until May of the following year when the Israeli air force bombed Beirut. During that time the PLO had not once broken the ceasefire and no Israeli from the Galilee settlements had even been wounded by the Palestinians.[4] To pretend that the PLO really posed a serious threat to northern Israel is merely ridiculous; so is the suggestion that the invasion was in retaliation for the attempted assassination of the Israeli ambassador in London. Each of these assertions, immediately put forward by Israeli spokesmen, was a weak and unconvincing pretext for a war that had obviously been prepared long in advance.

In its previous wars Israel's main enemy had been the armies of the neighbouring Arab countries. In this, its fifth and bloodiest campaign so far, there was only one real enemy: the Palestine Liberation Organisation. Although Syria's army, stationed in the Beqa'a valley south-east of Beirut, was involved in some fighting with the advancing Israelis, and although its air force sustained some heavy losses, the Syrian role in the war was a peripheral one.

On 6 June an Israeli army of 30,000 men surged across the Lebanese frontier, brushed aside the United Nations peace-keeping force UNIFIL, and engaged the Palestinians on three fronts. After heavy hand-to-hand fighting Beaufort Castle was captured and shortly afterwards the Israelis took the town of Nabatiya. On the coast Tyre and Sidon were bombed from the sea and air and further north the town of Damour was besieged. Although bitter fighting continued behind their lines during the following weeks, the Israelis were on the outskirts of Beirut by 10 June. The devastation had been astounding. Israel subsequently claimed that great care had been taken to avoid civilian casualties, but it was hardly a claim that could be taken seriously by Western television audiences. You only had to look at news bulletins and see the debris of shattered Sidon to realise the extent of Israeli 'care'. Most of Tyre had similarly been razed, as well as the large refugee camp of Ain el-Hilweh. A fortnight after the invasion had started, the International Red Cross estimated that 14,000 people had been killed and 20,000 wounded, the great majority of them Lebanese and Palestinian civilians who had been the victims of Israeli air attacks. 'Operation Peace for Galilee' had become simply a massacre although Israel and its apologists in the West continued to deny it. The Israeli embassy in London made the incredible claim that throughout the whole operation 'the Israel defence forces took maximum precautions to ensure that the civilian population would not be harmed'.[5] It is difficult to think of any other country calling itself liberal and democratic which has invaded its neighbour, massacred the civilian population at a ratio of sixty to one (about sixty dead Arabs for every dead Israeli soldier) and has then had the effrontery to claim that it has been doing its utmost not to hurt civilians.

Although Begin's declared war aim had been to clear the Palestinians to an area twenty-five miles from the Israeli border, it soon transpired — as Israeli armoured columns raced towards Beirut — that this was merely another ruse to deceive world opinion. The aim was now the total expulsion of the PLO from Lebanon. If the Palestinians refused to go, Begin and Sharon were fond of repeating, then the Israeli army would go into Beirut and eliminate them. Over the following weeks, while the United States tried desperately to arrange the evacuation of the guerrillas, Israel kept up the pressure by mounting a series of devastating aerial and artillery attacks on the districts of West Beirut.

The bombardment of Beirut was one of the most horrific events of recent history. Day after day Israeli gunners sat outside the city lobbing thousands of shells into the densely packed apartment blocks. From the sea the Israeli navy pounded the coastal districts while F-16 aeroplanes screeched overhead, terrorising the population and levelling whole buildings. According to the *Sunday Times*, among the targets hit by the Israelis in the two months following their arrival in Beirut were 'five UN buildings, 134 embassies or diplomatic residences, six hospitals or clinics, one mental institute, the Central Bank, five hotels, the Red Cross, Lebanese and foreign media outlets and innumerable private homes'.[6] Apart from the 6,000 PLO guerrillas in the besieged city there were some half million Lebanese and Palestinian civilians, and every day of the bombardment about 200 or 300 of them were killed. Many of them were burnt to death by phosphorous bombs. The Canadian ambassador, Theodore Arcand, said that the destruction was so comprehensive it 'would make Berlin of 1944 look like a tea party'.[7]

Throughout this savage attack Menachem Begin ranted about the momory of the Nazis and the history of the holocaust: in a letter to President Reagan he compared Arafat in Beirut to Hitler in his bunker. But to most people the comparison seemed inappropriate: if there was a parallel to be drawn it was with Warsaw in 1944.

As the bombardment went on day after day, the international community looked on incredulously, mesmerised by the savagery of the Israeli action. The EEC, the UN Security Council and other bodies made ritual condemnations while the United States remonstrated weakly with its protégé and was brusquely snubbed. The most feeble reaction of all came from the Arab world which seemed petrified into silence and inaction. Beirut, the birthplace of Arab nationalism and for long the intellectual and commercial capital of the Arab world, was being pulverised by a brutal foreign army while the Arab states did nothing. Palestine, the sacred cause upheld for decades by the Arab nation, was suddenly abandoned and no Arab army came to help the beleaguered PLO garrison in West Beirut. For the Arabs it was a shameful and humiliating episode, one that marked the decadence of the Arab nationalist ideal and one that is bound to have repercussions throughout the Arab world.

The future of the region, and particularly of Lebanon itself, will depend on the true nature of Israel's war aims. It has long been clear that the object of the invasion was not simply to clear the PLO out of south Lebanon, or even to expel them from the country altogether. Israeli generals have often boasted that they could take on all the Arab armies at the same time and still destroy them, and the chief of staff has even claimed that he could defeat the armed forces of the Soviet Union.[9] It is therefore frivolous to claim that the PLO constituted a military threat to Israel and *for that reason* had to be destroyed. The war against the PLO was waged because Israel believed that the defeat of the organisation would shatter Palestinian nationalism for ever and make the annexation of the West Bank a comparatively straightforward task.

But behind the invasion there may have been other and more complicated causes as well. Shortly after the first assault Israeli spokesmen went into action to declare that their state did not covet a single inch of Lebanese soil. It is too early to judge the veracity of the remark but anyone who has been studying the statements of Israeli spokesmen over the years will be instantly reminded of the claim made by Levi Eshkol at the beginning of the 1967 war: Israel, said the prime minister, had no intention of annexing 'even one foot of Arab territory'. Three weeks later Arab Jerusalem and the surrounding villages were formally annexed, two years later the colonization of the West Bank and Gaza was begun, and fourteen years afterwards the Syrian Golan Heights were declared a part of Israel. Begin may or may not annex areas of Lebanon but the historical precedents are not good. Ben Gurion and Dayan had spent years urging their government to annex southern Lebanon as far as the Litani river but they did not prevail. In those days of Labour Party administrations in the 1950s Israel was a ruthless and uncompromising state. But compared with what it has become today it was moderate and reasonable, just as Ben Gurion and Dayan, two of the toughest politicians the twentieth century has produced, are moderate and almost 'dovish' when placed side by side with Begin, Sharon and Shamir.

It is too early to predict what Israel will finally do in Lebanon, and possibly its leaders have not yet made up their mind. No doubt they are waiting to see how much they can get away with. If neither the Americans nor anyone else stops them, they may annex southern Lebanon and channel the valuable Litani waters into northern Israel. As I have said, the Litani has long been an objective of Zionist policy, and engineering schemes for its diversion were drawn up many years ago.[10] However, if sufficient international pressure is exerted, it is possible that Israel will withdraw its army after installing a client regime in Beirut based on the Maronite Phalangist Party. Either way, yet another slice of Arab territory will have passed into Israeli control and yet another of Zion's expansionist dreams will have been fulfilled.

Looking at the invasion with as wide a perspective as it is now possible to have, it seems clear that Israel had two separate objectives: to take control, direct or indirect, of at least a part of Lebanon, and to shatter the Palestinian nationalist movement. Of the second aim, *The Observer* said in a leading article: 'Mr Begin and General Sharon had clearly planned a massacre, an attempt to destroy not only the PLO guerrillas as a fighting force but to break the political aspirations and will of the Palestinians as a nation or people.'[11] Dr Nahum Goldman, one of the pioneers of Zionism and a man who was for years president of both the World Jewish Congress and the World Zionist Organization, went even further: 'the apparent aim is to liquidate the Palestinian people — which you cannot do to four million people.'[12] And you cannot. The Israelis have expelled the Palestinians from their homes in 1948, in 1967 and in 1982. The have bombed their pitiful refugee camps on countless occasions presumably because they believe that if they go on killing Palestinians then one day Palestinian nationalism will disappear. But of course the opposite happens and the brutality of repression merely drives more people into open resistance.

It is impossible for the Palestinians to make peace with the present Israeli government, no matter how many concessions they make, because the Israelis do not accept that the Arabs have any right to any part of Palestine. If some Palestinians are going to continue living within the boundaries of historic Palestine then it is clear that they must do so on sufferance, because Israel allows them to do so, and not because it is their right. Begin has never accepted the UN Partition Plan and he and his party will never accept that Palestinians have a right to the state which the UN proposed for them in 1947. I am convinced that behind this rigid and inhuman attitude towards the Palestinians there sits an uneasy conscience, a deep-seated realisation in many Israelis that they dispossessed the country's inhabitants in 1948 and have treated them abominably every since. But most Israelis do not admit these things because to do so would be to question the legitimacy of their own position today. So they take the opposite way and do everything they can to vilify the Palestinians and to dehumanize them, to treat them as if they were beasts undeserving of the world's attention. That is why no Israeli official can refer to the Palestinians without calling them 'terrorists', 'animals' or 'bastards'.[13] That is why, for them, no compromise can ever be made with Palestinian nationalism.

This attitude was well illustrated by the reaction to Yasser Arafat's implicit recognition of Israel when he signed a statement prepared by US congressmen accepting 'all United Nations resolutions relevant to the Palestinian question'.[14] For a resistance leader to recognise a state which has usurped every inch of his homeland and driven more than half his people into exile is a uniquely moderate step. But there was no corresponding moderation on the Israeli side. The only useful thing the PLO could do, said the spokesman of the Israeli foreign ministry, was to disappear.[15] Palestine no longer existed and therefore there was no point in it having a liberation movement.

For years it has been obvious that Israel will never make peace with the Arabs unless compelled to do so. It is now more obvious than ever. Israel faces no immediate and substantial military threat from them and is unlikely to do so for a very long time. If no pressure is exerted on its government to come to terms with the Arabs, it will spend the next few years colonizing the remaining areas of the West Bank as a prelude to the annexation of the last remnants of Arab Palestine. Israel will then consist of all of Palestine, a part of Syria and perhaps parts of Lebanon and even Jordan as well. It will have become the most successful settler state since the United States exterminated the Red Indians of the American plains.

Whether this situation comes about or not depends on the United States, because no other country either has or can have a similar degree of control over Israel. As the late President Sadat used to say, in the Middle East labyrinth America has 99 per cent of the cards. However, because of the nature of its internal politics, it has so far refused to play them. In the next year or so the United States will have to make a crucial decision. If it allows Israel to retain its conquests, it will be jeopardising the survival of the West's Arab friends in the Middle East and inviting further wars and another oil embargo. If it finally accepts the UN principle of 'the inadmissibility of the acquisition of territory by war'[16] and persuades Israel to renounce its expansionist ambitions, it will be bringing peace to the area, safeguarding its own interests and, by persuading Israel to behave responsibly, securing the state's long-term future. It will also, partially and belatedly, be doing

something to alleviate the sufferings of the Palestinian people and
to compensate for the part played by America in their long and
unredeemed agony.

August 1982

Bibliography

Ibrahim Abu-Lughod (Ed), *The Transformation of Palestine,* North Western University Press, Evanston, 1971

M.F. Abcarius, *Palestine,* Hutchinson, London, 1946

Musa Alami (Ed), *The Future of Palestine* (Reprint), Hermon Books, Beirut 1970

Richard Allen, *Imperialism and Nationalism in the Fertile Crescent,* Oxford University Press, New York, 1974

Adnan Amad (Ed), *Israeli League for Human and Civil Rights* (The Shahak Papers), Near East Ecumenical Bureau for Information and Interpretation, Beirut, 1973

Amun, Davis, Sanallah, Elrazik and Amin (Ed), *Palestinian Arabs in Israel: Two Case Studies,* Ithaca Press, London, 1977

George Antonius, *The Arab Awakening: the story of the Arab national movement,* Khayats, Beirut, 1938

Uri Avnery, *Israel Without Zionists: A Plea for Peace in the Middle East,* Macmillan, London, 1968

Nevill Barbour, *Nisi Dominus: A Survey of the Palestine Controversy,* George G. Harrap, London, 1946

Xavier Baron, *Les Palestinians: Un Peuple,* Le Sycomore, Paris, 1977

Gabriel Ben-Dor (Ed), *The Palestinians and the Middle East Conflict,* Turtledove, Ramat Gan, 1976

David Ben-Gurion, *Israel: A Personal History,* Funk and Wagnalls, New York, 1971

Elmer Berger, *Who knows better must say so!* American Council for Judaism, 1955

Nicholas Bethell, *The Palestine Triangle: The struggle between the British, the Jews and the Arabs 1935-48,* Andre Deutsch, London, 1979

Robert Brenton Betts, *Christians in the Arab East,* SPCK, London, 1979

Robert Briscoe with Alden Hatch, *For the Life of Me,* Little, Brown and Company, Boston, 1958

J.S. Buckingham, *Travels in Palestine,* Longman, Hurst, Kees, Orme and Brown, London, 1821

John Bulloch, *Death of a Country: The Civil War in Lebanon,* Weidenfeld and Nicolson, London, 1977

John Bulloch, *The Making of a War: the Middle East from 1967 to 1973*, Longman, London, 1974

E.L.M. Burns, *Between Arab and Israeli*, George G. Harrap, London, 1962

Henry Cattan, *Palestine in International Law*, Longman, London, 1973

Henry Cattan, *Palestine, the Arabs and Israel*, Longman, London, 1969

Henry Cattan, *Palestine, the Road to Peace*, Longman, London, 1970

Gerard Chaliand, *The Palestinian Resistance*, Penguin, London, 1972

Erskine B. Childers, *The Road to Suez*, MacGibbon and Kee, London, 1962

Abner Cohen, *Arab Border Villages in Israel*, University Press, Manchester, 1965

John Cooley, *Green March, Black September: The Story of the Palestinian Arabs*, Frank Cass, London, 1973

C.R. Conder, *Palestine*, George Philip and Son, London, 1889

John H. Davis, *The Evasive Peace: A Study of the Zionist–Arab Problem*, John Murray, London, 1968

Davis, Mack and Yuval – Davis (Eds), *Israel and the Palestinians*, Ithaca Press, London, 1975

Jonathan Dimbleby, *The Palestinians*, Quartet, London, 1979

Peggy Duff (Ed), *War or Peace in the Middle East?* Spokesman, London, 1978

Abba Eban, *My country: The Story of Modern Israel*, Weidenfeld and Nicolson, London, 1972

Fouzi El-Asmar, *To be an Arab in Israel*, Institute for Palestine Studies, Beirut, 1978

Amos Elon, *The Israelis: Fathers and Sons*, Weidenfeld and Nicolson, London, 1971

Frank H. Epp, *The Palestinians: Portrait of a People in Conflict*, McClelland and Stewart, Toronto, 1976

Mrs Stewart Erskine, *Palestine of the Arabs*, George G. Harrap, London, 1935

Robin Fedden, *Syria and Lebanon* (3rd edition), John Murray, London, 1965

Geoffrey Furlonge, *Palestine is My Country: The Story of Musa Alami*, John Murray, London, 1969

Maxim Ghilan, *How Israel lost its Soul*, Penguin, London, 1974

Martin Gilbert, *Exile and Return: The Emergence of Jewish Statehood*, Weidenfeld and Nicolson, London, 1978

Sir John Glubb, *Peace in the Holy Land: An historical analysis of the Palestine Problem*, Hodder and Stoughton, London, 1971

Sir John Glubb, *A Soldier with the Arabs*, Hodder and Stoughton, London, 1957

A. Goodrich-Freer, *Arabs in Tent and Town*, Seeley, Service and Co. Ltd., London, 1924

A. Granott, *The Land System in Palestine: History and Structure*, Eyre and Spottiswode, London, 1952

Sami Hadawi, *Bitter Harvest: Palestine 1914–1967*, New World Press, New York, 1967

Jean-Pierre Haddad, *Le Combat du Liban*, Henri Couchon, Paris, 1977

Mohamed Heikal, *Sphinx and Commissar: The Rise and Fall of Soviet Influence in the Middle East*, Collins, London, 1978

Mohamed Heikal, *The Road to Ramadan*, Collins, London, 1975

The Complete Diaries of Theodor Herzl, Herzl Press and Thomas Yoseloff, New York, 1960

David Hirst, *The Gun and the Olive Branch: The Roots of Violence in the Middle East*, Faber and Faber, London, 1977

Albert Hourani, *Minorities in the Arab World,* Oxford University Press, London, 1946

Harry Howard, *The King—Crane Commission,* Khayyats, Beirut, 1963

Michael Hudson, *The Electoral Process and Political Development in Lebanon,* New York, 1962

Doreen Ingrams, *Palestine Papers 1917—1922: Seeds of Conflict,* John Murray, London, 1972

Michael Ionides, *Divide and Lose: The Arab Revolt of 1955—1958,* Geoffrey Bles, London, 1960

Tareq Y. Ismael, *The Arab Left,* Syracuse University Press, New York, 1976

Halim Said Abu-Izzedin (Ed), *Lebanon and its Provinces,* Kayyats, Beirut, 1963

G.H. Jansen, *Zionism, Israel and Asian Nationalism,* Institute for Palestine Studies, Beirut, 1971

Sabri Jiryis, *The Arabs in Israel,* Monthly Review Press, New York, 1968

Sabri Jiryis, *Democratic Freedoms in Israel,* Institute for Palestine Studies, Beirut, 1972

Christina Jones, *The Untempered Wind: Forty Years in Palestine,* Longman, London, 1975

Dov Joseph, *The Faithful City: The Siege of Jerusalem, 1948,* the Hogarth Press, London, 1961

Paul A. Jureidini and William E. Hazen, *The Palestinian Movement in Politics,* D.C. Heath and Co., Lexington, 1976

A.W. Kayyali, *Palestine: A Modern History,* Croom Helm, London, 1978

A.W. Kayyali (Ed), *Zionism, Imperialism and Racism,* Croom Helm, London, 1979

Walid W. Kazziha, *Palestine in the Arab Dilemma,* Croom Helm, London, 1979

Leila Khaled, *My People Shall Live: The autobiography of a Revolutionary,* Hodder and Stoughton, London, 1973

Walid Khalidi (Ed), *From Haven to Conquest: Readings in Zionism and the Palestine Problem until 1948,* Institute for Palestine Studies, Beirut, 1971

Jon Kimche, *Seven Fallen Pillars: The Middle East, 1915—1950,* Secker and Warburg, London, 1950

Jon and David Kimche, *Both Sides of the Hill: Britain and the Palestine War,* Secker and Warburg, London, 1960

Khalid Kishtainy, *Palestine in Perspective,* Palestine Research Centre, Beirut, 1971

Arthur Koestler, *Promise and Fulfilment,* Macmillan, London, 1949

Arthur Kutcher, *The New Jerusalem,* Thames and Hudson, London, 1973

Felicia Langer, *With my own eyes,* Ithaca Press, London, 1975

Felicia Langer, *These are my brothers,* Ithaca Press, London, 1979

Walter Z. Laqueur (Ed), *The Middle East in Transition,* Routledge and Kegan Paul, London, 1958

Harry Levin, *Jerusalem Embattled,* Victor Gollancz, London, 1950

Alfred M. Lilienthal, *What Price Israel?* Institute for Palestine Studies, Beirut, 1969

Netanel Lorch, *Israel's War of Independence, 1947—1949,* Hartmore House, Hartford, 1968

Kennett Love, *Suez: The Twice-Fought War,* McGraw Hill, New York, 1969

Luke and Keith Roach, *The Handbook of Palestine and Transjordan,* Macmillan, London, 1930

Peter Mansfield, *The Arabs,* Allen Lane, London, 1976

Peter Mansfield, *The Middle East* (4th edition), Oxford University Press, London, 1973

Moshe Ma'oz (Ed), *Palestinian Arab Politics,* Jerusalem Academic Press, Jerusalem, 1975

John Marlowe, *The Seat of Pilate,* Cresset Press, London, 1959

Christopher Mayhew and Michael Adams, *Publish it not . . .: The Middle East Cover-up,* Longman, London, 1975

Moshe Menuhin, *The Decadence of Judaism in Our Time,* Institute for Palestine Studies, Beirut, 1969

M.R. Mehdi, *A Palestine Chronicle,* Alpha Publishing Company, London, 1973

James Morris, *The Hashemite Kings,* Faber and Faber, London, 1959

H.V. Muhsam, *Bedouin of the Negev: Eight Demographic Studies,* Jerusalem Academic Press, 1966

George T. Murray, *Lebanon: The New Future,* Thomson Rizk, Beirut, 1974

Nafez Nazzal, *The Palestinian Exodus from Galilee 1948,* Institute for Palestine Studies, Beirut, 1978

Jorgen Nielsen, (Ed), *International Documents on Palestine 1972,* Institute for Palestine Studies, Beirut, 1975

Francis E. Newton, *Fifty Years in Palestine,* Coldharbour Press, Wrotham, 1948

Laurence Oliphant, *Haifa or Life in Modern Palestine,* William Blackwood and Sons, Edinburgh, 1887

Roger Owen (Ed), *Essays on the Crisis in Lebanon,* Ithaca Press, London, 1976

Don Peretz, *Israel and the Palestine Arabs,* The Middle East Institute, Washington, 1958

Stewart Perowne, *The One Remains,* Hodder and Stoughton, London, 1954

Polk, Stamler and Asfour, *Backdrop to Tragedy: The Stuggle for Palestine,* Beacon Press, Boston, 1957

Y. Porath, *The Emergence of the Palestinian−Arab National Movement 1918−1929,* Frank Cass, London, 1974

Y. Porath, *The Palestinian Arab National Movement 1929−1939: From Riots to Rebellion,* Frank Cass, London, 1977

William Quandt, Fuad Jabber, Ann Mosely Lesch, *The Politics of Palestinian Nationalism,* University of California Press, Berkeley, 1973

Fahim I. Qubain, *Crisis in Lebanon,* The Middle East Institute, Washington, 1961

Yitzhak Rabin, *The Rabin Memoirs,* Weidenfeld and Nicolson, London, 1979

Riad El-Rayyes and Dunia Nahas, *Guerrillas for Palestine,* Croom Helm, London, 1976

Maxime Rodinson, *Israel and the Arabs,* Penguin, London, 1968

Carlos P. Romulo, *I Walked with Heroes,* Holk, Rinehart and Winston, New York, 1961

Edward Said, *Orientalism,* Routledge and Kegan Paul, London, 1979

Edward Said, *The Question of Palestine,* Routledge and Kegan Paul, London, 1980

Elie Adib Salem, *Modernisation without Revolution: Lebanon's Experience,* Indiana University Press, Bloomington, 1973

Kamal S. Salibi, *Crossroads to Civil War: Lebanon 1958−1976,* Ithaca Press, London, 1965

Kamal S. Salibi, *The Modern History of Lebanon,* Weidenfeld and Nicolson, London, 1965

Rosemary Sayigh, *Palestinians: From Peasants to Revolutionaries,* Zed Press, London, 1979

Walter Schwarz, *The Arabs in Israel,* Faber and Faber, London, 1959

Sarah Searight, *The British in the Middle East,* East—West Publications, London, 1979

Israel Shahak (Ed), *The Non-Jew in the Jewish State,* 2 Bartenura Street, Jerusalem, 1975

George Adam Smith, *The Historical Geography of the Holy Land* (25th edition), Fontana Library of Theology and Philosophy (reprint), London, 1966

Sir Edward Spears, *Fulfilment of a Mission: Syria and Lebanon 1941–1944,* Leo Cooper, London, 1977

Desmond Stewart, *The Middle East: Temple of Janus,* Hamish Hamilton, London, 1972

Desmond Stewart, *Turmoil in Beirut,* Allan Wingate, London, 1958

Richard P. Stevens, *Zionism and Palestine before the Mandate: A phase of Western Imperialism,* Institute for Palestine Studies, Beirut, 1972

W.F. Stirling, *Safety Last,* Hollis and Carter, London, 1953

Louise E. Sweet (Ed), *Peoples and Cultures of the Middle East* (Vol. 2) Natural History Press, New York, 1970

Christopher Sykes, *Cross Roads to Israel: Palestine from Balfour to Begin,* Collins, London, 1965

Alan R. Taylor, *Prelude to Israel: An Analysis of Zionist Diplomacy 1891–1947,* Philosophical Library, New York, 1959

A.L. Tibawi, *Anglo-Arab Relations and the Question of Palestine,* Luzac Co, London, 1977

A.L. Tibawi, *A Modern History of Syria, including Lebanon and Palestine,* Macmillan, London, 1969

Fawaz Turki, *The Disinherited: Journal of a Palestinian Exile,* Monthly Review Press, New York, 1972

Brian Van Arkadie, *Benefits and Burdens: A Report on the West Bank and Gaza Strip Economies Since 1967,* Carnegie Endowment for International Peace, Washington, 1977

Chaim Weizmann: Excerpts from his Historic Statements, Writings and Addresses, The Jewish Agency for Palestine, New York, 1952

Edmund Wilson, *Black, Red, Blond and Olive,* OUP, London, 1956

N.A. Ziadeh, *Syria and Lebanon,* Ernest Benn, London, 1957

Notes

Introduction

1 J.S. Buckingham, *Travels in Palestine*, Longman, Hurst, Kees, Orme and Brown, London, 1821. From the introduction.
2 Memorandum to Lord Curzon. Public Record Office, FO 371/4183.
3 Quoted in Moshe Menuhin, *The Decadence of Judaism in Our Time*, 2nd impr., Institute for Palestine Studies, Beirut, 1969, pp. 64–5.
4 Interview with Frank Giles in *The Sunday Times*, 15 June 1969.
5 *Ha'Aretz,* 9 September 1974. Quoted in David Hirst, *The Gun and the Olive Branch,* Faber and Faber, London, 1977, p. 265.
6 See 'George Walker at Suez' in Trollope's *Tales of All Countries,* Chapman and Hall, London, 1863.
7 Quoted in M. F. Abcarius, *Palestine,* Hutchinson, London, 1946, p. 19.
8 Redcliffe N. Salaman, 'The Prospects of Jewish Colonization in Palestine', *Contemporary Review,* No. 653 (May 1920).
9 Letter of 30 May 1918, quoted in Doreen Ingrams, *Palestine Papers 1917–1922: Seeds of Conflict,* John Murray, London, 1972, pp. 31–2.
10 Most of these were fund-raising films for Zionist groups such as the United Jewish Appeal and the Jewish National Fund. Titles include *This Is the Land* (1935), *Built in a Day* (1938), *The Future Can Be Theirs* (1948), etc.
11 Quoted in Taylor Downing, *Palestine on Film,* C.A.A.B.U., 1979.
12 Edmund Wilson, *Black, Red, Blond and Olive,* O.U.P., New York, 1956, pp. 462–3.
13 Arthur Koestler, *Promise and Fulfilment,* Macmillan, London, 1949, pp. 199–200.
14 Speech in the Knesset, 11 March 1978.
15 George Bernard Shaw, *John Bull's Other Island,* Constable & Co., London, 1907, pp. xxxiv–v.

Chapter 1

1   Maxime Rodinson, *Israel and the Arabs,* transl. M. Perl, Penguin, Harmondsworth, 1968, p. 216.

2   Census of Palestine, October 1922. Quoted in H.C. Luke and E. Keith-Roach, *The Handbook of Palestine and Trans-Jordan,* 2nd ed., Macmillan, London, 1930, p. 37.

3   Census of Palestine, October 1922. Quoted in H.V. Muhsam, *Bedouin of the Negev: Eight Demographic Studies,* Jerusalem Academic Press, Jerusalem, 1966, p. 10.

4   Laurence Oliphant, *Haifa, or Life in Modern Palestine,* William Black-wood and Sons, Edinburgh, 1887, pp. 184—5.

5   Census of Palestine, October 1922. Quoted in Luke and Keith-Roach op. cit., p. 37.

6   C.R. Conder, *Palestine,* George Philip and Son, London, 1889, pp. 117—18.

7   Oliphant, op. cit., pp. 163 and 167.

8   Official estimate. Quoted in Albert Hourani, *Minorities in the Arab World,* O.U.P., London, 1947.

9   Such as the Ghassanids and the Bani Salih. See Khalid Kishtainy, *Palestine in Perspective,* Palestine Research Center, Beirut, 1971, p. 38.

10   See A. Granott, *The Land System in Palestine: History and Structure,* Eyre and Spottiswoode, London, 1952.

11   See Rosemary Sayigh, *Palestinians: From Peasants to Revolutionaries,* Zed Press, London, 1979, p. 32.

12   Ibid., p. 36.

13   See Luke and Keith-Roach, op. cit., p. 262.

14   Kishtainy, op. cit., p. 97.

15   Public Record Office, FO 195/1264, No. 10, 30 July 1879.

16   See *Palestine: Report on Immigration, Land Settlement and Development* by Sir John Hope Simpson, H.M.S.O., London, 1930 (Cmd 3626.)

17   Most of the information on Palestinian domestic architecture come from T. Canaan, 'The Palestinian Arab House: Its Architecture and Folklore', *Journal of the Palestine Oriental Society,* vol. 12 (1932).

18   See the description in Frances Newton, *Fifty Years in Palestine,* Cold-harbour Press, London, 1948, pp. 33—7.

19   See Henry Rosenfeld, 'From Peasantry to Wage Labor and Residual Peasantry: The Transformation of an Arab Village', in Louise E. Sweet, (ed.) *Peoples and Cultures of the Middle East,* vol. 2, Natural History Press, New York, 1970.

20   Y. Porath, *The Emergence of the Palestinian-Arab National Movement 1918—1929,* Frank Cass, London, 1974, p. 14.

21   Taysir Nashif, 'Palestinian Arab and Jewish Leadership in the Mandate Period', *Journal of Palestine Studies,* No. 24 (Summer 1977).

22   Sarah Searight, *The British in the Middle East,* rev. ed., East-West Publications, London, 1979, p. 211.

23   Oliphant, op. cit., p. 310.

24   Quoted in Porath, op. cit., p. 14.

25   Oliphant, op. cit., pp. 116—18.

26   Conder, op. cit., p. 21.

27   Oliphant, op. cit., p. 114
28   Newton op. cit., p. 56.
29   C.F. Volney, *Travels through Syria and Egypt in 1783, 1784 and 1785,* quoted in Kishtainy, op. cit., p. 92.
30   Kishtainy, op. cit., p. 78.
31   Ibid., p. 81.
32   Oliphant, op. cit., p. 320.
33   This particular one comes from Ada Goodrich-Freer, *Arabs in Tent and Town,* Seeley, Service and Co. Ltd, London, 1924, p. 86.
34   See Luke and Keith-Roach, op. cit., p. 59.
35   See Sayigh, op. cit., p. 51.
36   O seller of grapes. . .
                            Tell my mother, tell my father.
                            The Bedouin have captured me.
              I used to clean the house and cut wood for fuel,
                   And I used to draw water for my mother.
              I used to rock to sleep the child of the gazelle
                                In a golden cradle.
                   Now I am rocking the son of the Bedouin.
                 In a cradle of *dahriyye* [untranslatable]
                          After wearing silken clothes
                          I now wear coarse garments.
      Quoted in St. H. Stephan, 'Palestinian Nursery Rhymes and Songs', *Journal of the Palestine Oriental Society,* vol. 12 (1932).
37   This is a clearly an impossible figure to fix accurately. The lower number is given in Eliahu Elath's 'The Bedouin of the Negev', *Journal of the Royal Asian Society,* vol. 45 (1958), p. 127. Higher figures, relying on British sources, are given by H.V. Muhsam, op. cit., pp. 7 and 10.
38   Muhsam, op. cit., p. 25.
39   Elath, op. cit., p. 128.
40   Quoted in Elath, op. cit., pp. 128—9.

Chapter 2

1   Quoted in John Nicolis Booth, 'The Moral Case for the Arabs', *Middle East Newsletter,* September 1969.
2   See Abba Eban, *My Country: The Story of Modern Israel,* Weidenfeld and Nicolson, London, 1973, p. 262.
3   H.C. Luke and E. Keith-Roach, *The Handbook of Palestine and Trans-Jordan,* 2nd ed., Macmillan, London, 1930, p. 211.
4   Conversation with the author in Jerusalem, February 1979.
5   A.W. Kayyali, *Palestine: A Modern History,* Croom Helm, London, 1978, p. 15.
6   Y. Porath, *The Emergence of the Palestinian-Arab National Movement 1918—1929,* Frank Cass, London, 1974, p. 20.
7   Ibid., p. 162.
8   Summary of the Inter-Allied Commission (King—Crane Commission),

quoted in Harry Howard, *The King—Crane Commission,* Beirut, 1963, p. 100.

9   See,, for example, George Adam Smith, *The Historical Geography of the Holy Land,* 25th ed., Hodder & Stoughton, London, 1931; reissued, Collins, London, 1966, p. 27, and Porath, op. cit., p. 5.

10 Porath, op. cit., p. 5.

11 *Ha'Olam,* vol. 5 (1911), quoted in Moshe Pearlman, 'Chapters of Arab—Jewish diplomacy', *Jewish Social Studies,* vol. 6 (1944).

12 Quoted in Neville Mandel, 'Turks, Arabs and Jewish Immigration into Palestine, 1882—1914', in A. Hourani (ed.), *Middle Eastern Affairs,* No. 4, Oxford, Oxford University Press, 1965, P. 102. (St Antony's Papers, No. 17.)

13 Khalil al-Sakakini, quoted in Porath, op. cit., p. 28.

14 T. Herzl, *The Complete Diaries of Theodor Herzl,* ed. R. Patai, transl. H. Zohn, Herzl Press and Thomas Yoseloff, New York, 1960, vol. 2, p. 581.

15 Bernard A. Rosenblatt, 'Zionism at the Peace Conference', *The Public* (Chicago), 1 February 1919.

16 Israel Zangwill, 'Before the Peace Conference', in *Asia* (New York), February 1919.

17 Quoted in Doreen Ingrams, *Palestine Papers 1917—1922: Seeds of Conflict,* John Murray, London, 1972, p. 56.

18 Ibid., pp. 56—7.

19 Ibid., p. 58.

20 Ibid., pp. 85—6.

21 C. Weizmann, *Chaim Weizmann: Excerpts from his Historic Statements, Writings and Addresses,* Jewish Agency for Palestine, New York, 1952, p. 48.

22 Herzl, op. cit., vol. 1, p. 88.

23 Quoted in Kayyali, op. cit., p. 163.

24 Ibid., p. 207.

25 *Davar,* 29 September 1967.

26 Remarks made at a meeting of the Royal Institute of International Affairs, reproduced in Arnold J. Toynbee, 'The Present Situation in Palestine', *International Affairs: Journal of the Royal Institute of International Affairs,* vol. 10, No. 1 (January 1931).

27 Quoted in Mrs Stewart Erskine, *Palestine of the Arabs,* George G. Harrap, London, 1935, p. 167. A slightly different version of the remark is given by Porath, op. cit., p. 366.

28 Erskine, op. cit., p. 166.

29 Frances Newton, *Fifty Years in Palestine,* Coldharbour Press, Wrotham, 1948, p. 143.

30 See Christina Jones, *The Untempered Wind: Forty Years in Palestine,* Longman, London, 1975, pp. 50—1.

31 Quoted in Nevill Barbour, *Nisi Dominus: A Survey of the Palestine Controversy,* George G. Harrap, London, 1946, p. 97.

32 Ibid., p. 100.

33 See Mandel, op. cit., p. 201 passim.

34 Cited in Barbour, op. cit., p. 118.

35   Y. Porath, *The Palestinian Arab National Movement 1929–1939: From Riots to Rebellion,* Frank Cass, London, 1977, p. 87.

36   Ibid., pp. 83–4. Information from the Department of Statistics of the Jewish Agency. The same figures are given in Rosemary Sayigh, *Palestinians: From Peasants to Revolutionaries,* Zed Press, London, 1979, p. 37.

37   Porath, *The Palestinian Arab National Movement 1929–1939,* p. 86.

38   Sir John Chancellor to Lord Stamfordham, 27 May 1930. By kind permission of Sir Christopher Chancellor.

39   Israel Zangwill, 'The Return to Palestine', *New Liberal Review,* December 1901, p. 627.

40   Quoted in L.M.C. van der Hoeven Leonhard, 'Shlomo and David, Palestine, 1907', in Walid Khalidi (ed.), *From Haven to Conquest: Readings in Zionism and the Palestine Problem until 1948,* Institute for Palestine Studies, Beirut, 1971, p. 116.

41   See *Palestine: Report on Immigration, Land Settlement and Development* by Sir John Hope Simpson, H.M.S.O., London 1930 (Cmd 3626).

42   Chancellor to Lord Stamfordham, 27 May 1930.

43   Sir John Chancellor to Lord Wigram, 29 June 1931. By kind permission of Sir Christopher Chancellor.

44   Chancellor to Lord Stamfordham, 27 May 1930.

45   For accounts of this episode, see Barbour, op. cit., pp. 117–8, and W.R. Polk, D.M. Stamler and E. Asfour, *Backdrop to Tragedy: The Struggle for Palestine,* Beacon Press, Boston, 1957, pp. 237–8.

46   See Simpson, op. cit.

47   Quoted in Polk, Stamler and Asfour, op. cit., p. 333.

48   Toynbee, op. cit., p. 53.

49   Kayyali, op. cit., p. 137.

50   See Barbour, op. cit., p. 162.

51   See David Hirst, *The Gun and the Olive Branch: The Roots of Violence in the Middle East,* Faber and Faber, London, 1977, p. 25.

52   Luke and Keith-Roach, op. cit., p. 341.

53   W.F. Stirling, *Safety Last,* Hollis and Carter, London, 1953, pp. 114–15.

54   Laurence Oliphant, *Haifa, or Life in Modern Palestine,* William Blackwood and Sons, Edinburgh, 1887, p. 69.

55   Stirling, op. cit., pp. 115–16.

56   Chancellor to Lord Stamfordham, 27 May 1930.

57   Freya Stark, *East is West,* John Murray, London, 1945, p. 103.

58   *Ha'Aretz,* 15 November 1969. Quoted in Hirst, op. cit., p. 63.

59   Quoted in Frank C. Sakran, *Palestine Dilemma: Arab Rights versus Zionist Aspirations,* Public Affairs Press, Washington, 1948, p. 204.

60   Note on map Illustrating Territorial Negotiation – between H.M.G. and King Hussein, Public Record Office, FO 371/4352.

61   *Parliamentary Debates (Hansard),* ser. 5, House of Lords, vol. 53, col. 655. Quoted in Barbour, op. cit., p. 107.

62   Chancellor to Lord Stamfordham, 27 May 1930.

63   Porath, *The Palestinian Arab National Movement 1929–1939,* op. cit., p. 49.

64   *Statistical Abstract of Israel, 1974,* Central Bureau of Statistics, Jerusalem, table v. 71, p. 123.

65   Ibid.
66   Quoted in Kayyali, op. cit., p. 174.
67   Ibid., p. 204.
68   Tom Bowden, 'The Politics of the Arab Rebellion in Palestine, 1936–39',
      Middle Eastern Studies, vol. 11, No. 2 (May 1975), p. 169.
69   Conversation with the author in Jericho, February 1979.
70   Khalidi, op. cit., app. 4, pp. 846–9.
71   Porath, *The Palestinian Arab National Movement 1929–1939,* op. cit.,
      pp. 261–73.
72   *Parliamentary Debates (Hansard),* ser. 5, House of Commons, vol. 347,
      col. 1967. Quoted in Michael Ionides, *Divide and Lose: The Arab Revolt
      of 1955–1958,* Geoffrey Bles, London, 1960, p. 44.

Chapter 3

1   Kermit Roosevelt, 'The Partition of Palestine: A Lesson in Pressure
      Politics', *Middle East Journal,* vol. 2, No. 1 (1948), pp. 1–16. Reprinted
      in Walid Khalidi (ed.), *From Haven to Conquest: Readings in Zionism
      and the Palestine Problem until 1948,* Institute for Palestine Studies,
      Beirut, pp. 515–26 and 727–9.
2   Carlos P. Romulo, *I Walked with Heroes,* Holt, Rinehart and Winston,
      New York, 1961, pp. 285–9. Reprinted in Khalidi, op. cit., pp. 723–6.
3   Report of Sub-Committee 2 to the Ad Hoc Committee on the Palestinian
      Question, U.N. document A/AC 14/32, 11 November 1947.
4   Ibid.
5   Robert Briscoe with Alden Hatch, *For the Life of Me,* Little, Brown and
      Company, Boston, 1958, p. 266.
6   Menachem Begin, *The Revolt,* transl. S. Katz, ed. I.M. Greenberg,
      W.H. Allen, London, 1951, p. 335.
7   Dov Joseph, *The Faithful City: The Seige of Jerusalem, 1948,* Simon and
      Schuster, New York, 1960, p. 218.
8   Government of Israel, *Refugees in the Middle East: A Solution in Peace,*
      Israel Information Service, 1967.
9   See David Hirst, *The Gun and the Olive Branch,* Faber and Faber,
      London, 1977, p. 124.
10   See N. Lorch, *The Edge of the Sword: Israel's War of Independence
      1947–1949,* Putnam & Co: Ltd, London, 1961, pp. 87–9; reprinted in
      Khalidi, op. cit., pp. 756–60; and Erskine Childers, 'The Wordless Wish:
      From Citizens to Refugees', in Ibrahim Abu-Lughod (ed.), *The Trans-
      formation of Palestine,* Northwestern University Press, Evanston, 1971,
      p. 179.
11   Y. Allon, 'The Zionist Settlement Movement as a Military Factor in the
      Israel War of Liberation', transl. I. Halevy-Levin, ed. A. Fishman, in
      Dov Knohl, *Siege in the Hills of Hebron: The Battle of the Etzion Bloc,*
      Thomas Yoseloff, New York, London, 1958, p. 376. Quoted by Childers,
      loc. cit.

12   For the stength of the Zionist forces, see David Ben-Gurion, *Israel: A Personal History,* transl. by N. Meyers and U. Nystar, New York, Funk and Wagnalls, 1971, p. 93; Netanel Lorch, *Israel's War of Independence, 1947–1949,* Hartmore House, Hartford, 1968, p. 31; Joseph, op. cit., pp. 29, 31; and *A Survey of Palestine: Prepared in December 1945 and January 1946 for the Information of the Anglo-American Committee of Inquiry,* Government Printer, Jerusalem, 1946, (especially the suppl.).

13   Joseph, op. cit., p. 31.

14   See Nafez Nazzal, *The Palestinian Exodus from Galilee, 1948,* Institute for Palestine Studies, Beirut, 1978.

15   Ibid., p. 18.

16   See Khalidi, op. cit., app. 9-B, p. 867.

17   Sir John Glubb, *A Soldier with the Arabs,* Hodder and Stoughton, London, 1957, p. 84.

18   Ibid., p. 94.

19   Ibid., p. 234.

20   Jon Kimche and David Kimche, *Both Sides of the Hill: Britain and the Palestine War,* Secker and Warburg, London, 1960, p. 268. Quoted by Childers, op. cit., pp. 201–2.

21   Quoted in Moshe Menuhin, *The Decadence of Judaism in Our Time,* 2nd impr., Institute for Palestine Studies, Beirut, 1969, p. 226.

22   Quoted by Erskine Childers in a letter to the *Spectator,* 9 June, 1961.

23   Letter to the author, 10 May 1979.

24   Erskine Childers, 'The Other Exodus', *Spectator,* 12 May 1961, pp. 672–5. Reprinted in Khalidi, op. cit., pp. 795–803.

25   In letters to the prime minister of Egypt and other Arab governments, 8 March 1948.

26   Geoffrey Furlonge, *Palestine Is My Country: The Story of Musa Alami,* John Murray, London, 1969 p. 157.

27   Progress Report, U.N. document A/648, 1948, p. 14.

28   *Palestine Post,* 23 April 1948.

29   Kimche and Kimche, op. cit., pp. 227–8.

30   Quoted in Nazzal, op. cit., p. 105

31   Ibid., pp. 33–7, 107.

32   Ibid., p. 95.

33   Ibid., pp. 105–8.

34   Letters of 8 November 1948. Quoted in Eyal Kafkafi, 'A Ghetto Attitude in the Jewish State', *Davar,* 6 September 1979.

35   Jacques de Reynier, 'Deir Yassin', transl. by Institute for Palestine Studies, in Khalidi, op. cit., p. 764.

36   Jon Kimche, *Seven Fallen Pillars: The Middle East, 1915–1950,* Secker and Warburg, London. 1950, pp. 217–18.

37   Quoted by Childers, in Abu-Lughod, op. cit., p. 186.

38   Begin, op. cit., p. 165. Quoted by Childers in Abu-Lughod, op. cit., p. 189.

39   Reynier, op. cit., p. 765.

40   Harry Levin, *Jerusalem Embattled,* Gollancz, London, 1950, p. 160.

41   Leo Heiman, in *Marine Corps Gazette* (Tel Aviv), June 1964.

42   *Ha Sepher Ha Palmach,* vol. 2, p. 286; cited in Hirst, op. cit., p. 41.

43   Reported in the *New York Times,* 23 October 1979.

44   Quoted in Menuhin, op. cit., p. 491, and Childers, in Abu-Lughod, op. cit., p. 184
45   Report to the U.N. secretary-general, 16 September 1948.
46   U.N. General Assembly resolution 194 (III) of 11 December 1948.
47   U.N. Security Council, *Official Records,* suppl. 108 (S/949), August 1948, pp. 106−9.
48   Menuhin, op. cit., p. 198.
49   D. Ben-Gurion, 'Israel among the Nations', in State of Israel, *Government Year-Book 5713 (1952),* Government Printer, Jerusalem, 1952, p. 38. Quoted by Childers, in Abu-Lughod, op. cit., p. 165.
50   James G. McDonald, *My Mission to Israel, 1948 − 1951,* New York, 1951; cited by Childers, in Abu-Lughod, op. cit., p. 196.
51   Moshe Dayan in 'Face the Nation', C.B.S., 11 June 1967.

Chapter 4

1   Fawaz Turki, *The Disinherited: Journal of a Palestinian Exile,* 2nd ed., Monthly Review Press, New York, 1974, p. 94.
2   See Jabra I. Jabra, 'The Palestinian Exile as Writer', *Journal of Palestine Studies,* No. 30 (Winter 1979).
3   Arif al-Arif, *al-Nabka,* Beirut, Sidon, 1956−60, vol 5, pp. 1122− 6. Taken from U.N.R.W.A. documents of 25 November, 1952.
4   Elmer Berger, *Who Knows Better Must Say So: Letters of an American Jew,* 2nd ed., Institute for Palestine Studies, Beirut, 1970, p. 43.
5   Quoted in Edward Hagopian and A.B. Zahlan, 'Palestine's Arab Population: The Demography of the Palestinians', *Journal of Palestine Studies,* No. 12 (Summer 1974), p. 55.
6   Bassem Sirhan, 'Palestinian Refugee Camp Life in Lebanon', *Journal of Palestine Studies,* No. 14 (Winter 1975), p. 92.
7   Turki, op. cit., p. 41.
8   Sirhan, op. cit., p. 101.
9   Turki, op. cit., p. 183.
10   Jabra I. Jabra, op. cit., p. 85.
11   *Annual Statistical Abstract 1978,* Central Statistical Office, Ministry of Planning, Kuwait, 1978, table 23, p. 23.
12   Ibid., table 325, p. 367.
13   Figures of the Central Statistics Department, Minsitry of Planning, Abu Dhabi, December 1978.
14   See Hanan Mikhail Ashrawi, 'The Contemporary Palestinian Poetry of Occupation', *Journal of Palestine Studies,* No. 27. (Spring 1978), pp. 77−101.
15   Ibid., p. 89.
16   The poem is reproduced, in a slightly different translation, in Fouzi El-Asmar's own book, *To Be an Arab in Israel,* Institute for Palestine Studies Beirut, 1978, pp. 198−9.

Chapter 5

1   Fouzi El-Asmar, 'To be an Arab in Israel', in U. Davies, A. Mack and
     N. Yuval-Davis (eds), *Israel and the Palestinians,* Ithaca Press, London,
     1975 p. 198. The other references for El-Asmar are, unless stated, to his
     book *To Be an Arab in Israel,* see note 3.
2   Walter Schwarz, *The Arabs in Israel,* Faber and Faber, London, 1959, p. 58.
3   Fouzi El-Asmar, *To Be an Arab in Israel,* Institute for Palestine Studies,
     Beirut, 1978, pp. 14, 24.
4   Ibid., p. 17.
5   Tawfiq Zayyad, 'The Fate of the Arabs in Israel', *Journal of Palestine
     Studies,* No. 21 (1976), p. 97.
6   *Ha'Aretz,* 30 April 1958.
7   Quoted in Sabri Jiryis, *The Arabs in Israel,* The Fifth of June Society,
     Beirut, 1969, p. 31.
8   Reported in *Ha'Aretz* and *Yedi'ot Aharonot,* 25 October 1972.
9   *Parliamentary Debates (Hansard),* ser. 5, House of Commons, vol 861,
     col. 502.
10   Davis, Mack and Yuval-Davis, op. cit., p. 200.
11   Don Peretz, *Israel and the Palestinian Arabs,* Middle East Institute,
     Washington, 1958, p. 96.
12   Quoted in H. Amun, U. Davis and N.D. San'allah, 'Deir al-Asad: The
     Destiny of an Arab Village in Galilee', in *Palestinian Arabs in Israel:
     Two Case Studies,* Ithaca Press, London, 1977, pp. 4—5.
13   *Yedi'ot Aharonot,* 10 October 1975.
14   *Yedi'ot Aharonot,* 2 February 1979.
15   Davis, Mack and Yuval-Davis, op. cit., p. 211.
16   El-Asmar, op. cit., p. 35.
17   Ibid. pp. 46—8.
18   Davis, Mack and Yuval-Davis, op. cit., p. 210.
19   Ibid.
20   El-Asmar, op. cit., pp. 48—9.
21   Zayyad, op. cit., p. 99.
22   Jiryis, op. cit., p. 29.
23   Israel Shahak (ed.), *The Non-Jew in the Jewish State,* 2 Bartenura St,
     Jerusalem, 1975, p. 3.
24   Ibid., p. 135.
25   El-Asmar, op. cit., pp. 83—5, 91.
26   Ibid., p. 103.
27   Israel Shahak, op. cit., p. 63.
28   Amun, Davis and San'allah, op. cit., pp. 51—2.
29   Ibid., p. 56.
30   Shahak, op. cit., p. 22.
31   *Davar,* 3 September 1973.
32   *Yedi'ot Aharonot,* 10 October 1975.
33   Zayyad, op. cit., p. 95.
34   Joseph L. Ryan S.J., 'Refugees within Israel: The Case of the Villagers of
     Kafr Bir'im and Iqrit', *Journal of Palestine Studies,* vol. 2, No. 4
     (Summer 1973), p. 59.

35   Ibid., p. 60.
36   Ibid., pp. 61–2.
37   Ibid., p. 62.
38   *Jerusalem Post,* 18 January 1979.
39   Amun, Davis and San´allah, op. cit., pp. 9, 13.
40   See Eliahu Elath, 'The Bedouin of the Negev', *Journal of the Royal Central Asian Society,* vol. 45 (1958), p. 131, and Walter Schwarz, op. cit., p. 158.
41   Elath, op. cit., p. 132.
42   Cited in an article by Harry Wall in the *Jerusalem Post,* 23 February, 1979.
43   Ibid.
44   Schwarz, op. cit., p. 40 and *Israel and Palestine,* No. 51 (August 1976), p. 1.
45   Schwarz, op. cit., p. 99.
46   Peretz, op. cit., p. 143.
47   *Ha´Aretz,* 4 April 1969. Quoted in David Hirst, *The Gun and the Olive Branch,* Faber and Faber, London, 1977, p. 221.
48   *Jerusalem Post,* 31 January 1979.
49   *Jerusalem Post,* 13 February 1979.
50   See Mohammed Mehdi, *A Palestine Chronicle,* Alpha Publishing Company, London, 1973, for a complete list of villages destroyed since 1948.
51   Amun, Davis and San´allah, op. cit., pp. 13, 64.
52   *Israel and Palestine,* No. 51 (August 1976), p. 3.
53   *Ha´Aretz,* 8 June 1979.
54   El-Asmar, op. cit., pp. 24–5.
55   Walter P. Zennar, 'Some Aspects of Ethnic Stereotype Content in the Galilee: A Trial Formulation', *Middle Eastern Studies,* vol. 8, No. 3 (October 1972), p. 409.
56   Davis, Mack and Yuval-Davis, op. cit., p. 202.
57   Sabri Jiryis, *Democratic Freedoms in Israel,* Institute for Palestine Studies, Beirut, 1972, pp. 83–4.
58   El-Asmar, op. cit., p. 78.
59   Jiryis, op. cit., p. 87.
60   Ibid, pp. 88–9.

Chapter 6

1   *Newsweek,* 5 February 1979.
2   Resolution 2253 (ES-V), 4 July 1967.
3   Quoted in Michael Adams, 'Bulldozers the Symbol of Israeli Mastery', *Guardian,* 4 March 1968.
4   Conversation with the author in Jerusalem, February 1979.
5   See David Hirst, 'Homes for the Boys', *Guardian,* 26 April 1972.
6   *International Herald Tribune,* 21 April 1975.
7   Reported in the *Daily Star* (Beirut), 28 July 1972.
8   *Daily Star* (Beirut), 28 December 1973.
9   Arthur Kutcher, *The New Jerusalem,* Thames and Hudson, London, 1973, p. 54–5.

10   Sammy Khalil Mar'i, 'Higher Education among Palestinians, with Special
     Reference to the West Bank', in Gabriel Ben-Dor (ed.), *The Palestinians
     and the Middle East Conflict: Studies in their History, Sociology and
     Politics,* Turtledove, Ramat Gan, 1978, p. 436.
11   Ibid., p. 437.
12   Shimon Shamir, Rina Shapiro, Elie Rekhess, Shira Tibon, and Israel
     Stockman, 'The Professional Elite in Samaria', in Ben-Dor, op. cit.,
     pp. 467−8.
13   Conversation with the author in Jerusalem, February 1979.
14   Felicia Langer, *With My Own Eyes: Israel and the Occupied Territories
     1967−1973,* Ithaca Press, London, 1975, p. 4.
15   See the Supplement to the Report of the Director-General of the Inter-
     national Labour Office, Geneva, 1979, paragraph 14. The same figure is
     given in a report in the *Jerusalem Post,* 31 January 1979.
16   Ian Black, 'Peace or No Peace, Israel Will Still Need Cheap Arab Labour',
     New Statesman, 29 September, 1978.
17   See, for example, *The Significance of Some West Bank Resources to Israel,*
     Economics Department of the Royal Scientific Society, Amman,
     February, 1979; Brian Van Arkadie, *Benefits and Burdens: A Report on
     the West Bank and Gaza Strip Economies since 1967,* Carnegie
     Endowment for International Peace, Washington, 1977; and Jamil Hilal,
     'Class Transformation in the West Bank and Gaza', reprinted in *Journal
     of Palestine Studies,* No. 22 (Winter 1977), pp. 167−175.
18   *Jerusalem Post,* 23 May 1978.
19   See Elizabeth Monroe, 'The West Bank: Palestinian or Israeli?', *Middle
     East Journal,* vol. 31, No. 4 (Autumn 1977).
20   Paul Quiring, 'Israeli Settlements and Palestinian Rights. Part 1', *Middle
     East International,* September 1978, pp. 10−12.
21   See Ann Lesch, 'Israeli Settlements in the Occupied Territories', *Journal of
     Palestine Studies,* No. 25 (Autumn 1977), pp. 26−47; and No. 29
     (Autumn 1978), pp. 100−19.
22   Martin Woollacott, 'Water Row Begins To Spill Over', *Guardian,* 23 May
     1979; see also Colin Smith, 'The Israeli Water Theft', *The Observer,*
     20 May 1979.
23   Paul Quiring, 'Israeli Settlements and Palestinian Rights. Part 2', *Middle
     East International,* October 1978, pp. 12−15.
24   Conversation with the author, Jericho, February 1979.
25   See the report in the *Jerusalem Post,* 30 January 1979.
26   See *The Market of Arab Children in Israel,* Israeli League for Human and
     Civil Rights, Tel Aviv, 1978.
27   John Reddaway, *Facing the Facts of Israeli Occupation,* a talk given to the
     Council for the Advancement of Arab-British Understanding in the
     House of Commons, 9 May 1978.
28   E.C. Hodgkin, 'Grim Reports of Repression in Israeli-occupied Lands',
     The Times, 28 October 1969.
29   Conversations with the author in London and Hebron, September 1978
     and February 1979.
30   See, for example, *International Review of the Red Cross,* No. 114
     (September 1970); a communiqué published by Amnesty International in

Paris on 24 May 1978; 'Israel and Torture', *The Sunday Times,* 19 June 1977; and the report of the National Lawyers Guild 1977 Middle East Delegation, *Treatment of Palestinians in Israeli-Occupied West Bank and Gaza,* National Lawyers Guild, New York, 1978.

31   Michael Adams, 'Israel's Treatment of the Arabs in the Occupied Areas', in Abdul-Wahhab Kayyali (ed.), *Zionism, Imperialism and Racism* Croom Helm, London, 1979, p. 133.

32   Ian Black, 'Punishment for the West Bank', *New Statesman,* 29 June 1979.

33   Adnan Amad (ed.), *Israeli League for Human and Civil Rights* (The Shahak Papers), Near East Ecumenical Bureau for Information and Interpretation, Beirut, 1973, p. 213.

34   *Jerusalem Post,* 2 February 1979.

35   Ann M. Lesch, 'Israeli Deportation of Palestinians from the West Bank and the Gaza Strip, 1967–1978', *Journal of Palestine Studies,* No. 30 (Winter 1979), pp. 101–31.

36   Ibid., p. 112.

37   'Israel and Torture', *The Sunday Times,* 19 June 1977.

38   *Ha'Aretz,* 3 August 1979.

Chapter 7

1   John Cooley, *Green March, Black September: The Story of the Palestinian Arabs,* Frank Cass, London, 1973, p. 139.

2   William B. Quandt, Fuad Jabber, Ann Mosely Lesch, *The Politics of Palestinian Nationalism,* University of California Press, London, 1973, p. 108.

3   See, for example, Leila Khaled, *My People Shall Live,* Hodder and Stoughton, London, 1973, p. 122.

4   Quandt, Jabber and Lesch, op. cit., p. 104.

5   Fawaz Turki, *The Disinherited: Journal of a Palestinian Exile,* 2nd edn, Monthly Review Press, New York, 1974, p. 142.

6   8 June 1974. Quoted in *Pravda,* 27 January 1977.

7   From a conversation with the author in Beirut, 18 April 1979.

8   Sir John Bagot Glubb, *A Soldier with the Arabs,* Hodder and Stoughton, London, 1957, p. 152.

9   Turki, op. cit., p. 144.

10   *Palestinian Leaders Discuss the New Challenges for the Resistance,* Palestine Research Center, Beirut, 1974, p. 13.

11   See the P.F.L.P. bulletins of July–August 1974 and July–August 1975, published by the Foreign Relations Committee of the Popular Front for the Liberation of Palestine.

12   *New York Times,* 1 May 1978.

13   Communiqué of the Baghdad Conference, November 1978.

14   Quoted in Frank H. Epp, *The Palestinians: Portrait of a People in Conflict,* McClelland and Stewart, Toronto, 1976, p. 141.

15   Fawaz Turki, 'To Be a Palestinian', in U. Davis, A. Mack and N. Yuval-

          Davis (eds.), *Israel and the Palestinians,* Ithaca Press, London, 1975,
          p. 195.
16   David Hirst, *The Gun and the Olive Branch,* Faber and Faber, London,
          1977, p. 304.

Chapter 8

1   Arnold J. Toynbee, 'The Present Situation in Palestine', *International
          Affairs: Journal of the Royal Institute of International Affairs,* vol. 10,
          No. 1 (January 1931).
2   Y. Porath, *The Palestinian Arab National Movement 1929–1939,* Frank
          Cass, London, 1977, p. 209.
3   Quoted in Riad el-Rayyes and Dunia Nahas, *Guerrillas for Palestine,*
          Croom Helm, London, 1976, p. 120.
4   Quoted in John Bulloch, *The Making of a War: the Middle East from
          1967 to 1973,* Longman, London 1974, p. 116.
5   Information from *Statistical Yearbook, 1951,* the Jordanian Department of
          Statistics. Quoted in A.B. Zahlan, 'Palestine's Arab Population',
          Journal of Palestine Studies, No. 12 (1974), p. 57.
6   Quoted in Yitzhak Rabin, *The Rabin Memoirs,* Weidenfeld and Nicolson,
          London, 1975, p. 157.
7   *Al-Ahram,* 9 December 1977. Quoted in Walid Kazziha, *Palestine in the
          Arab Dilemma,* Croom Helm, London, 1979, p. 103.

Chapter 9

1   Quoted in Tewfiq Khalaf, 'The Phalange and the Maronite Community',
          in Roger Owen (ed.), *Essays on the Crisis in Lebanon,* Ithaca Press,
          London, 1976.
2   From a speech at the fifteenth annual conference of the Phalangist Party
          at Chtoura, 22 September 1972.
3   Cable from the National Assembly of Eqypt to the Chamber of Deputies
          Lebanon, 10 December 1972.
4   From a statement on 2 June 1972.
5   Jean-Pierre Haddad, *Le Combat du Liban,* Henri Conchon, Paris, 1977,
          p. 26.
6   Quoted in *Le Monde,* 28 July 1976.
7   From a conversation with the author in the Cedars, March 1975.
8   Haddad, op. cit., p. 37.
9   From a speech on 19 July 1976.
10   From a article in *The Times,* 5 May 1976.
11   Quoted in *Al-Bayrak,* 3 May 1976.
12   *The Times,* 5 May 1976.
13   Quoted in Haddad, op. cit. p. 136.

Chapter 11

1   Galia Golan, 'The Soviet Union and the P.L.O.', in Gabriel Ben-Dor
    (ed.), *The Palestinians and the Middle East Conflict,* Turtledove, Ramat
    Gan, 1978, pp. 229, 232.

2   Quoted in Baruch Hazan, 'Involvement by Proxy – Eastern Europe and the
    P.L.O. 1971–1975', in Ben-Dor, op. cit., p. 331.

3   'Mao Tse-Tung Urges Arabs Boycott West', *Arab World* (Beirut), 6
    April 1965.

4   Lilian Criag Harris, 'China's Relations with the P.L.O.', *Journal of
    Palestine Studies,* vol. 7, No. 1 (Autumn 1977), p. 123.

5   Ibid.

6   See Ali Mazrui, 'Black Africa and the Arab–Israeli Conflict', *Middle
    East International,* September 1978, pp. 13–15.

7   Ibid., p. 14.

8   See U.N. General Assembly Resolution 3236 (XXIX) of 22 November, 1974.

Epilogue

1   See Michael Bar-Zohar, *The Armed Prophet*, Weidenfeld & Nicolson, 1967,
    p. 139.

2   Ibid. (Hebrew edition), Am Oved, Tel Aviv, 1977, vol. 3 pp. 1234–5.

3   Quoted in Livia Rokach, *Israel's Sacred Terrorism,* Association of Arab-
    American Graduates, 1980, pp. 28–9.

4   See the leading articles in *The Times,* 10 and 14 June 1982.

5   Letter to *The Times*, 19 June 1982.

6   *Sunday Times,* 8 August 1982.

7   Ibid.

8   The text was widely quoted. See for example *The Observer,* 8 August 1982.

9   General Eytan made this claim in *Ha'aretz,* 28 December 1979.

10 See the article by Thomas R. Stauffer, 'The Lure of the Litani', in *Middle
    East International,* 30 July 1982.

11 *The Observer*, 13 June 1982.

12 Interviewed by Walter Schwarz in the *Guardian*, 18 June 1982.

13 See for example the remarks by Israeli officials in *Newsweek,* 14 June 1982,
    and the *Guardian*, 17 June 1982.

14 This statement was signed by Arafat and witnessed by a group of American
    congressmen in Beirut on 25 July 1982.

15 See the article by David Lennon, 'Israel's blunt rejection', in *Middle East
    International*, 30 July 1982.

16 UN Security Council Resolution 242.

Issy

Since leaving Oxford in 1974, where he read Modern
History, David Gilmour's work has taken him to most
regions of the Middle East. During the early part of
the Lebanese civil war he worked at the Institute for
Palestine Studies in Beirut and later moved to Cairo.
While doing research for this book, he travelled
through Jordan, Syria, Lebanon, Israel, the Occupied
Territories and the countries of the Arabian Gulf. He
now lives with his wife and two children in London
where he works as a journalist. He is a contributor to
a number of magazines including *The New Statesman,
New Society* and *Middle East International*.

DISPOSSESSED
The Ordeal of the Palestinians
DAVID GILMOUR

SPHERE BOOKS LIMITED
30-32 Gray's Inn Road, London WC1X 8JL

First published in Great Britain by
Sidgwick & Jackson Ltd in 1980
Copyright© 1980, additional material 1982 by David Gilmour
Published by Sphere Books Ltd 1982

Set in Times

Reproduced, printed and bound in Great Britain by Collins,
Glasgow

To Slwa Es Said

ACKNOWLEDGEMENTS

This book could not have been written without the co-operation of hundreds of Palestinians whom I have met and talked to during the last five years. It would be impossible to thank here all the people who have helped me and the following is only a list of those — Palestinians and others — from whom I have received particular help and hospitality: Musa Alami, Muhammad Jarallah, Israel Shahak and Rouhi al-Khatib from Jerusalem; Ahmed Tuqan and Antun Atalla from Amman; Hatem Abu Ghazaleh and his family from Gaza; Tawfiq Zayyad, Selim Jubran and Atallah Mansour from Nazareth; Yusuf Rida from Nablus; Ali Sa'ad from Damascus; Abdul Mohsin Kattan and Khaled al-Hassan from Kuwait; Nabil Hijazi, Zaki Nuseibeh and Ibrahim Ibrahim from the United Arab Emirates; and Leila Baroody, Walid Jumblatt, Sami Alami and members of the Es Said, Dimechkie and Abul Jubain families from Beirut. I would also like to thank Sir John Glubb for his information on Jordan and Sir Christopher Chancellor for permission to quote from his father's papers. I am particularly grateful to John Reddaway, Robert Swann, Philip Mansel and Elfi Pallis who read the manuscript and gave me valuable advice on its contents; to Phyllida Ashton, who advised me on the transliteration of Arabic names, and to Hillary Metwally who twice typed it all out.

March 1980   D.G.